Kelsae

A HISTORY OF KELSO
FROM EARLIEST TIMES

❁

ALISTAIR MOFFAT

BIRLINN

For Jack and Ellen Moffat
with love

This edition published in 2006 by
Birlinn Limited
West Newington House
10 Newington Road
Edinburgh
EH9 1QS

www.birlinn.co.uk

First published in 1985 by Mainstream Publishing, Edinburgh
© Copyright Alistair Moffat 1985 and 2006
Index Copyright © Adam D. Bisset 1985

ISBN10: 1 84158 457 6
ISBN13: 978 1 84158 457 7

British Library Cataloguing-in-Publication Data
A catalogue record for this book is available from the British Library

Printed and bound by Antony Rowe Ltd, Chippenham

Contents

Preface to the Birlinn Edition

History is a story of loss and gain, and of solidity and fluidity. The original meaning of the Greek word *histor* was something like 'eye-witness', especially in a trial or investigation of any sort. History was what you saw or what others reported they themselves had seen. As dating formalised and the past lengthened into decades, royal reigns, centuries, ages, millennia, the meaning of history changed. It became an enquiry. And much was lost.

Unlike Julius Caesar, historians no longer fought in the battles they recorded and described, or, like Herodotus and Thucydides, spoke to people who had watched great events unfold before them. The authority of more modern historians derived not from the sense of having been, seen and conquered but from a promise to get the facts straight and in the correct order. What was gained was perspective, a stronger sense of the sequence of history, how one thing happened and led to another. And also volume. Once historians had slipped out of the need to have been there and seen it, an avalanche of history rumbled down to bury us in facts, dates, places, people and all the paraphernalia of the past.

Facts became central, solid certainties around which the mists of history swirled. Interpretation and the points of view of people who weren't there became important, and although no-one seriously disagrees that William the Conqueror conquered, how and why he did it are a matter of seemingly endless speculation. History appears now to be constantly fluid, in an eternal process of being rewritten and re-understood.

Kelsae has not been rewritten, although I was tempted. A few blunders (one of them hilarious) have been removed and the text updated here and there. But it is largely the same book I wrote in the early 1980s and the one I had been thinking about for a long time before that. Re-reading it, I see how old-fashioned it is, indeed how unfashionable it is. There isn't much in the way of interpretation and analysis. I tried to get at as many of the facts as seemed germane and sort them in the right order. And then at the end of the book there is a riot of colour as a group of Kelsonians remembered the twentieth century in their town. These were real historians – eyewitnesses – and theirs is the best bit of the book, the part I enjoyed re-reading most. The stuff that goes before them is really their introduction, a necessary context for what they have to say.

But it is written, more or less, in the style of the old histories. Of course I did not personally witness many of the events in Kelso's thousand-year story, but I relied on the memories and records of as many people as I could find who had, as well as sources written at the time or soon after the events they described. That meant a fair bit of translation, and a lot less interpretation. And through the whole of the text, I never lost sight of what I myself could see. Kelso is what this book is all about, the physical shape of the town itself, its streets, its buildings, its bridges and ferries, and its river. Kelso is what I witnessed as I grew up, and the place seemed to become part of my way of understanding the rest of the world. More than home, it was a home-place, a mental street-map which I never lost and which I unconsciously used as a template to lay over new experiences in strange places. In many important ways this book turned into a personal enquiry. I wanted to know how Kelso got to be the way it is.

In the twenty years since *Kelsae* was published, some important parts of the town's life have changed. Kelso's population has risen slightly and remained at just over 6,000. And over the last forty years there has been an increase of around 2,000, proportionately an enormous rise of 50 per cent. Against a background of general depopulation this is a substantial achievement, both in terms of the provision of housing and of jobs. Although the magnetic draw of large supermarkets has had its usual baleful effect, Kelso Square and the streets leading off it are still busy, a good place to shop and to get a blether. In the 1960s it was certainly possible to eat a homely sort of lunch at Stempel's or a nervous, hushed dinner at one of the hotels, but Kelso now has some good restaurants, and pubs which do a lot more than *do food*. Social habits have changed in the last twenty years or so, and local people now think nothing of going out regularly to eat in a local restaurant. That has given the centre of the town more colour and cheer.

The current structure of local government allows Kelso's Community Council little real power and the office of Honorary Provost is ceremonial. But it is important nevertheless. In small places, symbolism matters and a worthy provost, like the present incumbent, supplies focus and occasionally a clear Kelso voice. But as James Stewart said in his interview at the end of the book, the town lost a great deal when the town council was abolished in the early 1970s.

Elsewhere there has been gain, the identity of the town rediscovering ancient lustre. The early medieval fair of St James was recently revived and gains strength as it finds its place in the annual calendar at the end of September. After a break of seventy years – scarcely more than a pause for breath for an institution at least nine centuries old – its renewal adds substantially to the life of the town. After the demise of the royal burgh of Roxburgh in the sixteenth century, the nearest was Jedburgh and its officials claimed jursidiction over St James' Fair until it faded away in the 1930s. But no prior approval is needed in the twenty-first century from the royal burgh of Jethart, thank you very much!

Other facets of Kelso's identity have seen loss. The distinguished name of Kelso Rugby Football Club will never again appear in an international match programme at Murrayfield or any of the other great stadia around the world. Very sadly, rugby has professionalised and its international players now turn out for city or district teams, their identity much diluted by the hire of non-Scots or pseudo-Scots. No longer will rugby heroes walk down Kelso's streets as they used to. In the early 1960s the great Basher Hastie scored a try against France on the Saturday and on the following Monday morning cycled through the town and up to his work at Kelso Station. My Gran waved her stick at him, demanding to know why he hadn't remembered to touch down behind the French posts to make certain of the extra points. Glory has become remote, something that happens on television and not the achievement of neighbours, or hulking prop-forwards frightened of old ladies with sticks.

Rugby was an enormously important piece of Kelso's sense of itself. Starved of the talented players historically produced by the town and its farming hinterland, the team does its best in the second division, roughly where a town of 6,000 might expect to be: no better, no worse. And yet once we were kings, champions. In the mid 1980s a highly gifted Kelso XV won the Scottish Rugby Championship twice in a row, beating all-comers and regularly fielding half a dozen Scotland players and a couple of British Lions. That will never happen again. No more photographs of awkward young men with their Scotland caps and jerseys will go up on the clubroom walls.

Re-reading the text of *Kelsae*, I found myself in the uncomfortable position of reviewing my own book. Strange, because it's a position I've often longed to be in – purple adjectives marshalled, clouds of literary and historical glory trailing: the man is a genius!

But now that the opportunity has at last presented itself, I find myself much inhibited. 'It was the best I could do at the time' is the most I can come up with. It sounds lame, like an excuse, a pre-emptive response to criticism. But it's not intended that way. It really was the best I could do. I've written ten history books since *Kelsae* (I notice that their focus seems to be constantly widening; *Kelsae*, *The Borders*, *Celtic Scotland*, *Prehistoric Scotland* and now a great tome on the peoples of the North Sea) and some of them contain the odd excruciating paragraph. *Kelsae* probably does too. But I don't really care. When I had finished the book, I had one overriding feeling: it made me want to come back home, home to Kelsae, bonnie Kelsae.

Alistair Moffat
November 2005

Introduction

WHEN I embarked seriously on this project I thought that since Kelso is a small place it might make only a small book. I forgot that Kelso is a very old place with a continuous history. That has made for a bigger book.

The first four hundred years of Kelso's story are written in Latin — the homemade, everyday sort turned out by the monks of Kelso Abbey's scriptorium. They wrote on precious vellum and parchment and to save space they used a kind of Latin shorthand which I found extremely difficult to unravel. Once I had cracked the code I found behind it a terse, elegant but remarkably consistent style. Because they wrote attractively and clearly about their experience in Kelso, I have included, in translation, much of what the monks had to say. They caught the flavour of their time far better than anyone writing at five hundred years distance.

I have also used material in Scots, English, French and Italian, and I've done so not to be flashy but because it was necessary. Kelso was an important place in the Middle Ages both in a national and international context. Allowing for the differences in the amount of communication, Kelso was much more famous before 1500 than after.

I have indicated in the text where most of my sources come from but I've avoided footnotes and a bibliography because this is not that kind of book. To all the authors from whom I've stolen material, and not mentioned their names in the text, thank you.

The limits of the book (its limitations are obvious) are the modern parish boundaries of Kelso. I have tried to write something about the important places and the events that occurred inside the parish and have generally excluded anything that happened outside. This is an emphatically local history.

The balance of the book may seem odd. Where sources are scarce, as in the mediaeval period, I have written at greater length than, say, for the nineteenth century. I did this because much of mediaeval Kelso has disappeared: Wester Kelso, the conventual buildings around the Abbey, the greater part of the Abbey Kirk itself, and most spectacularly the entire town of Roxburgh.

Whereas early Kelso required explanation and exposition, mainly because the sources are few and not in English, the latter period sometimes did not. If you are interested in, say, Floors Castle or Kelso Rugby Club, good histories already exist.

I was also concerned with the look of the town, how it was laid out and how it developed. Bits of history that were important in their time but have left no mark on Kelso are not to be found here. For example, the rebellion of 1715 was obviously pivotal to Scotland's history in a general way but the aspect of it that engaged me was that the Earl of Dunfermline chose to proclaim the Old Pretender at Wester Kelso's market cross, and not in the Square. The subsequent fortunes of the Old Pretender interested me not at all, whereas the specific choice of the cross as the place to proclaim him is vitally important.

Many local histories tell you more about the person who wrote them than the place. I hope this one does the reverse. To this end I've written it in a direct style. People interested in Kelso want the facts, in my view, and not my feelings about them.

But where feelings do have a place in this book is in the last chapter. Mrs Helen Pettigrew, Rodger Fish, James Stewart, Jack Moffat, Will Ker, Sandy Blair, Donald Scott and Alan Smith have shared their personal memories of the town in its recent past. Most of these people have lived in Kelso all their lives. What they have to say is precious. It is the best sort of history because it is absolutely authentic. In one sense the rest of the book is their introduction as it tries, by quoting chunks of past experience, to be authentic at second hand, to be real.

I have called the book 'Kelsae' because that is the name I knew it by as a child, the name people shout from the terracing at Poynder Park and the name my parents use for the town they live in.

Kelsae is a beautiful place, a place worth knowing about.

Alistair Moffat
Edinburgh
September 1985

Part One

KELSO ABBEY AND ITS FOUNDATION CHARTER

---

1 David I moves his Abbey from Selkirk to Kelso

THE RECORDED history of Kelso began in 1113, at Selkirk. David Earl of
Tweeddale and Northampton (later to become David I of Scotland)
brought 13 monks from the Abbey of Tiron in France to found a new
monastery at Selkirk. David gave the French monks extensive lands in the
Tweed valley, revenues in his burghs of Roxburgh and Berwick, from his
own household, and some property in his English earldom of
Northampton. It was common practice in the Middle Ages to set down all
of these gifts in a document or charter which the monks could produce as
evidence for their ownership of land or services. The foundation charter of
Selkirk Abbey is no exception, as it notes down in careful detail the names
of all the places where the Abbey held property, and its exact geographical
limits, along with all the other gifts and services it received. This charter
gives the first historical glimpse of the Scottish Border country in the 12th
century. The villages of Sprouston, Midlem, Bowden and Redden must all
have been going concerns in 1113 when David gave parts of them to Selkirk
Abbey, and his burghs of Roxburgh (which has now completely
disappeared) and Berwick were undoubtedly thriving towns with weekly
markets and a sizeable merchant population.

Earl David also held a strong castle at Roxburgh. Known as Marchidun
or Marchmont, it was situated at strategically important crossing-points of
both the Teviot and the Tweed and it acted as protection for the town of
Roxburgh. Soon after he became King of Scotland in 1124 David decided,
on the advice of John, Bishop of Glasgow, to move his Abbey of Selkirk to a
new site at a place called Kelso. He did this so that he could concentrate
power in southern Scotland in one centre around Roxburgh. Kelso was
certainly thought of as no more than a suburb of Roxburgh, although it was

the location of an earlier church called St Mary's. Before 1128, when the Abbey of Selkirk was moved and became the Abbey of Kelso, the church of St Mary had been in the diocese of the Bishop of St Andrews. Bishop Robert was persuaded to give this church to the monks in 1128 probably as a temporary home for the abbey and certainly as a site where the building of the new foundation could begin.

In order to avoid confusion over the transplantation of the monks from Selkirk to Kelso, David I re-issued the foundation charter in the name of Kelso, re-organised his gifts of land to suit the new location and on 3 May 1128 in the presence of the royal family and Scotland's nobility, the Abbey Kirk of Kelso was founded. That act marks the beginning of the continuous history of Kelso.

Here are the opening sentences of the foundation charter translated from the Latin:

> David by the grace of God King of Scots, to all the faithful sons of Holy Mother Church, greetings. Let it be known to everyone, now and in the future, that when I was an Earl I founded a certain monastery at Selkirk as an abbey in honour of the Virgin Mary and Saint John the Evangelist [I did this] for the salvation of my soul and those of all my ancestors and successors. But when I had succeeded to the kingdom by divine mercy after the death of my brother King Alexander, on the advice and counsel of John Bishop of Glasgow of venerated memory, I transferred the aforementioned monastery, because the previous site was not suitable for an abbey, to the area around Roxburgh, to the church of the Virgin Mary which lies on the bank of the River Tweed, in place which is called Kelso.

2 Kelso before 1128

There is some slight evidence that there was a much earlier settlement at Kelso, apart from the fact that the church of St Mary pre-existed the foundation of the Abbey. The historian Nennius, recording events which happened around 600AD, mentions that Mynyddawy, Prince of Dunedin (Edinburgh?), raised a war-band to go down into Yorkshire on a raiding foray. Apparently he took with him a warrior called Catrawt of Calchvynyd. Now the origin of the name 'Kelso' comes from the fact that the town stands on a chalky heugh — something that is remembered in the modern street-name of Chalkheugh Terrace — and early references in mediaeval documents variously appear as Calkou, Calchehoh or Celchehov. In the language spoken in south-eastern Scotland around 600AD Calchvynyd means chalk heugh and Catrawt's raid may be the very earliest historical appearance of Kelso.

3 *An important and wealthy Abbey*

What is certain is that after David I's foundation in 1128 Kelso became almost immediately one of the most important churches in Scotland. Within the royal conurbation of Roxburgh, Kelso Abbey represented a vital arm in the government of southern Scotland. While David exerted military control over the area from his great castle, and dominated economic affairs through his royal burgh, he used the Abbey for the administration of this important part of his new kingdom and, of course, to act as a spiritual focus. In his charter the young king made it clear that he was bestowing large gifts on Kelso for religious reasons; he believed, like all christians in the Middle Ages, in the existence of Heaven and Hell and equally in his earthly power to accumulate virtue in a sincere effort to avoid the latter. Put simply, David thought that his patronage of Kelso would ensure his place in Heaven after his death.

Nevertheless, it is in the context of David's concentration of royal power at Roxburgh that the early history of Kelso is best seen. The king's lavish generosity to the Abbey guaranteed its place in the ecclesiastical politics of mediaeval Scotland, but more generally as David's first foundation in an unfamiliar kingdom —indeed his Abbey at Selkirk was the very first import of any of the reformed Benedictine monastic orders in Britain — Kelso and its abbots found themselves at the centre of government in twelfth century Scotland. In order to grasp how this came about it is necessary to first look at two things: the organisation of the Abbey, and the roots of its power — Kelso's landed wealth.

The foundation charter again:

> This church [St Mary's] was in the bishopric of Robert Bishop of St Andrews who, for the love of God and of me, has given it to my abbot and monks, released, quit and freed from every subjection and exaction. That is, in order that the abbot and monks of the aforementioned church might have oil and holy water from whatever bishop they wish, either in Scotland or in Cumbria, so that they might undertake the ordination of their own abbot and monks, and any other business of the church.

The River Tweed formed the boundary between the bishoprics of St Andrews and Glasgow and, although Kelso fell within the former, it is clear that David wanted to assert the independence of the new abbey from the outset. The source of the oil and holy water was more than just a matter of form: if the Bishop of St Andrews had been the bishop who supplied these then that would allow him a direct interest in the choice of the abbot of the monastery. If the monks elected a candidate who was not to the bishop's liking he could withold the oil needed to anoint the new abbot and the water needed to bless the election, thereby effectively preventing the proper sanctification of the monks' choice. By allowing the monastery to seek oil and water from the bishop of their own choice David ensured a free and independent election.

That freedom preserved one of the central ideas of the monastic community. Withdrawal from the world and the self-containment needed to achieve that was essential to the Rule of St Benedict, the code followed by the Order of Tiron, the origin of Kelso's monks. The Tironians had adopted, in a reformed interpretation, the tenets of poverty, chastity and obedience in their pursuit of a life devoted to the worship and contemplation of God. Both their independence and the remoteness they had initially chosen at Selkirk were vital to the community in their efforts to measure up to this ideal.

At the height of its power the abbey probably had around 40 monks and a number of novices, who were young men training for holy orders. The Order of Tiron was especially noted for its emphasis on crafts and each monk was expected to practise some manual skill. Although this was seen by St Bernard, the founder of Tiron, as primarily a device to combat idleness and the leisure to think evil thoughts, it must have seemed an attractive feature to David I. In general, monks were wealth-creating subjects since they acted like efficient corporations which managed property well, and the Tironians with their skills may have seemed to the young king as more productive than most.

Here is the first grant of property made to the monks in the foundation charter:

> I [David] have truly given to this church in perpetual gift the village of Kelso with its proper boundaries by land and by water, freed, quit and released from every exaction.

This sentence is all that is known about Kelso before 1128. It contains two bits of information. Evidently Kelso was more than just a church which had belonged to the bishopric of St Andrews. 'Villa', the Latin word used to describe the place, can be translated as 'village', that is, more than a farm and certainly less than a burgh. Kelso was probably a small hamlet that clustered around the church of St Mary.

Prior to 1128 Kelso was seen as some kind of administrative entity. It had 'proper boundaries by land and water' that were legally recognised in the foundation charter and, although the text does not explicitly say so, these boundaries sound like the limits of Kelso Parish. Before the Reformation Kelso Parish was much smaller than it is now and comprised only that part of the modern parish which lies to the north of the Tweed. That would explain the mention of a water boundary.

David I goes on to give details of what he expects in return for his gifts:

> And so that I might hear the service of God in that church on feast days or on other days as often as I like, I have given in perpetual and free gift all my offerings and those of the people who were with me.

The cost of material grants to ecclesiastical bodies could not possibly be compensated for by the economic advantages of giving land to wealth-producing subjects. David says that he gives 'free gifts' and by that he means that he expects nothing material in return. Usually when the king granted land to a layman, he specified certain services that he wanted as a condition of the grant. For example, fighting men or knights were given pieces of land in return for doing military service for the king, or providing hospitality in the form of food and drink for the royal court, or paying sums of cash. All that David expected from the monks of Kelso was the right to hear the divine service in the Abbey Kirk whenever he liked. He gave away so much land belonging to the crown 'in free and personal gift' that David I became known as 'Ane Sair Sanct for the Croon'.

4 Kelso's property at Ednam

Two and a half miles to the north-east of Kelso, the village of Ednam provided a vital temporary service to the new monastery. In 1105 King Edgar of Scotland (David I's elder brother) had given the 'waste of Ednam' to a man called Thor Longus. He built a church there which he gave to the monks of Durham along with some land and it was dedicated to St Cuthbert, their patron saint. Thor brought the waste of Ednam under cultivation 'with his own stock' but he had to have his corn ground at the king's mill in the village. Ednam Mill is still working today and there can be few mill-wheels that have turned for nearly 900 years. The royal ownership of Ednam Mill may have been a burden to Thor Longus and the church of St Cuthbert, but it was a boon to Kelso Abbey which, at that early point, could not grind its own corn. Here is what David gave the monks out of his mill at Ednam:

> And in Ednam at the mill 12 chalders [about 400 bushels] of barley each year, and from the moor of Ednam the right to dig peat for burning, from [an area bounded by] a ditch which runs down from another moor with the road on the

15

right as it crosses Ednam moor right up to where three big stones stand on either side.

That is the description of a place by people who knew it already. The natural resource of peat as heating and cooking fuel was important to everyone, not just the monks in their draughty church at Kelso. The precision with which their peat-cutting rights are set down presumes the close interests of other consumers who took their fuel from Ednam moor and it is a good example of the great care taken in drafting charters that concerned land and the rights to it. Working on the shaky assumption that the road referred to is the modern road running from the east (from Edenmouth) into the village and the likelihood that the moor lay within the parish of Ednam, the moor described here may be the high ground around the farm of Ferneyhill. That would make it a convenient source of peat for the monks since it lay nearest to the abbey.

5 Kelso and Roxburgh

In addition to the everyday needs for barley (mainly for the brewing of beer) and fuel, the new monastery also required hard cash if it was to build and furnish the great Abbey Kirk envisaged by their founder. In the early twelfth century burghs were the concern of the king and it was within David I's power to grant Kelso substantial revenues from its near neighbour on the opposite bank of the Tweed, Roxburgh:

> And in the burgh of Roxburgh forty solidi [shillings] each year from the taxation, and all the churches and schools of the same burgh with all their appurtenances. And one toft next to the church of St James and another in the new burgh. And land which belonged to Walter Cementar. And from the mills twenty chalders of both meal and grain, and a seventh part of the fishing.

It is clear that Roxburgh was a flourishing town in 1128 and a rich source of income for the abbey. The story of Roxburgh belongs in a separate chapter but suffice it to say here that it must have served as a centre for all kinds of resources for the monks. Not only did it provide scarce cash but it also would have contained skilled workmen of all trades who could be employed in the building of the monastery.

6 Lands south of the Tweed

On the southern bank of the Tweed Kelso Abbey had some of its most fertile lands. The monks owned property stretching from Heiton in the west right up to the English border at the Redden Burn. They held the church of St Michael (which the Ordnance Survey map places near the grandstand in the present-day Border Union showground) and some land which Herbert de Maccuswel had given them. His name is remembered in that stretch of the Tweed called the Maxwheel, where the river turns to flow eastwards below Kelso Bridge. The modern village of Maxwellheugh is simply his name combined with the local word for a hill or a height. The Abbey also owned the Chapel of St Thomas a Becket which lay at the head of Wooden Burn. It looks today as if the church stood in a field immediately to the south of Wooden House. As late as the sixteenth century the estate of Wooden was known as St Thomas Chapel Lands.

The land down by the River Tweed has always been good farming country and, in the foundation charter, David I made sure that his new abbey was well provided with productive properties near at hand:

> And in Sprouston [I give] one carucate of land [more than 100 acres] and 20 acres and measures attaching to the carucate, and three acres of pasture. And the church of that village and the land attaching to the church. Lord John, Bishop of Glasgow, gives and at the same time confirms it by his episcopal authority.

This kind of possession later became known as an abbey grange, intended to be the source of produce for the monks' own consumption. Sprouston was in the bishopric of Glasgow and in the same way that Bishop Robert of St Andrews was persuaded to give up Kelso to the abbey, John of Glasgow gave the church to the monks. Incidentally, he is the same man who advised King David to move the Tironians from Selkirk to Kelso.

7 The Wool Trade through Berwick

Returning to the Foundation Charter, one of the most significant grants made by David I was in the port of Berwick. Here is the relevant passage:

> And in Berwick one carucate of land and one measure next to the church of St Laurence, and another measure in the burgh. And forty solidi a year from the taxation of the same burgh. And a half of the fishing called Berwickstream and a seventh part of the mills.

Berwick was the outlet for the export of raw materials from the Tweed valley and Kelso's relationship with the thriving seaport sets the abbey in the context of international trade as it existed in the Middle Ages. In contrast to the local economy around Kelso itself, there was a busy export

17

trade of raw wool to the densely populated manufacturing area of Flanders or northern Belgium. Although coarse cloth was made all over the Borders (including Kelso) at that time, the technology needed to weave fine fabrics was concentrated in Flanders and northern Italy and, by the twelfth century, Flemish merchants had set up links with wool growers in Scotland and England. The Tweed valley produced wool in bulk off the backs of the short-haired sheep that grazed on the foothills of the Cheviot and Lammermuir Hills. Kelso Abbey had extensive holdings of sheep grazing and by the thirteenth century they probably owned more than 7,000 head. The revenue from the sales of wool to the Flemings is not recorded and in fact the Kelso documents are not very informative about the workings of the wool trade. A great deal has to be guessed at from scanty source-material.

The Abbey ran sheep ranches in both the Lammermuirs and the Cheviots. Around the village of Yetholm they owned grazings at Shotton and Colpinhope, at Primside and up the beautiful Bowmont Valley the monks held great tracts of the land known as Molle or Mow. In the twelfth century the valley was densely populated and intensively cultivated. The maze of ancient names for small bits of land, and the number of named owners testifies to the comparative fertility of the Bowmont Valley. A legal case, settled in 1185, gives an idea of how the monks operated their holdings.

Eschina of London, the wife of Henry of Mow, confirmed that Kelso Abbey owned the church at Mowhaugh. For the sake of the soul of her daughter, buried at the abbey, she granted to 'the chaplain and the men of the monastery residing at Mowhaugh' the rights to common pasture for their sheep and the right to take fuel and timber from her woods. Later, she had cause to question the exercise of these pasture rights and in the course of patching up the disagreement the documents reveal that the abbey regularly grazed more than 700 sheep in the Bowmont Valley. It seems that the abbey employed shepherds and estate-workers (conversi) under the supervision of the chaplain of Mowhaugh Church. After the sheep-shearing, the monks used the services of their workers and tenants to transport the fleeces to Kelso and thence to market at Roxburgh. Since there are no records of Kelso's men carrying wool from Roxburgh to Berwick, it is possible that the Flemings organised that part of the trade themselves.

Clues to the route the Flemings might have followed from the central Borders to their ships at Berwick are to be found in the Kelso charters. In the reign of Malcolm IV, Hye of Simprim gave the Abbey of Kelso the little church at that place. By 1251 David de Bernham, Bishop of St Andrews

(Simprim being in his bishopric), allowed Kelso to take over the church completely and he specified that the income from it should be used 'to give strangers hospitality'. In the Middle Ages the Latin word *peregrinus* meant a traveller, a pilgrim or a foreigner, and when Bishop David gave Simprim Kirk to Kelso he made repeated references to *peregrini* and the fact that they needed looking after. Now, David de Bernham was a reforming bishop who tried to ensure that the church attended to its primary Christian duties, such as giving shelter to travellers. The references to *peregini* point to the likelihood that Simprin lay on a well-travelled road. The hamlet of Simprim lies about halfway between Kelso and Berwick on the route by the northern, and Scottish, bank of the Tweed. Documents concerning the abbey's men at Redden and the carrying duties they owed Kelso give information about the length of time it took in the twelfth century to make a journey, with merchandise, between Kelso and the port of Berwick. Apparently it took two days to complete the trip, one way. That would make Simprim a handy place to break the journey and rest for the night. There is more evidence to help build up a picture of a busy commercial highway between Kelso/Roxburgh and Berwick. In 1415 someone recorded, in Scots instead of Latin, a note of the boundaries of the abbey's church at Simprim. Here is a part of that document:

> South of the green meadow upon the burn brae, which is the resting-place for the abbot's carts when they come from Berwick.

The description refers to the bit of land between Milne Graden and Simprim on the ridge on the north side of the Tweed. The document, although it was written more than a century after the height of the wool trade between the Borders and Flanders, testifies to a long-standing practice of breaking the return journey from Berwick to Kelso. The mention of the 'abbot's carts' might mean that when the raw wool was offloaded at the port, the monks used the empty carts to bring back salt and coal from Berwick. Both these commodities were, and still are, in abundant supply on the coastline around the village of Scremerston. Another piece of documentary evidence lends support to the idea of a well-used road between Berwick and Roxburgh/Kelso. James II issued a series of detailed ordinances in 1455 for the protection of the Border country and in particular, he was anxious that the 'the est passage betuix Roxburghe and Berwik' should be adequately defended.

When David I gave Kelso lands and rights in his burgh of Berwick, he was granting the monks an interest in the most prosperous town in Scotland at that time. Their property shows how great their involvement in the trade of Berwick was. They received forty shillings from the customs paid by merchants who used the port, rented several shops in the main streets and also owned rights to fish for salmon at the mouth of the Tweed. This last was and is still a prosperous business and the extent of the fishings held at Berwick by different individuals is the subject of dozens of detailed charters. Fish was the main source of protein in the monks' diet since, being good husbandmen, they would rather kill a salmon than a productive mammal.

More than simply a property-owner, Kelso had a big stake in the flow of trade through Berwick. Not only did their shepherds provide the raw wool but they also had interests at Roxburgh (the inland commodity market), they helped maintain part of the trade-route and they also took a cut at the point of export.

8 Other Properties

In the central Borders King David had been very generous to his monks; they owned all the land attached to the villages of Bowden, Midlem and Whitlaw, and they held thirty acres at Lilliesleaf. This is land which appeared in the original charter for the foundation of the abbey at Selkirk and its proximity to the old site means that David probably intended it to act as a convenient source of produce for the monks much in the way that Sprouston and Redden fulfilled that function after 1128.

Kelso still retained property at Selkirk and the documents detail 'a certain parcel of land lying between the road which comes down from the castle, above the old abbey'. Even though the monks only stayed at Selkirk for fifteen years, they managed to build an abbey church of some kind, although the likelihood is that it was only a wooden structure.

The Foundation Charter goes on to list Kelso's property at Duddingston (known in the twelfth century as 'Traverlene') and as far away as Renfrew. One of David's more interesting gifts was land he owned as Earl of Northampton at a place called Hardingstone and this could only have been of use to the monks as a money rent at a time when they had need of hard cash. When they were settled at Kelso, he exchanged Hardingstone for land at Duddingston. When Jedburgh Abbey was founded, David again used this piece of land in Northampton to sustain the new foundation.

The final section of the Foundation Charter details huge gifts in kind made by the king to Kelso. They are an excellent illustration of the sort of goods that were highly valued in the twelfth century and they show that not all of the abbey's great wealth was tied up in land.

And a tenth of the animals, pigs and cattle each year from the four parts of Galloway which I held when King Alexander was alive, and a tenth of the cattle of Tweeddale each year. And half of the hides of all the beasts slaughtered for my kitchen and that of all my successors. And the same share of the suet and tallow as [they have] of the hides, and all the skins of the lambs and rams. And a tenth of the deerskins [bucks and does] taken by my huntsmen.

I give these products of my kitchens and my slaughtered beasts to them [the monks] from that land which I held when King Alexander was alive. And in Karsah a salt-works. And all this I confirmed to the aforesaid monastery, its abbot and monks so that they may hold it freely and peaceably and by perpetual right. And so that none of my successors shall presume to demand anything of the aforesaid church except for prayers for the salvation of their souls.

Witnessed by Henry, son of the King, and others.

Thus concludes the Foundation Charter of Kelso Abbey. It represents a tremendous array of gifts and something which made Kelso immediately extremely wealthy and a place of central importance in mediaeval Scottish politics. For the rest of its long history Kelso was never again to exert such influence as it had in the first two centuries of its existence. The removal of the Tironian monks from Selkirk to their new home beside the Tweed happened because David I wanted to concentrate power at his burgh of Roxburgh. In order to present a complete picture of Kelso in this early period, it is necessary to turn now to the history of the town that lay across the river from the new abbey and which has now completely disappeared.

21

Part Two

---

1 A New Town

WHEN HE became Earl of Tweeddale in 1107, David I began to develop his inheritance. Not only did he introduce religious orders like the Tironians at Selkirk, he also sought to establish effective military control over the huge tracts of land he owned. David had been brought up as a Norman and had been knighted at the court of the English King Henry I where he doubtless observed the way in which the Norman conquerors (the conquest had taken place only thirty years before) had consolidated their hold on England. Because there were very few Normans and very many English, the conquerors had chosen to pattern the country with strong castles, garrisoned with soldiers who could exert a measure of control over the surrounding countryside out of all proportion to their numbers.

David did not have to conquer Tweeddale, he owned it by hereditary right and did not encounter the hostility the Normans had in England. But nevertheless he needed to use his manpower resources wisely if he wanted to change the nature of the land he governed. His Norman incomers had to be one of the main agents for that change, and the two characteristically Norman ways in which David developed his earldom were the creation of strong castles and the building of thriving towns around them.

The site of Roxburgh must have looked like the obvious place for a stronghold to the young Earl David. Bounded very closely by the River Teviot on its south side and by the Tweed only a short distance to the north, the long oblong mount that was to become Roxburgh Castle rose to a height of seventy to eighty feet, dominating the undulating landscape around it. To the east of the castle the two rivers Teviot and Tweed join to make a peninsula of the area where David built his new burgh, thus ensuring that it would be well defended by water. Although there is a in the seventh century that Roxburgh acquired its modern name. The old style of 'Marchidun' means in Old Welsh 'the horse-fort' or, better, the cavalry fort, but that place-name was discarded, probably in the 630s or 640s. By that time Anglian warbands, striking out from their principal base at Bamburgh, had taken the citadel of Edinburgh and almost certainly overrun the Tweed Valley. A warlord known as 'Hroc', or 'The Rook' took Marchidun and renamed it 'Hroc's burh', the Rook's Fortress, or Roxburgh.

The town first appears on record in 1113 in the foundation charter of Selkirk Abbey. David addressed this document 'To all his French, English and Scottish friends' and it was witnessed by twenty-four people including David's son Henry and three of his chaplains. Out of the remaining number, ten were men who had come over from Normandy with William the Conquerer in 1066 and had subsequently been given land by him. Amongst these witnesses were Robert de Brus, Robert de Umfraville and Robert Corbet — all of whom received land in the Border country, all of whom were French-speaking and all new to the area. In addition, there are two other men simply called Radulf the Englishman and Aimar the Frenchman. This list of witnesses to Earl David's first important act in Scotland shows the strength of foreign penetration in the Border country in the early twelfth century and the context in which the young earl began to develop his inheritance. Two decades later the names of several of the townspeople of Roxburgh come to light. Some time before he died in 1152 Earl Henry, David I's son, confirmed the lands of Beatrix de Beauchamp in the burgh of Roxburgh. She was the wife of another of the king's important Norman vassals, Hugo de Morville, and she had originally acquired the land in question from a man with a French name, Roger Janitorius. During this period David also sought to build up the volume of trade passing through his port of Berwick and the early names of townspeople there are mainly French (e.g. Bernard de Baliol) or Flemish (Jordan Flandrensis).

All of this adds up to a strong indication that David's new castle and town at Roxburgh were primarily the creation of newcomers to the Borders, the French and English friends who witnessed the Selkirk charter.

One of the other signatories to the foundation charter was Gospatric, formerly Earl of Northumbria. He had lost his English earldom but was given extensive lands by King Alexander I in East Lothian and Berwickshire. In the early twelfth century Gospatric had the title of *vicecomes* or sheriff of Roxburgh which meant that he was the royal governor of the castle and David I's representative in his absence. This ensured a continuing administrative set-up when the king's court was held elsewhere in Scotland.

Gospatric died in 1138, the year that David I chose to move against King

Stephen of England. David massed his army at Roxburgh and invaded England down the ancient Roman highway of Dere Street, which began its journey across the Cheviots only seven miles from the burgh. This military operation underlines the strategic importance of Roxburgh's location. Not only was the site inherently strong but it also lay very near the junction of two mediaeval roads, and it controlled a relatively low crossing point of the Tweed — probably the last before the bridge at Berwick. This made Roxburgh a convenient place to assemble an army for operations in both England, and later, Scotland. In addition Roxburgh's position had important ramifications for the growth of the town as an economic centre.

Turning to ecclesiastical affairs, the year 1125 saw Roxburgh as the scene of a church council that signalled the beginning of a long conflict over the question of the independence of the church in Scotland. The venue for the council was the Chapel of St John the Evangelist inside Roxburgh Castle's walls, and the business of it was conducted by the Papal Legate, John of Crema. Pope Honorius had sent Cardinal John to mediate in a dispute between the Scottish Bishops and the Archbishop of York, who at that time claimed supremacy over the Scottish church. York had been trying to assert its right, as an archbishopric, to take a decisive role in the appointment of Scotland's bishops and major ecclesiastics. In the twelfth century Scotland did not have its own archbishop and York was the nearest. The leading churchmen on the Scots' side was Bishop John of Glasgow, the man who advised King David to move the Tironians from Selkirk to Kelso. He refused to subject himself to the Archbishop of York at the council of Roxburgh and ultimately he seems to have won his case.

John was again at the Chapel of St John the Evangelist at Roxburgh in 1127. He witnessed the formal declaration by Robert, Bishop of St Andrews, that the Scottish church of Coldingham should remain in the possession of the English bishopric of Durham.

These two episodes serve to illustrate how Roxburgh could be the stage for events vital to the assertion of the independence of the Scottish church, even before David I added to the town's role in religious affairs when he established his colony of monks on the site of their new monastery across the Tweed at Kelso.

All of these facts, suppositions and historical episodes tend to support the contention that Roxburgh was largely the creation of David, first as Earl of Tweeddale and later as King of Scotland. Unlike Selkirk or Kelso Abbey, the town does not have anything like a foundation charter to act as a handy starting-point for its history. But it does seem that David used his English and French friends to develop the site into an important centre. He also organised the royal administration of Roxburgh and his lands around it into a sheriffdom which was first held by an Englishman. He also used the Chapel of St John the Evangelist in his castle to forward the claims of the independent church of Scotland.

Roxburgh was evidently a busy place, a town that would have been well known to many people in mediaeval Scotland; and yet nothing remains of it and very little can be learned about it from surviving documentary sources. However, something tangible does remain of the castle and it is appropriate to turn now to the initial reason for Roxburgh's existence, its military function as a stronghold.

2 *Roxburgh Castle*

Although Roxburgh Castle was never abandoned between 1125 (when it is first explicitly mentioned — the Selkirk charter of 1113 only names the burgh) and 1550 when it was finally destroyed, only a few fragments of masonry are left. These lie mostly on the south side of the site by the River Teviot. Roxburgh was a large castle and it is surprising that so little of it has survived, even taking into account the energy of the stone-robbers from across the Tweed at Kelso.

The stone and wooden ramparts of the castle may have largely disappeared, but it is still possible to see something of the man-made defences that lie outside the enclosure at the top of the mount. Submerged in the Teviot between the policies of Springwood on one bank and the west end of the castle-mount on the other, there is a series of large boulders lying in a curved line against the current. It is probable that these formed the foundations of a mediaeval dam or cauld which could divert water (when needed) into the man-made moat that runs around the foot of the mount right up to the east end of the castle, eight hundred feet away. The level of the moat seems much too high to allow this to happen now. But, bearing in mind that the castle walls on the north and west sides of the site were all cast down, it seems likely that the force of gravity has ensured that their resting-place is beneath the grassy bottom of the moat, making its level much lower than at present. The big boulders that make up the cauld have regular gaps between them to allow the river current to pass through normally, but when the moat needed topping up those gaps could have been easily dammed to divert the Teviot's water around Roxburgh Castle for an hour or two. That was certainly the opinion of one member of the English raiding party that destroyed Kelso Abbey in 1545. His name was Bartholomew Butler and he reported to his superiors that he thought this method of filling the moat was a practical proposal. Doctor Christopher Douglas, writing much later in the Statistical Account for Scotland of 1792, shared Butler's view adding, probably erroneously, that there existed a drawbridge over the moat.

Moving into the castle itself, the earliest building to come on record is the aforementioned Church of St John the Evangelist. Like the early Church of St Margaret on Edinburgh's Castle rock (also the earliest building on record in that castle), St John's was probably for use by the king, his sheriff and the soldiers who garrisoned Roxburgh. Most Norman castles had a central tower or *donjon* surrounded by an enclosing wall and Roxburgh was no exception. Called the Douglas Tower or the Bell Mount, it was the other important building inside the castle. It was this tower that David I imprisoned Malcolm Macheth, a Scots nobleman who had been the unsuccessful leader of a rebellion against the king. David kept him locked up at Roxburgh for twenty-three years. Macheth was of royal descent and therefore could not be killed, but was too politically dangerous to be set free. In 1154 Macheth was joined by his grandson Donald, who had also risen in revolt and had been captured at Whithorn in Galloway. The two men shared imprisonment in the Douglas Tower for three years until Malcolm Macheth died in 1157, probably Roxburgh Castle's longest continuous resident.

In 1174 David I's grandson, William the Lion, allowed himself to be captured by the English. He had invaded northern England and after an indifferent campaign, King William was taken by a small force of English knights who surprised him while he laid seige to Alnwick. The leader of the English knights, Ranulf Glanvill delivered up the hapless Scots king to Henry II of England. William was taken off to Falaise in Normandy where Henry forced him to accept English supremacy over his kingdom of Scotland, and to give up as surety for this the castles of Edinburgh, Berwick and Roxburgh. An English garrison took over the castle and probably exacted the cash and goods needed to maintain it and its new defenders from the surrounding burgh of Roxburgh. The first English occupation of the castle ended in 1189 when Roxburgh passed back into the control of the Scots king.

For more than a century Roxburgh Castle stood at the centre of Scottish politics. It acted as a royal court on several occasions and many of the king's recorded acts ended with the phrase 'at Roxburgh' and the date of the document. Legal matters were often dealt with at the castle and, in 1231, the Justiciar of Lothian held proceedings to settle local disputes in Roxburghshire. This can have been only one of many such sessions. In 1255 the strength of Roxburgh was recognised when the English faction at the quarrelling Scottish court kidnapped the young Alexander III and held him prisoner at Roxburgh. The English King Henry III was entertained there at that time with his entire retinue in attendance.

In the winter of 1282 Roxburgh Castle was the scene of a royal marriage between Lord Alexander, the son of Alexander III, and Margaret de Dampiere, daughter of the Count of Flanders. The marriage had been agreed and arranged the year before and the contract concluded in the Treaty of Roxburgh. The fact that the ceremony took place inside the castle walls, and not at Kelso Abbey, indicates that the Church of St John the Evangelist was still in use at the end of the thirteenth century. Lord Alexander died young in 1284 and the succession to the crown of Scotland became the subject of international concern. Edward I of England took a close interest in this and as overlord of the Scottish kings (as a result of the submission of William the Lion a century earlier) he began a process of interference which culminated in the Wars of Independence. By the end of the thirteenth century, Roxburgh Castle was once again occupied by the English.

In 1313 their occupation was brought to a swift end by a daring and famous assault. Sir James Douglas, better known as the Black Douglas, took back the castle by scaling the walls on its south side. The exploit was related by the poet, John Barbour, in his epic 'The Bruce'.

The Black Douglas assembled sixty of his men and, using their black cloaks to disguise their shape, they crept, like cattle in the dark, along the path that runs between the castle and the Teviot. They climbed the castle mount until they reached the foot of the walls and using hooked scaling ladders, they gained the battlements and overcame the guards. Barbour goes on:

> Then straightaway they went to the tower
> Where all the folk were, at that hour,
> singing and dancing at their ease,
> Or playing games, as they might please.

Douglas's men stormed into the hall and 'mercilessly slew' the feasting crowd, but then:

> The Warden saw how went the strife.
> (Sir Guillemin de Fiennes his name)
> And to the tower now he came
> With others of his company,
> And barred the entrance hastily.
> The rest, that then were left outside,
> Were taken prisoner or died,
> Unless perchance some leapt the wall.

That night held the hall,
Despite the chagrin of his foe,
His men were pausing to and fro
Throughout the castle all the night
Till on the morrow day was light

The warden in the tower stayed;
The greatest valour he displayed.
And seeing that, except the tower,
The castle was in Douglas' power
He strove with all his might to hold
The tower; but the archers bold
Sent arrows in such quantity
That thereby sore distressed was he
But, none the less, another day
He kept his enemies at bay.

Sir Guillemin eventually surrendered the tower to the Scots in return for safe conduct for himself and his men to England. Roxburgh Castle was of such strategic importance to the Scottish king that it was necessary to destroy it so that it did not fall into English hands. Barbour finishes off the episode:

When (the castle was taken) King Robert sent
His brother Edward, with intent
To tumble all the castle down,
Both walls and tower, to the ground.
A full great company took he;
And there they worked so busily
That very soon both tower and wall
Right to the ground were tumbled all.

The tower that held out for a day (while the rest of Roxburgh Castle had fallen to the Scots) was almost certainly the *donjon* where Malcolm Macheth was imprisoned in 1134. In honour of its captor it became known as the Douglas Tower and along with the feasting hall (which must have been adjacent to the Douglas Tower if Barbour's account is correct) and St John's church, it was one of three buildings inside the walls that stand out in the early sources.

The only other solid piece of information about the area inside the castle walls, during the period before the Wars of Independence, is contained in a charter of Earl Henry, son of David I. Along with some land in the burgh of Roxburgh, Henry gave the Church of St John *unam mansuram terrae infra castrum* — a piece of land inside the castle. The term *mansura* usually refers to a plot of land for the specific purpose of building a house. If the chaplain of St John's did in fact use his land inside the castle for that purpose, then that makes a total of four buildings that can be identified at Roxburgh Castle before the end of the thirteenth century: the Douglas Tower, the feasting hall, the Church of St John the Evangelist and its priest's manse.

3 Repairs and Renovations

After the famous Scottish victory at Bannockburn in 1314, Roxburgh Castle, on the frontier between the two nations, continued to be a focus of political activity. Edward Baliol, the son of King John Baliol, had a very real claim to the throne of Scotland and it was from Roxburgh that he proclaimed his cause. He intrigued continually with Edward III of England and after the disastrous battle at Halidon Hill in 1333 the castle passed back into English hands. In 1342 Alexander Ramsay took Roxburgh for the Scots king but by 1356 it was again occupied by the English and was to remain so for more than a century.

As a result of this very long occupation, it is a set of English records that give the first detailed picture of Roxburgh castle, or at least a substantial part of it. In 1378 a master mason, an Englishman called John Lewyn, rebuilt a bit of the castle for the new king, Richard II. The contract for the job and Lewyn's estimates for the cost of it have been preserved. They were written in Old French and here is a translation of the first section of the contract:

> This contract is made between the King and John Lewyn, master mason. It testifies that Lewyn will do the following works at Roxburgh Castle. That is: a stone and lime wall fortifying the side of the castle [starting] from the Watchtower end and towards the north and south right up to the other wall of the castle. And [Lewyn will build] three towers, one of them fifty feet in height above the ground, and the walls of these towers shall be six feet thick. Of these three towers, one will be in the middle while another will join on to the old wall of the castle in the north and the third will join it in the south. The middle tower will have a gate and two vaulted rooms, each of which will be twenty feet long and eleven and a half feet wide. Above the gate and the two rooms will be a hall forty feet long. There will be three fireplaces in the hall and above it there will be a private room with a fireplace.
>
> There will be a barbican [gatehouse] in front of the gate, ten feet long inside with a vaulted archway. The walls of the barbican will be five feet thick and a total height of twelve feet above and below the ground, and they will be fortified inside and outside. In the tower on the south wall there will be a vaulted larder and above it a vaulted kitchen with three fireplaces, and above the kitchen a private room with one fireplace. And in the tower in the north wall there will be four rooms, each one on top of the other with a private room

and a fireplace. Two of the four rooms will be vaulted. There will be dwelling houses [barracks?] along the walls between the towers, these will be twenty-four feet in length and eighteen feet wide. And the wall between the middle tower and the other two towers will be thirty feet high and all of ten and a half feet thick (so that there can be) vaulted passage-ways four and half feet wide in the middle of the wall leading from the middle tower to the other two towers.

And John Lewyn will build up to a height of thirty feet the old walls of the castle on both sides [north and south] that is, from the two towers in the south, and in the north right along to the *donjon* [Douglas Tower]. In the middle of each of these walls there will be a turret ten feet higher than the built up wall and there will be similar turrets, each six feet square, in the battlements.

The contract goes on to list materials needed by Lewyn, give details of his bill of around 1100 marks and finally ends with the clause that he is not bound to do this work if war starts with the Scots.

From this account it is obvious that the English king was prepared to spend a significant amount of money on Roxburgh to keep it in battle condition. Nevertheless, by 1416 the castle was again in need of repair. Henry V appointed two commissioners to survey the castle and list its particular defects. They were Sir John Clavering and Robert Harbotell and they seem to have known the site better than John Lewyn because their report is full of names for the fortifications of the castle, whereas the earlier contract does not even specify the area that will be repaired. However, many of the names used by Clavering and Harbotell have disappeared and the picture of Roxburgh Castle that they describe can only be guessed at. Here is a translation of their report, from the Latin:

To begin with, a wooden turnpike [turnstile-type gate] at the entrance of the West Gate has decayed. At Billop's Tower the wooden parapet of the same wall in the same place [as the gate] has decayed and needs to be mended. This castle should have two iron gates; one at the entrance of the castle and the other at the *donjon* called the Douglas Tower. The roof-covering and parapets of this tower because they have been blown away by the wind right down to the rafters. A tower on Teviot-side should be repaired. A new wall should be built from the Douglas Tower down to the Teviot. The base of the wall from the Douglas Tower to the East Gate and the parapet of the tower are on the point of falling unless speedily repaired. The base of Stokhouse Tower is completely broken apart and the tower is on the point of falling. There are two posterns [small gates] above Teviot-side that should have iron gates. The base of the Round Tower towards Teviot-side is completely broken apart and the parapet on this tower has decayed so much that soldiers can neither defend themselves nor the castle unless it is speedily repaired. The wall from the Round Tower to the Stannegarret [Barbican — see Lewyn's contract] is ruined and full of holes, and on the point of falling unless repaired quickly. It is necessary to have a new wall from Westpostern up to Teviot-side to safeguard the castle. The foundations of the Postern Tower are completely broken and need to be mended and there needs to be a new buttress at that tower. The foundations of the tower at Westhead are completely broken and on the point of falling. There should be a new tower at Brown's Stable because there is a dangerous place where one man could climb up and enter without a ladder. The Neville Tower is ruinous and almost broken down because of decayed roofing, and the parapet of this tower is decayed. The base of the Long Wall is breached and ought to be repaired. The Draw-Well, which Sir Robert de Umphraville recently repaired, is completely broken because of decayed timbering, because the timbering of this spring is completely rotted. There is in this castle a Hall of eight roof-couples without walls, covering or beams and the whole timber work is completely decayed. And there is neither artillery nor munitions nor victuals or any of the things necessary for the safeguarding of the castle. And neither soldiers nor servants of the king [of England] dare to linger there for long unless the castle is quickly repaired. And there certainly ought to be a mill inside the castle for grinding the corn there. And John [Clavering] and Robert [Harbotell] state that there are many defects in this castle which should be speedily repaired for the fortification and safeguarding of this castle.

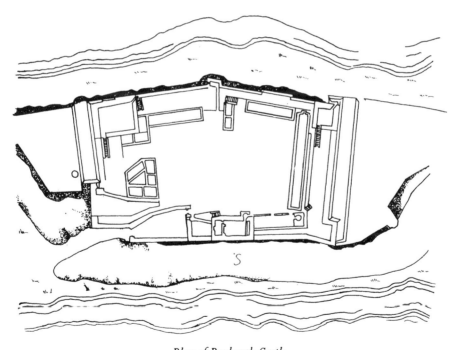

Plan of Roxburgh Castle

These repairs were not carried out immediately and Roxburgh Castle had to wait until 1419 for the work of re-fortification to begin in earnest. The following year 500 stones of iron were sent up from England to make the iron gates recommended by Clavering and Harbotell, and the castle was provisioned and manned against the Scots.

4 James II killed at the seige of Roxburgh Castle

The English king held Roxburgh until 1460 when a huge army led by James II attacked the castle. James used large cannons to break down the walls, and it was while one was firing that it exploded. A piece of the cannon struck James II and killed him. Queen Mary arrived from Edinburgh with the young James III to carry on the seige until the Scots finally took Roxburgh and it was 'doung to the ground'. James III was crowned at Kelso Abbey after the castle was secured and destroyed.

5 The Decline of the Castle

In 1488 Roxburgh Castle was probably only a ruin of little military importance with no garrison of Scots or English soldiers. James IV granted to Walter Ker of Cessford the *castrum et locum castri vocatum le Castlested*, that is, the castle and the area of the castle known as the Castlestead. This seems to suggest that at best Roxburgh was reduced to a tower (probably the Douglas Tower) and an enclosing wall around the site of the old castle. Certainly the king can have attached little strategic importance to Roxburgh if he could give it away to Walter Ker whose own stronghold was only eight miles to the southwest.

The English invaded Scotland in 1545 under the Earl of Hertford and devastated much of the Border countryside including the great abbeys of the area. King Henry VIII wanted to consolidate his military position in the south of Scotland and he instructed Hertford to examine the site of the 'castell of old Rockesburghe, being within a quarter of a myle of Kelso.' Hertford reported that it was 'altogether ruyned and fallen downe . . . it is one of the strongest seates of a fortresse that I have seen. And, forasmoch as it has been in your Highnes porgenytors handes herestofore, I wold the rather wishe that your Majeste shuld make a forte there, which is farr the stronger seate and moch more propice place than Kelso'. By October 1547 work on the building of the fort was well advanced and a plan of it was made by a surveyor called Rydgeway. His plan has come down to us in the collection of the Duke of Rutland and it is the only plan of the castle in existence. The fort only covered part of the site of the old castle leaving the western and eastern ends outside its walls. There are only one or two place-names on the Rutland plan and it is very difficult to relate it to the survey done by Clavering and Harbotell in 1416 and the building work outlined by John Lewyn in 1378. Nevertheless, it is possible to organise a conjectural reconstruction of Roxburgh Castle at the time of its greatest importance if all three sources are taken together.

Beginning at the West Gate, it is likely that it was always where Rydgeway places it on his plan and it was protected by two towers. The 1416 survey notes a Postern Tower which may be the 'Mownt' next to the 'Base Cowrtte' of 1547 and Billop's Tower was probably to the north of the Base Cowrtte. There are some remains of the West Gate visible today. The East Gate of the castle was the main concern of John Lewyn's contract and the 'Round Tower towards Teviot-side' of 1416 was probably his central tower. The Barbican built by Lewyn is possibly the 'Stannegarret' of 1416 — the name meaning a watchtower or lookout to the north, the direction of any likely attack by the Scots and the direction from which James II was firing that fatal fusillade. The French word used in Lewyn's contract is *veille* which means watch-tower. This eastern part of the castle is not formally included in the Rutland plan, but there is a slight hint of the Round Tower's existence in Rydgeway's drawing of the outer defence works on the east of his plan. Today there are visible remains of both the Round Tower and the Barbican perched on the Kelso end of the castle site. Very little indeed has survived of the northern curtain wall, because that was the side most exposed to artillery fire in contrast to the south side which has had to suffer much less depradation. Only a large tree-covered mound shows where the Douglas Tower once stood and it is the highest part of the site. In the southern wall it is still possible to see where the two postern gates mentioned in the 1416 survey are. There is also a noticeably thicker part of the southern wall which may be the location of the south-eastern tower of the fort of 1547.

By the year 1544 Roxburgh Castle had reached a sorry state. Some reivers based at Wark Castle were in the Kelso area on the lookout for plunder. Here is a report of part of their expedition:

> On the 29th of August the horsemen of Wark rode into Scotland, and lay in the cornfields beside Old Roxburgh, to the number of forty men, or thereabouts, and the rest kept their horses. So they seized the Lord of Cesford's goods that came forth out of the castle, and forth out of the byres beside the castle to the number of 23 kye and oxen, 12 horses and mares.

Good only for the stabling of horses and for cow byres — and not the safest of protection at that — Roxburgh Castle had sunk to its lowest ebb.

Doubtless a careful archaeological dig would reveal a great deal about Roxburgh Castle and exchange all of this conjecture for some hard facts. The locations would be found of the Church of St John, the feasting hall, the priest's house, the Neville Tower and all the other features of what was one of the greatest castles of mediaeval Scotland.

6 The Burgh of Roxburgh

There are some ruined walls and towers left to suggest the shape and scale of Roxburgh Castle, but nothing whatever remains of the mediaeval town that lay on the haugh-land to the east. Even though Roxburgh was one of the four most important burghs in Scotland during the twelfth and thirteenth centuries with four churches to serve it, schools for its children, a royal mint, and a sizeable population, it has entirely disappeared. There is now no trace of any building, not one stone left standing upon another. Aerial photography shows nothing: no tell-tale changes in the colour of the grass and certainly no outlines of any large structures or the circuit of Roxburgh's mediaeval walls show up at any season of the year. It is an extraordinary disappearance for a town that was, during the reign of David I, as important a burgh as Edinburgh, Dunfermline or Berwick.

Perhaps because nothing can now be seen of it the history of Roxburgh has been largely ignored. Yet it is possible to discover a good deal about what it was like in its prime by reading through the written records left by the monastic foundations made by David I and his subjects in the Border country. The four great abbeys of Kelso, Dryburgh, Melrose and Jedburgh had all been given property in or revenue from Roxburgh.

The town first comes on record in 1113 with David I's foundation of the Abbey of St Mary and St John at Selkirk. Roxburgh was as prosperous a place as the (then Scottish) burgh of Berwick, or at least the king believed that it was because David I granted the same revenue from each town to the new abbey. When, in 1128, he moved Selkirk's monks down the Tweed to Kelso, the place was clearly thought to be a mere suburb of Roxburgh. 'Selkirk Abbey was moved to Kelso beside Roxburgh' the records say, so that David could concentrate power around his favourite burgh.

7 The Wool Trade

Situated at the confluence of the Tweed and Teviot at points where both rivers could be crossed, Roxburgh stood in a pivoted economic position. The town grew up at the centre of the international trade in the raw wool produced on the Border sheep ranches, many of which were managed by the great abbeys. Wool merchants came from as far away as Flanders and Northern Italy to buy the wool needed to supply their expanding cloth-making industries. Much of it was exported by sea through Berwick where the Flemings maintained a place of business known as the Red Hall. When this was burned by the English in 1296 there were thirty Flemings living there. German merchants also had a trade centre in Berwick which they called the White Hall, and there is some slight evidence that a similar centre existed in the town of Roxburgh. It was known as the Black Hall and it appears in a document dated 1330, when it belonged to Margaret de Auldton, the wife of a wealthy burgess of Roxburgh, Roger de Auldton.

The only two tangible remains of the old town of Roxburgh serve to further emphasise the close connections between it, the wool trade and Flanders. In the western porch of Kelso Abbey, the Galilee Porch, there are two tombstones that were taken from the churches of Roxburgh before they were obliterated. On one there is a carving of a pair of sheep shears and, on the other side of the stone, the inscription 'Here lies Johanna Bulloc who died in the year of Our Lord 1371. Pray for her soul'. Johanna was the wife of a merchant, Robert Bulloc, whose business is symbolised by the sheep shears on the tombstone.

Johanna's bodily remains lie somewhere beneath the haugh in the place that was the graveyard of the Church of St James. The second stone is also from the fourteenth century but it came from a different cemetery, that of the Franciscan Church of St Peter. It was originally quarried from the distinctive *pierre bleu* limestone which comes from the area around Tournai in Flanders. The tombstone was made for a man whose name is not now readable but the word 'mercer' or cloth merchant can still be made out. The lettering is done in the Lombardic style and the name of Roxburgh is misspelt, suggesting that the stone was carved as well as quarried in Flanders. It is perhaps no accident that the only survivals from the old town of Roxburgh are two testaments to one of the main reasons for its early development, the wool trade. The high incidence of the surname Fleming around Kelso is another reminder of the merchants who sailed the North Sea to buy the wool from the backs of Border sheep.

8 Roxburgh's Churches and the Site of the Town

By the early part of the thirteenth century Roxburgh's thriving population required four churches to cater for its spiritual needs. These would probably have all been of stone construction with cemeteries around them, which makes their total obliteration all the more surprising. Graveyards usually show up on aerial photographs as regularly placed rectangular shapes and stone foundations, being difficult to destroy and awkward to dig out of the ground, often show up very readily.

The earliest-mentioned Church of St John the Evangelist was inside the castle walls (although its priest did own property in the town) and it served the garrison and the frequently noble, and occasionally royal, visitors to Roxburgh Castle. The churches of St James and Holy Sepulchre both seem to have been parish churches used by the ordinary inhabitants of the burgh, while the fourth of Roxburgh's places of worship was a Franciscan Friary dedicated to St Peter. The location of all these churches is recorded in written sources and, in the absence of any maps of the mediaeval town, they can be used as reference points around which the jigsaw of Roxburgh might be assembled.

It is certain that the burgh lay to the east of the castle on the flat-topped ridge known as Kay Brae. All the documentary evidence implies that this is the site, although there exists no explicit statement to that effect. An old map of Floors estate, made in 1798, does offer corroboration. It identifies an oblong area to the east of the castle on Kay Brae as 'High Town', an unmistakeable reference to mediaeval Roxburgh.

The ridge on which the town lay runs on a west to east axis from the east gate of the castle, falling away on three sides down to the flat haugh which is bounded by the Tweed to the north and east and the Teviot to the south. The three churches outside the castle give an idea of the eventual scale of the settlement. St James, the most frequently mentioned of Roxburgh's churches and the last to go out of existence (in 1649), lay to the north of Kay Brae, between it and the Tweed. In the nineteenth century its cemetery was discovered (and Johanna Bulloc's tombstone) when the ground was being levelled for horse-racing. The church's name was perpetuated in St James' Fair which was held annually on 5 August as recently as the 1930s on the piece of haugh-land known to local people as the Fairgreen. The Church of Holy Sepulchre is mentioned only once in documents relating to Dryburgh Abbey and it seems to have been more centrally situated in the town, on the south side of the main street.

9 *The Franciscan Friary of St Peter*

Much more is known about the Franciscan Friary of St Peter at Roxburgh. The Franciscans came into being in the early thirteenth century as part of a movement towards the reform of the catholic church. Inspired by the example of St Francis, they were a preaching order who were sustained only by the giving of alms, in an attempt to safeguard the purity of their lives. Called the Greyfriars after the colour of their habit, the Franciscans made for the centres of population in Western Europe where their preaching could be most effective.

In 1231 they arrived at Berwick, probably the largest burgh in Scotland at that time. The following year King Alexander II gave land in Roxburgh for the building of a Friary. The site was to the south of the town walls, between them and the Teviot as it runs eastward to join the Tweed. No trace remains of the Friary that was dedicated to St Peter but its name is remembered in 'Friars Cottage', a house that stands by the bridge over the Teviot, and the southern part of the haugh was known first as 'Friars Farm' and later as 'Friars Haugh'. The Statistical Account of 1794 adds a little more information:

> [There] . . . stood a convent of the mendicants of the order of St Francis. Within these few years, a fine arch of their church remained, and other parts of the building, which are now almost wholly effaced. This monastery was consecrated by William, Bishop of Glasgow, in the year 1235.

Bishop William also mediated in a dispute that Kelso Abbey had with the incoming Friars, and the following document records how the affair was settled:

> To all the faithful in Christ, greetings. Be it known to your whole community that in the year of Grace 1235, on the morning of May 4th, there appeared before us at Roxburgh, Herbert, Abbot of Kelso and Friar Martin, Warden of the Friars Minor in Scotland. And they came to an agreement concerning the consecration of a cemetery attached to the Church of St Peter. We, being satisfied that the Friars Minor are privileged to bury their former brethern, wherever they possessed certain houses [friaries], and none others . . . We consecrated the cemetery on the same day, under the provision that the rights of the monks of Kelso over their churches should suffer no prejudice.

Evidently Abbot Herbert was worried that Kelso's monopoly of the business of burials, exercised at Roxburgh through her dependent churches, might be broken, and William of Glasgow went to some trouble to reassure him.

In 1296 the Warden of Roxburgh Friary, Adam Blunt, played a historic part in the beginnings of the Wars of Independence. On behalf of King John Baliol, he delivered a document to Edward I at Berwick which denied the supremacy that the English king had tried to assert over Scotland. During his Scottish campaigns, Edward lodged twice at the Friary, in 1296 and in 1301.

King Robert the Bruce took an interest in the Franciscans and in 1332 he gave them cash as compensation for the theft of valuables and books, done, it is claimed, at the instigation of the monks of Kelso. An allowance was also made for the repair of the roof of St Peter's, but the materials intended for it were diverted to Berwick in a hasty attempt to shore up the town's fortifications against the impending invasion by Edward III. A year later it seems that English Friars had occupied St Peter's and in 1336/7 the English king paid them cash for the use of the ford of the Teviot for 205 days. This transaction makes it clear that the Friars controlled the ford of the rivers on the southern road out of Roxburgh, towards England. In order to safeguard their revenue from this source, the Friars must have built some sort of toll-gate on their bank of the Teviot. Today there is an old cauld about 100 metres south of Teviot Bridge, and that may be all that remains of the Friars' ford.

In 1460 the death of James II occurred during the seige of Roxburgh Castle. It is recorded that the king was brought first to the Friary of St Peter where he received the last rites of the church. A mass was celebrated on the anniversary of the king's death and endowment was made to the Friars for this express purpose. If St Peter's was the nearest church to the scene of the fatal accident that befell James II, it is likely that it happened on the Roxburgh side of the Tweed, and not where tradition places the event, on the Floors side of the river. Both St James' and Kelso Abbey itself would have been nearer, if James II was wounded on the north side of the Tweed.

After 1460 the fortunes of Roxburgh Friary waned along with those of the town and Kelso Abbey. Like the latter the Friary is listed as one of the places burned by Hertford in 1545 and in 1547 it was still in ruins. At that time, an English captain called Bulmer found work for his soldiers in building a guard-house at the gate of the Friary, and in roofing over part of the church as stabling. Bulmer probably created this military post out of the ruins of St Peter's to command the ford of the Teviot and thereby prevent a surprise attack on Roxburgh Castle.

The last warden of Roxburgh Friary was Henry Cant and when he died in 1564 the Kers of Cessford, who were gradually taking over the area of Old Roxburgh, bought the rights to run the ford and the ferries over the Teviot. The ferries continued in use until the completion of the present bridge over the Teviot in 1794.

10 Walls, a New Town and a Bridge

Both the Teviot and the Tweed gave Roxburgh's site natural defences but, nevertheless, mention is made of both walls and ditches constructed to protect the town from attack. There was a West Gate and a wall between the steep castle slopes and its moat, and the Tweed in the north. On its southern and eastern flanks there was a wall encircling the burgh — the Friary is described as lying 'outside the walls of Roxburgh'. To the north and east of Kay Brae the documents tell of the growth of a *novus burgus* or new town as the population of Roxburgh quickly expanded. This may have focused on the Church of St James which was dedicated during the same period as the new town is mentioned. At all events it was rapidly absorbed into the original settlement since no further reference is made to the *novus burgus* after 1150.

Much later, in 1330, developments on the north side of Roxburgh appear on record again. This time it concerns the building of a bridge over the Tweed. There has been much conjecture over the early existence of a bridge between Roxburgh and Kelso, and the more frequent mention of ferries has persuaded some that those supplied the only means of crossing the Tweed. In 1330 the computation of rents owed in Roxburgh to the royal court makes provision for the rebuilding of a bridge over the Tweed. This work was evidently carried out because three years later Sir Andrew Murray was trapped 'on the narrow bridge' by Edward Baliol's men as he attempted to capture the town for David II, Baliol's rival. When Roxburgh was under English control in 1369, Edward III directed the burgh of Berwick to pay forty marks for the repair of the bridge at Roxburgh, and in doing so the king was probably trying his best to restore working trading links between both towns. But by 1398 Roxburgh's bridge had again suffered. The peace commissioners between England and Scotland heard a bill of complaint against Sir William Stewart and the son of the Earl of Douglas for breaking down the bridge at Roxburgh. In 1411 the bridge was broken again and perhaps it is a measure of the economic decline of the burgh that there is no record of it being repaired.

The tremendously destructive English expeditions of 1545 and 1547 give valuable information about what Roxburgh's bridge may have looked like and where it stood. The same small army that re-fortified the Friary set up their camp nearby in that part of the haugh known as Vigorous Haugh (after a burgess of Roxburgh, Thomas de Vigurus who owned land there). The English had in their number a man called William Patten, who later wrote down what he saw during the campaign in a book *The Expedicion into Scotland*. He relates how impressed the English commanders were with the defensive qualities of Roxburgh Castle's site and the haugh-land around. He goes on:

> Over this [the Tweed] between Kelso and Roxburgh there has been a great

stone bridge, with arches, which the Scots in time past have broken, so that we should not come to them.

Sixteen days after he had observed this, Patten described how the English army struck their camp. Apparently they were travelling east:

This morning, soon after seven of the clock, my lords passed over the Tweed here. The best place for getting over (which was against the west end of our camp, and not far from the broken arches of the broken bridge) was set with great stones in the bottom so uneven of ground that . . . many of our footmen and horsemen were greatly in peril . . . many carriages were overthrown . . . and one or two drowned.

Patten's account provides two valuable pieces of information and one telling observation. Roxburgh bridge was made of stone and it was an arched bridge. Some idea of what it looked like can be got from the two late mediaeval bridges at Berwick and Dumfries. More important is the clue to its location. Patten puts the ruined bridge to the west of the English encampment which makes it north-west of the site of the town of Roxburgh. That means that Wester Kelso probably developed as a bridge-end settlement much in the way that Tweedmouth grew up at the southern end of Berwick's bridge during the same period.

There is a faint echo of this arrangement in the wooden briges that used to be specially built over the Tweed for St James' Fair on 5 August. Because of the extent of Floors Estate, the temporary bridge had to be built from the Cobby over the haugh. At the Kelso end stalls were often set to catch trade from the people travelling over the bridge to the fair at Roxburgh.

11 The Royal Mint and the Schools

Although it is no longer possible to plot the location of Roxburgh's royal mint, there is one scrap of information about the length of time it was in production. In the mid-twelfth century Scottish silver pennies were minted at Roxburgh (and not at Kelso as some historians claim) and these were among the first Scottish coins to come into circulation. A large coin hoard was found at Mellendean on the south bank of the Tweed opposite Kelso, and one might reasonably have expected to find locally minted coins well represented. However, out of the 890 coins discovered, by far the majority were English (704) in origin, while 103 came from mints in Flanders and only 65 were Scottish coins. Most of the money was dated around 1296 and it seems that by this date Roxburgh's mint had ceased to operate. The origins of the coins also give a good indication of the directions of local trade and as ever England was proving to be Scotland's most active trading contact.

Very little is known about the schools at Roxburgh apart from the fact that there was more than one and that, in 1241, Thomas was rector of them. He was doubtless a priest whose livelihood was provided by Kelso Abbey. It is possible that the schools were attached to Roxburgh's two parish churches, St James' and Holy Sepulchre.

12 Roxburgh's Streets

Three of the street names in the old town have come down to us. The 'Headgate' is probably the same street as 'King's Street' which is the most frequently cited address in Roxburgh. The merchant, Roger de Auldton, had occasion in 1330 to set down various bits of information about his property in the town. He was giving part of it to the Church of St James and to be sure that all parties were clear about what he owned, he gave the exact location of his 'burgages' or town properties. Here is a translation from Roger's deed to the Church of St James:

> [I give] three burgages of mine in the town of Roxburgh in the street called King's Street. One of these lies on the southern side of the street between the land of Uchtred Miller on the west and the land of Robert Sellar on the east. The second burgage lies on the northern side of the street with land belonging to Uchtred Miller on either side. The third burgage lies on the northern side of the street with the land that used to belong to Harvey of Heiton on the west and on the east the land of the priest of St John's Church [inside the castle].

It is clear from this that King's Street/Headgate ran from east to west along the top of the ridge from Kay Brae up to the east gate of Roxburgh Castle. It is easier to visualise this arrangement if one thinks of the Headgate and King's Street as being similar to Edinburgh's Castle Hill and High Street as they run from the gate of Edinburgh Castle down the ridge that lies to the east of it. Although on a smaller and less dramatic scale, it is feasible that Roxburgh was rather like mediaeval Edinburgh in layout.

The other surviving street-name from Roxburgh is Market Street. Margaret de Auldton inherited town property from William Pelliparius, a burgess of the old burgh. His lands were:

> One tenement lying in Market Street between the tenement of William Bosvill in the north and the tenement of the Abbot of Melrose in the south. And one tenement lying behind the shops and the tenement of Richard of Killor on the west. And one tenement lying behind the shops and between the

> tenement of Richard of Kelso on the south and John Knoicce on the north side.
> And also one tenement in King's Street lying on the south side between the
> tenement of the chaplain of Roger de Auldton on the east and the tenement of
> Roger, son of Uchtred Miller on the west.

So, Market Street ran south to north, probably down the northern slopes of Kay Brae towards the Tweed and St James' Church. If the street had run towards the Teviot, it would have come up against the property of the Franciscan Friary. Furthermore, being the site of Roxburgh's market, the street would have to be conveniently situated on the northern side of town for people bringing in their goods across the Tweed bridge.

The shops mentioned in the document were probably more like stalls, not permanently fixed in the street, and the town properties would have stood behind them, rather in the way the modern market is set up in Berwick. Market Street was certainly the location of Roxburgh's weekly market and also probably the place where the great annual Fair of St James was held.

13 St James' Fair

As well as its importance to the export trade in wool, Roxburgh lay on a busy land route from England into Southern Scotland. The connection between English commerce and the main town of the Border country was obviously strengthened greatly when the English occupied Roxburgh Castle during the reign of William the Lion, from 1175 to 1189, and the overwhelming preponderance of English coins in the Mellendean hoard adds weight to this view. St James' Fair probably started when English merchants could enjoy the military protection of their own king as they traded the wool and hides produced by the farmers and herdsmen of the Border country.

Because a new fair at Dumbarton (too far away simply to copy a neighbour's practices) was specifically given the customs or codes of practice used at St James' Fair, it is likely that Roxburgh held the most important fair in Scotland during the thirteenth century. It is clear that St James' Fair remained a royal fair even after the disappearance of the royal burgh of Roxburgh because it had to be the Provost of the royal burgh of Jedburgh (and not the baillies of the non-royal burgh of Kelso just across the Tweed) who came to the site of the old town to 'cry the fair' by ringing a bell to announce it. His hand-bell probably replaced the church bells of St James', the Fair Church.

The 1930s saw the last of the ancient fairs at Roxburgh. By that time

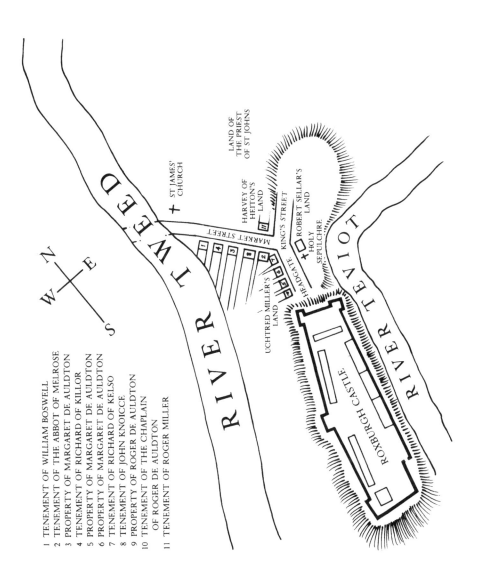

Plan of Roxburgh

1 TENEMENT OF WILLIAM BOSWELL
2 TENEMENT OF THE ABBOT OF MELROSE
3 PROPERTY OF MARGARET DE AULDTON
4 TENEMENT OF RICHARD OF KILLOR
5 PROPERTY OF MARGARET DE AULDTON
6 PROPERTY OF MARGARET DE AULDTON
7 TENEMENT OF RICHARD OF KELSO
8 TENEMENT OF JOHN KNOICCE
9 PROPERTY OF ROGER DE AULDTON
10 TENEMENT OF THE CHAPLAIN
    OF ROGER DE AULDTON
11 TENEMENT OF ROGER MILLER

RIVER TWEED

RIVER TEVIOT

ST JAMES'
CHURCH

LAND OF
THE PRIEST
OF ST JOHNS

HARVEY OF
HEITON'S
LAND

ROBERT SELLAR'S
LAND

KING'S STREET

HOLY
SEPULCHRE

MARKET STREET

HEADGATE

UCHTRED MILLER'S
LAND

ROXBURGH CASTLE

their main purpose was the trade in horses and ponies carried on by the gypsies (known locally as 'muggers' which seems to be a corruption of the word Magyar, a term sometimes used to mean gypsy although it really means Hungarian) who were allowed to camp on the Fairgreen only during the sales, at the beginning of August.

14 Roxburgh declines

The Wars of Independence made the Borders an area of prime military importance as armies crossed and recrossed it. Although Roxburgh had been burned at least thrice, in 1207, 1216 and 1243 (its buildings being mainly of wood and thatch, except for the castle and churches, a dry summer and a careless candle could combine to reduce the town to ashes) its gradual destruction began in earnest as sporadic Border warfare seriously eroded its economic importance. Politically the castle and town swung between English and Scots occupation, making its health and development in no-one's long-term interest. If the Scots were likely to attack and destroy the town at any time, there was no motive for the English to try to build up Roxburgh's trade and her wealth, and vice-versa. Quite simply, neither the English nor the Scots wanted Roxburgh to become too important in case they lost it.

Documents of the period of the Wars of Independence relate that the burgesses of Roxburgh swore allegiance to the English King Edward I, and in 1309 his son, Edward II, allowed them to raise a tax to pay for the complete walling-in of the town. This probably meant the replacement of the previous earthen ramparts and ditches with stone walls. In 1311 a small English garrison was sent to reinforce the burgesses against attack from the Scots but instead of helping to defend the burgh, the English apparently looted it and imprisoned some of the population. The Scots retook the castle and town in 1313-14, but it fell under English influence again in 1334. Eight years later, it was once again the Scots' turn to hold Roxburgh when Sir Alexander Ramsay expelled the English. After the battle at Neville's Cross in 1346 when David II was ransomed, Roxburgh again came under English domination and that was to last more than a century, until 1460 when James II was killed by a bursting cannon at the last full-scale seige of the castle.

Although they did not finally succeed in capturing the castle until 1460, the Scots did manage to burn the town twice, in 1377 and again in 1398. The fourteenth century saw the decline of Roxburgh with the militarisation of the Border. Even the burgh's weekly market suffered from competition across the Tweed, with the rising village of Wester Kelso near the wealthy abbey. Roxburgh's stone buildings doubtless fell prey to Kelsonian builders on the lookout for dressed, already quarried stone that lay only a short distance away. Despite the fact that the English restored the castle somewhat in the sixteenth century, the decline of the great mediaeval town of Roxburgh was almost complete by 1649, when its parish church of St James could muster only six communicants.

The 1330s was the only period after the Wars of Independence when any real attempts at renewing the burgh were made. Cash was raised from the population for the rebuilding of the Tweed Bridge in 1330. Seven years later, two grants of funds were made to Ednam Hospital and for the building of Roxburgh Hospital, now better known as Maison Dieu. The same year the priest of St John's in the castle received funds for the rebuilding of his church.

However, records dated 1501 give the strong impression of a deserted settlement. In assessing the rents owed in old Roxburgh (by this time known as 'Auld-Roxburgh') no reference is made to the streets or burgages as in the 1330s. Instead, the site is split up into five areas: Castlewait and Tounefield (belonging to the Kers), Castlemot, Orchart and Tounsteid (belonging to the Friary of St Peter). Even those names have now passed out of use, leaving no trace of where the town stood.

It is not quite true to say that absolutely nothing remains of any of Roxburgh's buildings. At the bottom of the path leading to the east gate of the castle, under the roots of a chestnut tree, the first few courses of a stone building are clearly visible. Since these courses are well below the ground level of the rest of the wooded ridge leading from the castle, it is likely that archaeology would reveal the remains of some of the mediaeval buildings in the Headgate or King's Street.

Part Three

KELSO ABBEY, 1128 to 1587

THE EXISTENCE of Roxburgh and its castle provided the background that David I wanted for his new foundation of Tironian monks and that is why he moved their settlement down the Tweed valley from Selkirk to Kelso. That is also the reason why a short account of the town and castle should come before the early history of Kelso itself — to set it in its proper context. The close proximity of the royal burgh of Roxburgh meant that the abbey became powerful and wealthy almost immediately, and David I's patronage of this, his first major religious endowment, and the reasons for it need to be looked at from the outset.

1 The Tironian Monks

David was obviously impressed by the Tironian order. He probably came to hear of them while he was a young man living at the court of the English king, Henry I. The order was founded by St Bernard the Less, a monk who had withdrawn from a fanatical preaching brotherhood to start his own monastic community in the wooded country around Tiron in Picardy, in northern France. In 1109, Bernard laid down new and stricter regulations for his monks to live by. Although their rule was based on the old ideas of Benedictine monasticism, it did include the new element of craftmanship. Each Tironian was required to learn and practise a trade of some kind: carpentry, smithing, milling or farming, for example. St Bernard insisted on this not only to keep his monks from the corrupting nature of idleness but also to develop the resources of what was initially a very poor community trying to survive in the forests of northern France.

How then did Earl David manage to find out about this remote new brotherhood? It seems likely that the agent for introducing the Tironians (and perhaps the idea of planting a convent of them at Selkirk, in David's earldom of Tweeddale) to David was his chaplain and tutor, John. Later to become Bishop of Glasgow and reviver of that diocese when his young master became King of Scotland, John seems to have had close connections with the abbey at Tiron. In 1136 he was out of favour with the papacy and it is interesting to note that Bishop John chose to exile himself to Tiron, where he spent two years before changing circumstances allowed his political rehabilitation in Scotland. In addition, it is significant that the first plantation of the new monks was at Selkirk, in what was later to be John's own diocese of Glasgow. Generally speaking, the early history of Kelso Abbey and its daughter-houses also evidences, at the very least, John's sustained interest in the order of Tiron.

On a practical level, the tradesmanlike nature of the new monks probably attracted the young David, anxious to build up his inheritance of the huge tract of land known as Tweeddale. Possibly also, the zeal and simplicity of the Tironians made them appear the most dynamic of the new orders, best able to survive at Selkirk which was, in 1113, little more than a wilderness. Certainly Earl David was enthusiastic about the monks of Tiron because in 1116 he undertook the arduous journey to the French monastery to visit St Bernard the Less himself. Sadly, the old man died only a few days before the arrival of the young Scottish earl.

Three years before his trip to Tiron, Earl David had already brought thirteen monks from France (the number thirteen is not an accident, it is an imitation of Christ and the twelve apostles) to Selkirk. As has been made clear, the Tironians were a reformed monastic order, amongst the earliest of the 'new' orders to be created out of the old and decaying structure of conventual life in France. But it needs to be emphasised that this foundation at Selkirk in 1113 was remarkable for one major reason: it was the first appearance in Britain of the new orders and it is a testament to David's enterprise that he made such a bold and risky choice in bringing them to his Scottish Border country.

2 Selkirk

He probably chose Selkirk because it had pre-existing religious associations. The early forms of the name *Selechirche* include the Old English word *circe* meaning a church, and the Old Norse word *sele* meaning a hall may be the first part of the name. It was not uncommon in the Borders to site new religious foundations in places with a history of ecclesiastical association. Both Jedburgh and Melrose (St Cuthbert had been linked with

Old Melrose for centuries) were holy places where twelfth century abbeys were founded, as indeed was Kelso, the location of the early church of St Mary.

3 Relations with Tiron

Ralph was the first Abbot of Selkirk. He reigned for three years until 1116 when the founder of the order, St Bernard the Less, died. The monks at Tiron elected Ralph to succeed him and a monk by the name of William was chosen to go to Selkirk to take over the leadership of the new community. When Earl David visited Tiron in 1116 it is likely that he brought William and another group of monks back to Scotland with him.

In 1119, William became the third Abbot of Tiron when his predecessor, Ralph, died suddenly. This again left Selkirk leaderless until the monks elected one of their number, Herbert, to be the new Abbot of Selkirk. He reigned for 28 years and gave the abbey some continuity of direction. The promotion of both Ralph and William from Selkirk to Tiron shows how close links were between daughter and mother house, and it shows how important the Tironians considered Selkirk to be since they seem to have sent their best men to run the new abbey. This first generation of monks in southern Scotland were, after all, Frenchmen and they must have been grateful to escape the relative harshness of the Scottish climate by returning to northern France.

Certainly the difficulties of travelling between Selkirk and Tiron made an impression on Abbot William. The journey is about 700 miles long and in mediaeval times it was done without benefit of made roads — in fact the quickest method of travel was probably by sea from Berwick to one of the Channel ports and thence inland to Tiron. At all events William had experienced the journey himself, and when he became abbot of Tiron he decided that the abbots of Selkirk need not make the trip to the annual chapter of the Tironian Order. Each year, all the abbots of Tironian monasteries were required to attend the annual general meeting, of the Order at the mother house of Tiron. Since the journey took so long from Selkirk — and William himself had presumably made it at least thrice — he allowed all his overseas abbots to attend only once every three years. As a footnote to this tale of toing and froing between the Borders and Northern France it is worth recording that the Abbey of Tiron was given a grant of one ship annually to call into any Scottish port and there to be free of customs duty. These taxes were a royal business and this is an example of David trying to make life easier for the Tironians and their efforts to communicate with their Scottish abbeys. Although the Abbey of Tiron had the grant changed to one of cash rather than immunity from customs, they obviously regarded it as important since there are two separate occasions in the thirteenth and fourteenth centuries when they had to remind the king that the cash had not been paid.

As Selkirk/Kelso became a wealthy and politically important abbey under the patronage of David I and his family, the abbots of the Scottish house began to think differently about their relationship with Tiron. The Chronicle of Melrose Abbey records in 1176 that John, Abbot of Kelso, was in dispute with Walter, Abbot of Tiron, about who should take precedence over the other. In effect, John was claiming that, although Tiron had been pre-eminent in the Tironian order as the mother house, the power and wealth of Kelso had raised it to a primary position. Political realities made it necessary for Walter of Tiron to recognise that John was his superior. No decision on this issue is recorded by the Melrose chronicler but some indication of John of Kelso's standing at the Vatican, the court where such disputes would be settled, can be gleaned from the fact tht in 1165 Pope Alexander III awarded John a bishop's mitre. That meant that the Abbot of Kelso had equal rank with a bishop and was accountable directly to the Pope. In the context of the Scottish church, that marked Kelso as a potent force, not just a convent of monks retiring in seclusion from the real world.

4 Kelso and the Independence of the Scottish Church

That pre-eminence had been the case from very early on in Kelso's history. When Abbot Herbert oversaw the move of Selkirk Abbey down to Kelso and into the centre of political life in Southern Scotland, it was clear that his patron, David I, intended the Abbots of Kelso to be important men. When he resigned from Kelso in 1147 Herbert became Bishop of Glasgow, succeeding John, the young king's teacher and mentor. He was consecrated bishop by the Pope Eugenius III at Auxerre in France. Herbert made the long journey to the papal court because the Scottish clergy and their king believed that it was vital to maintain direct relations with the Papacy in their efforts to establish an independent national church. The English Archbishops of York claimed jurisdiction over the Scottish clergy and especially in the business of appointing new bishops. When Herbert avoided York by going directly to the Pope for confirmation of his election as Bishop of Glasgow, he laid down a telling precedent which the Scots clergy were to build on later in the twelfth century. The monks at Kelso were at the centre of this fiercely fought political struggle as the most important monastery in the kingdom at that time.

5 Lesmahagow

In 1144 while Herbert was still abbot, Kelso founded its first daughter-house at Lesmahagow in Clydesdale. King David granted the church and lands to Kelso and they in turn dispatched a prior and a convent of monks to organise the new colony, much in the way that Tiron had sent monks to Selkirk thirty years before. Lesmahagow was the first of five Tironian monasteries to be created in Scotland either directly or indirectly from Kelso. It was never an independent convent, the Prior of Lesmahagow was always subject to the Abbot of Kelso and its revenues were always included in the rent roll of the abbey right up until the sixteenth century.

6 Earl Henry buried in the Abbey

A monk known as Arnold (or sometimes Ernald) became the fourth Abbot of Kelso in 1147. Six years later his abbey was the scene for a great state occasion when David I's only son, Early Henry, was buried there. His death was a great tragedy for the old king because Henry was not only earl of his father's English possessions of Northampton and Huntingdon, he was also the king-designate. That is to say, David and his son often acted jointly in giving charters or grants to religious houses, and rather than behaving simply as the great baron he was, he styled himself more like a deputy king. As such Earl Henry should have been buried at Dunfermline along with the rest of the Scottish royal family's ancestors. But David I chose instead to have his only son laid to rest at the Abbey of Kelso, underlining the old man's affection for the monks whom he had brought thirty years previously to the forest of Selkirk. The king's choice of Kelso for this solemn event also emphasises what must have been one of David's chief motives for bringing so many holy orders into his kingdom, and that was a simple religious faith. The abbeys he founded were for the salvation of his soul and those of his family and perhaps he thought it appropriate to bury his first and only son in the place where the first of his foundations eventually settled.

7 Abbot Arnold

In 1160 Abbot Arnold was elected to the bishopric of St Andrews and the manner of his appointment represented another stage in the struggle of the Scottish church for independence from York. In the absence of a Scots archbishop Arnold was consecrated by William, Bishop of Moray, who was acting in his capacity as Papal Legate, or as the Pope's proxy in Scotland.

That meant that like Abbot Herbert before him Arnold was in effect having his election sanctioned directly by the Pope. When he became the new Bishop of St Andrews, Arnold also assumed the office of papal legate in succession to William. Apparently this was done at the express wish of Pope Eugenius and it is an early indication of the Vatican's attitude to the see of St Andrews as a possible archbishopric.

The king's role in this matter was in the way of protecting his own interest. The appointment to high ecclesiastical offices was very important in mediaeval politics. The bishops and abbots were not only great and wealthy landowners (none more so than the abbot of Kelso) able to provide cash and fighting men for the king, but they were also in charge of the spiritual life of Scotland. Therefore it was in the royal interest that the appointment of Scots bishops be controlled inside the country and not by the English Archbishops of York, who after all were appointed by the English kings.

As soon as he became Bishop of St Andrews Arnold started work on the construction of the great cathedral, a necessary item in the effort to qualify as an archbishopric. By 1160 the building of the abbey church at Kelso would be far advanced, certainly sufficient for the architects of the new cathedral to imitate Kelso's simple style.

8 Thomas Dempster and the Mythical History of Kelso

The involvement of Kelso in high politics and the mediaeval architecture of Scotland was evidently not enough to make the abbots stand out as important figures for one historian. This was Thomas Dempster who in 1627 wrote a history of Scottish churchmen. According to Dempster Arnold wrote a treatise 'On the Right Government of a Kingdom'. Successive abbots wrote on the freedom of the Scottish church, appeals to the court of Rome, and in the late fifteenth century the prior Henry was said to be an intimate friend of the poet Angelo Poliziano and the philosopher Marsilio Ficino both of whom were at the court of Lorenzo dei Medici during the Florentine Renaissance. Henry, according to Dempster, translated the work of Palladius Rutulius on rural economy into Scots verse and carried on a long correspondence with the Florentine court. All this would have been remarkable, if any of it had been true. The extraordinary thing is that Dempster invented it all. He was a student at the University of Padua and a member of the Scottish nation there (Padua had long been an international university with each different group of foreign students organised into their nations). Perhaps Dempster felt inadequate in the company of so many cultured men like the French and Italians. Compared with the glittering intellectual achievements of the Italian Renaissance, life in backward, backwoods Scotland must have seemed unattractive as a background for Dempster. At all events he cured his inferiority complex by inventing what he considered a suitable cultured milieu for a student at Padua to come from. Dempster was one of the first of a long line of Scotsmen who were ashamed of their origins.

9 Kelso and Arbroath

In 1160 John was elected by his fellow monks as the fifth abbot of Kelso. He had been the Precentor of the Abbey, the man in charge of the church's music. The term 'precentor' actually means choirmaster and it looks as though Kelso had, by 1160, developed all the appurtenances of a great church — perhaps John's position as precentor means that the bulk of the building work on the kirk itself was finished or at least sufficiently advanced to allow a choir to sing at mass.

John's abbacy marked a period of expansion by Kelso. Two more Tironian abbeys were colonised from the mother-house at Kelso; in 1162 the man who founded Dryburgh Abbey, Hugh de Morville, set up another house at Kilwinning in Ayrshire. And in 1178 the important abbey of Arbroath was founded by King William the Lion who called upon Kelso to provide a colony of monks to begin the life of the church. Little is known about the history of Kilwinning but Arbroath ranks along with Kelso as one of the best-endowed abbeys in mediaeval Scotland. From the outset the relationship between mother and daughter house was clear; in the year of foundation, 1178, Kelso renounced any form of control she might have exercised over Arbroath. The new monastery was to be completely independent, responsible directly to Tiron itself and the King. In the same way that Kelso seemed to fill a vacuum in the central Borders, Arbroath quickly acquired much landed wealth from both the royal family and the great barons of Angus and the Mearns.

10 Roxburgh in English Hands

William the Lion had become King of Scotland in 1165 after the death of his brother, Malcolm IV. Both brothers had negiotiated with the English King Henry II for control of parts of northern England. When Henry proved yet again to be unresponsive to the Scots king's claims, William invaded Northumberland in 1174. He allowed the main body of his army to plunder the countryside while he remained with a small group of knights at Alnwick. He was surprised at dinner by the barons of Yorkshire commanded by Rannulf Glanvill and they carried the king away as their prisoner. This was to prove a dismal piece of bad luck for William. By the terms of the Treaty of Falaise he was forced to swear fealty to the English king for his kingdom while his barons and clergy were obliged in turn to acknowledge Henry II as their ultimate feudal overlord. This meant that the Scottish church, which had fought so hard for its independence under David I, was made subject to York. For a period of time after 1174 three Scottish castles were occupied by English garrisons. Roxburgh was among the named castles and the English remained in charge there for fifteen years until 1189. Having acknowledged the supremacy of York, and being overshadowed by the English soldiers at Roxburgh, the Abbot of Kelso must have felt that the emergence of his abbey in Scottish politics to be somewhat muted. And yet there is no evidence that the English occupation of Roxburgh hindered John's ambition. Not only did he claim that Kelso was to take precedence over its mother-house at Tiron, but John also tried to establish Kelso as the acknowledged superior amongst Scotland's monastic communities. No written evidence exists to confirm or deny any success he might have had in this aim, but there is no doubt about the Abbot of Kelso was the first of the Scots abbots to be given a mitre by the Pope. This award made to John by Pope Alexander III meant that the Abbot of Kelso had equal rank with Scots bishops and that he was responsible directly to the Pope for his abbey.

John of Kelso was, it seems, an ambitious man. He tried, and perhaps succeeded, in making Kelso supreme amongst Scots abbeys and monasteries, and supreme in the Tironian order. He sent out colonies of monks to other parts of the kingdom to found new houses, and he seems to have been the first Abbot of Kelso to go to the Papal court to plead his case for receiving the mitre. Despite the setback of William the Lion's capture and the English occupation of Roxburgh Castle, Kelso Abbey thrived under its fifth abbot.

11 Kelso Village and Kelso Parish

Just before and during the reign of Abbot John a few pieces of information about Kelso village and Kelso Parish come to light. Sometime between 1147 and 1152 David I issued a document confirming the gift of 'the village of Kelso with its proper boundaries by land and by water' to the abbey. Taken together with the fact that the church of St Mary definitely pre-existed the arrival of the monks at Kelso in 1128, it seems more likely that David is referring in this document to the boundaries of the parish of Kelso — although he calls it a village. The boundaries of the parish are nowhere explicitly defined but it is possible to build up a reasonably clear picture of where they ran at the beginning of the recorded history of Kelso by using bits of information gleaned from various land-grants made to the Abbey.

In 1159 the charter of Malcolm IV that confirmed the possesions of Kelso (it was usual for each succeeding king to reassure the abbeys and churches that he would honour the gifts made by his predeccessor) also brought the complete list of them up to date. In addition to the parish of Kelso, Malcolm's clerks note that the monks owned 'a piece of land which Gerold gave that lies next to the boundaries of the parish, and which runs down to the road leading to Nenthorn'. The donor was a man called Gerold de Thanu and reappears later in the Kelso documents as the father of Matilda de Burneville. Between 1200 and 1214 Matilda's husband, Robert de Burneville, gave more land to Kelso, 'The whole tenement that belongs to me in Brokesmouth which the monks held in that village before I came into my inheritence. That is, all the land at Brokesmouth once owned by my uncle Gerold (and which he gave to Kelso), and also the land which lies to the east of the road to Nenthorn.'

And one final piece of evidence to help complete the jigsaw. The Rent Roll of the Abbey in 1300 notes that Kelso owned the rights to fish in the Tweed 'from Brokesmouth down to the mouth of the Eden'.

The place-name of 'Brokesmouth' has passed out of use and no-one now knows where it was. The documents, however, do make it clear that it was somewhere on the north bank of the Tweed to the west of Kelso. It was also somewhere near the original piece of land given by Gerold de Thanu before 1159. That is on the Nenthorn side of Kelso Parish, on the road leading north-eastwards.

If the modern boundaries of the parish of Kelso are examined one can see that they start from an unnamed place a few hundred metres to the south of the farm of Stodrig. Now, there is a small stream running into the Tweed at that point, and if 'Brokesmouth' is another spelling of 'Brooksmouth', it may be that that was the place owned by Gerold and later by his son-in-law, Robert de Burneville. If it is, then it is certain that the modern parish boundary in that place is identical with the early mediaeval one. One further observation supports this arrangement. About a mile and a half from Brokesmouth/Brooksmouth the road to Nenthorn is crossed by the modern parish boundary at a place where the land 'runs down to the road', and at a point outside the parish but near enough to Kelso for the abbey to be supplied daily with agricultural produce from its property.

Besides this speculation there is more solid evidence to back up the theory that the modern parish boundary of Kelso, to the north of the Tweed, is not actually modern at all, but that it has not moved for 850 years. This involves the grant of some land in the neighbouring parish of Ednam made by King William the Lion sometime after 1165. He gave the abbey three carucates of land (a carucate is as much land as a team of oxen could plough in one day and it might have amounted to as much as 100 acres) and here is the document describing where the land is:

> Two and a half carucates of land near the boundaries of their [the monks] land of Kelso, on the north side of the peat-bog of Ednam, reaching from there along the boundary of the parishes [Kelso & Ednam parishes] to the southern bounds of Newton [Stichil] and from there along the parish boundary to the River Eden. Then along the Eden to the bridge on the west side of Ednam, and from there to the road leading to the hospital. And then to the forking of the road comes from the north side of the peat-bog and from there to where the boundary [of the 2½ carucates] started. This [goes] with the pasturage of a piece of land between the peat-bog and the boundaries of [the parish of] Kelso.
>
> [The other half carucate] lies on the east side of the quarry belonging to the abbey, between the fourteen acres of Paganus de Bosseville and the land belonging to the hospital on one side, and the peat-bog and the road leading down to Sprouston ford on the other side. And the fishing of the Tweed which used to belong to Ednam Parish from the boundaries of Kelso right up to the boundaries of Birgham.

Now that is a complex document even for someone who knows the area and it needs to be unpacked if it is to make sense. First, it is clear that the three carucates King William is giving all lie inside the parish of Ednam and that they are split into two parcels of land; one of 2½ carucates and another of ½ carucate. The larger piece of land lies to the north of the peat-bog of Ednam, that is the rising ground on which the modern farm of Ferneyhill now stands. The boundaries of the 2½ carucates begin on the north side of that high ground near the village of Ednam itself. They then run westwards to Newtonlees where the modern parish of Stichil has a southern flank, that is, the boundary runs from east to west. Then the limits of the 2½ carucates follow the boundary between Ednam and Nenthorn parishes down to the Eden before turning eastwards back towards Ednam itself, following the river. The directions proceed to the bridge on the other side of the village (where it still stands) and follow a road running to the north of the peat-bog. In fact the modern road from Ednam to Eden Hall does run up to a fork at Cliftonhill where the right fork goes down towards Ferneyhill before petering out.

So, the larger piece of land lay outside the parish of Kelso and inside Ednam in the southern part of that parish. It is best visualised as a long cigar-shaped area to the north of the River Eden. And the major point to extract from all this is that the mediaeval parish boundary between Kelso and Ednam ran along the Eden from below Newtonlees to a point just immediately west of the village.

The half carucate of land was situated down near the Tweed and its precise location completes the northern limits of Kelso Parish. There is visible evidence of very old quarry-workings along the left-hand side of the modern road leading from Kelso to Birgham, in the estates of Broomlands and Hendersyde. The document specifies that the quarries belonged to the monks and it is fair to assume that they were one of the sources for the stone needed to build Kelso Abbey. The modern parish boundary between Ednam and Kelso meets the Tweed's north bank just beyond the western tip of Sharpitlaw Anna where the extent of the quarrying also seems to end. In that place there is also a shallow part of the Tweed where it would be possible to ford it over to Sprouston. Furthermore the land of Paganus de Bosseville and the hospital (known as St Leonard's Hospital or Ednam Hospital, it probably was somewhere between Eden Hall and the village itself. Its main function was to provide lodging and to care for the sick and dying) were certainly in Ednam Parish and to the east of the quarries.

All of this necessarily lengthy excursus points to the fact the Kelso's parish boundary north of the Tweed has not changed since the twelfth century. It is important to establish this from the outset so as to define the area of this study — and to suggest the way in which the land was distributed around Kelso, and occasionally how it was used.

South of the Tweed the picture is relatively simple. A modern map will show Kelso Parish taking in the village of Maxwellheugh and the piece of haugh-land between the rivers Tweed and Teviot where the town of Roxburgh used to stand. Here is part of the First Statistical Account for Scotland, compiled in 1794. This section was written by Dr Christopher Douglas of Kelso; he begins:

> This district, formerly consisting of three parishes, viz. Kelso, Maxwell and St James . . . [situated] where the rivers Tweed and Teviot unite at Kelso. The former divides the parish nearly into two equal parts. St James lies between the two rivers; Maxwell on the south-east and Kelso on the north and west of both.

Maxwell Parish was probably served by St Michael's Church. It used to stand in what is now the Border Union Showground. There was also a chapel of St Thomas a Becket at the head of the Wooden Burn, and to the east the hospital known as Maison Dieu, a place-name that has survived. The Ordnance Survey map places another church, also St Thomas, about halfway between Maison Dieu and the Showground. This seems to be an incorrect attempt to locate the original chapel of St Thomas a Becket.

Territorially St James' was a tiny parish and it seems that, in contrast to other two more rural parts of Kelso Parish, it was an urban concern serving only the inhabitants of the town of Roxburgh. Its boundary follows the shape of the old town very closely.

So, by the middle of the twelfth century it seems that Kelso Parish north of the Tweed was well established as a distinct geographical entity with 'proper boundaries by land and by water'. The modern shape of Kelso was only altered before 1794 by the addition of two southern parishes that had become church-less.

12 A New Market

While the size of Kelso Parish, compared with the tiny urban parish of St James, would suggest a rural economy centred on a small village and its church (like Ednam), it was not long before the influence of the Abbey began to change that. The nature of the local economy could not fail to be affected by the arrival of the monks with their tremendous landed wealth. There is no doubt that Kelso began to expand. Here is part of a document issued by King William the Lion sometime between 1165 and 1171:

> From William, King of Scotland, to his Justiciar, his Sheriff and his burgesses of Roxburgh, greetings. Know that I give to God and the Church of St Mary of Kelso and the monks serving God there, for the soul of Count Henry my father, the souls of my ancestors and the salvation of my own soul, the right for the Abbot's men living in Kelso, on all weekdays, except the stated day of my market at Roxburgh, to buy in their own village fuel, timber and grain. And those bringing it in have the right to sell it to the villagers. The Abbot's men have the right to sell bread, ale and meat from their windows, and fish if it is brought in on the villagers' own carts or horses, and if they wish to sell it there from their own windows. Carts coming from other places carrying fish to Kelso can neither take it there nor sell it there unless they come to my market [at Roxburgh]. On the stated day of my market at Roxburgh they [the people of Kelso] are not allowed to buy anything in their village unless they come to my market where they can buy what they like from my burgesses according to their rules and customs.

This is a case of the king protecting his own market at Roxburgh from competition with the growing village of Kelso. It shows that the presence of the abbey had stimulated economic development at Kelso so much in only 40 years that the village was beginning to rival the town of Roxburgh as a trading centre, at least on a local level. Since the document given by

King William probably legitimised what had become regular markets at Kelso, it seems likely that these had been held for some considerable time before 1165.

13 Abbot Osbert and the Bishop of Rome

In 1180 Osbert succeeded John as Abbot of Kelso. He had been Prior of Lesmahagow, Kelso's first colony in the Clyde valley. Even though the abbey and its daughter-house were more than 70 miles apart, and that amounted to a long line of communication in the Middle Ages, it is obvious from Osbert's election that relations were close. And that the prestige of Lesmahagow was sufficiently high to allow its office of Prior to be a stepping-stone to the abbacy of Kelso.

Like his predecessor John, Osbert's reign was marked out in sharp changes of focus between international European politics and detailed local affairs around Kelso itself and the Tweed Valley. Almost as soon as he became abbot Osbert found himself in Rome with Jocelyn, Bishop of Glasgow, as part of a Scottish embassy to the papal court. William the Lion had resisted Pope Alexander III's attempts to have an Englishman made Bishop of St Andrews and had tried to have his own chaplain, Hugh, elected to the office. In an effort to force William into accepting the papal choice, Alexander excommunicated the king. This was a powerful weapon in an age that took the idea of salvation and damnation very seriously. By excommunicating him, the Pope had effectively expelled William the Lion from the church thereby condemning him to eternal damnation. Jocelyn of Glasgow and Osbert of Kelso were in Rome to try to lift William's excommunication. Luckily for them Pope Alexander III had just died and was replaced by Lucius III, a man more sympathetic to the Scottish cause. Not only did Lucius reinstate the king but he also gave the Abbot of Kelso another privilege. The Pope decreed that Kelso would not suffer from any sentence of excommunication unless it came directly from the Vatican. In 1201, two years before Osbert died, Innocent II confirmed Lucius' favours and added that no bishop or archbishop could excommunicate Kelso Abbey. And even if the whole of Scotland was forbidden to go to church for any reason, the monks at Kelso could celebrate mass, provided they did so discreetly, celebrating the divine offices in a low voice and with the abbey doors closed and without ringing the abbey bells. As a symbol of Kelso's direct dependence on the Vatican the monks had to pay a piece of gold or two pieces of silver each year to the Pope.

14 Kelso vs Melrose

Turning from international politics to matters of domestic concern,

Osbert's reign saw the rise of a serious dispute between the abbeys of Kelso and Melrose. When David I moved his colony of Tironian monks from Selkirk he had to reorganise their lands to suit their new site at Kelso. Most of this reorganisation took place around the Eildon Hills, the three-pointed hill that dominates the landscape of the central Border country, and it was made necessary by David I's foundation of the Cistercian Abbey of Melrose in 1136. Here is William the Lion's resolution of the dispute:

> [There has been] a dispute of many years standing between the houses of Kelso and Melrose concerning the boundaries between Melrose and Bowden, the lands of the monks of Kelso. At length the lord Pope Celestinus III has indicated to me by letter that he wishes me to enquire carefully and justly into the question of these boundaries, and to clear matters up. Cardinal John, at that time papal legate in my lands, was instructed to put the weight of his authority behind me.
>
> At length I came to Melrose in 1202 on the eighth day after Epiphany, and in the presence of many clergymen and lay people there was much talk about these boundaries. Both William [who was at that time Abbot of Melrose] and Osbert Abbot of Kelso obtained the agreement of their monks that they would refer the case to my arbitration and they swore to abide by my judgement on the boundaries, and to maintain firmly, completely and without violation what I said in my enquiry. I brought together the honest and ancient men of the countryside into my presence and I then put the enquiry into their hands.
>
> At length they came to my court at Selkirk on May 9th 1204. There in open court I pronounced their verdict to the clergy and laity of the lands in question. And it was the monks of Kelso who were bound by law to give up their lands. That is, to keep to the boundary made by my uncle, King David, which is marked by ditches on the top of Eildon Mid Hill. And I said that this was truly my judgement and that I am bound legally to the evidence of the honest and ancient men of the countryside. I wish the monks of Kelso to give up forever to the monks of Melrose two bovates of land, two acres and pasture for 400 sheep which the monks of Kelso used to hold. On that day discussion of the matter ended.

This was a dispute not about the transfer of lands to Melrose from Kelso's old holdings when the monks had first been settled at Selkirk, but rather about the precise geographical details of the transfer. It is interesting to see the king referring the case to the people who lived in that part of the Borders — the people who could remember the rearrangement of ownership made by David I and the precise places where the old king had caused the boundary to be marked. As is the case with Kelso Parish, these pieces of land were divided then by what is now the parish boundary between Melrose on the west and Bowden and Galashiels on the east.

William the Lion's court at Selkirk did indeed hear the last word on this dispute since no subsequent mention is made of it in the Kelso documents. Finally, it is astonishing to note the direct interest of Pope Celestinus and his legate in this affair. On the one hand Osbert of Kelso dealt with the Pope in the field of international politics over the question of the Scots king's excommunication, and on the other hand here is the Pope in Rome taking a direct involvement with the line of a boundary over Eildon Mid Hill.

15 First Kelsonians

Around the year 1200 Kelso Abbey received a gift of land from people who lived in the parish of Kelso. Their names are given —the first names of historical Kelsonians — as is that of a man who might legitimately be seen as the first Provost of Kelso. This is the full text:

> I, Arnold, son of Peter of Kelso, with the agreement of my wife Juheca, give to the Abbey of Kelso a messuage [a dwelling-house and its adjacent land] which belonged to my father in the village of Kelso. I do this for the salvation of my soul and the souls of all my family. I give this piece of land with toft and croft and all those things pertaining to it. And 3 solidi [shillings] a year taken from Ralph, provost [or burgess] of Kelso. And also [I give] a certain piece of land in the village of Kelso that belonged to Walter, son of Heck and Ingobald.

Although Kelso was becoming an important economic centre, there are no documents which show a dense town population like Roxburgh or Berwick. When land grants like the above are made it is not necessary to note carefully the exact location of property in relation to neighbouring properties. At this stage buildings in Kelso were probably fairly spread out, not yet having streets —rather like some Highland villages today.

16 The Abbey Mill

Most mediaeval town buildings were made out of wood and have, as a result, almost completely disappeared. That is true of mediaeval Kelso, except of course for the Abbey, and one other building. This was probably built of wood but later made of more permanent stone — the Abbey Mill. A fragment of this survives today, and on the site of the old mill the modern business of John Hogarth's Kelso Mill now stands. Mills need a fast current to turn their wheels and the monks set about building a cauld to direct the Tweed to their mill. Because their cauld was such a big undertaking (compared with the relatively minor business of constructing a cauld on the Eden for Ednam Mill for example) there is a tradition that Michael Scot, the Wizard, lent his magical powers to the project. In fact documents have survived to tell us a good deal about how the cauld was built. Along with the Mill which it served and the Abbey itself, the cauld is the only other part of mediaeval Kelso that survives.

From the outset the monks decided that a barrier needed to be thrown right across the Tweed, from the site of the mill across to where the town of Roxburgh stood. To get the correct angle for a fast current past the mill-wheel, they sought permission to begin their cauld from a piece of mediaeval Roxburgh just to the south of 'Vigorous Haugh'. This is now known as Crown Point, but in 1200 it belonged to Andrew Maunsel and he called it the Halech or simply 'the Haugh'. Here is the document that allowed the monks to start work:

> Let all the sons, present and future, of Holy Mother Church know that I, Andrew Maunsel, give and concede licence and liberty to the Abbot and monks of Kelso to build and hold in perpetuity their own mill-pond on the Tweed from that part of my land which I have on the eastern side of the town of Roxburgh. I give and confirm by this document however much land they wish in free and perpetual gift for the salvation of my soul and those of my ancestors and my heirs. This gift is witnessed by Walter, my son and heir. I and my heirs guarantee this against all men. Witnessed by John, Master Adam de Hereshill, Walter son of Andrew, Simon de Merkinstone, Walter son of Seher, William the Mercer, Servanus de Kelso, Robert de Wooler and many others.

From the list of witnesses, and the donor himself, this gift would seem to be almost a middle-class affair. The gift itself was not a huge tract of valuable land such as might be owned by a great lord, but was rather a small piece of town property that the monks required for a special purpose. Two of Andrew Maunsel's family are named; his son Walter and his brother Gerald. And there are no great men amongst the others; one is a cloth-finisher (William the Mercer) and another is a man from the opposite bank of the Tweed, Servanus de Kelso.

Having secured their building site, the monks needed materials to dam the river. At first they almost certainly used wood because there exists a later document from Lord Thomas de Gordon

> I give [the monks of Kelso] licence and liberty to take away enough wood, root and branch, to build the mill pond at Kelso and to repair it in perpetuity . . . providing that my body is buried in the cemetery of Kelso.

'Root and branch' implies that the monks needed a big pieces of wood to construct the cauld and when the work was underway it must have looked, in mediaeval terms, a building project of great scale and difficulty. The interval of time between Andrew Maunsel's gift (1200) and that of Thomas de Gordon (1255) is significant; the great cauld that spans the Tweed at Kelso took a very long time to build and the monks were careful to acquire gifts of materials to maintain properly the result of their labour.

17 The Abbey Cemetery

De Gordon's condition on his gift was that his body be buried in Kelso Abbey's cemetery. There are other references to the monks' place of burial and it is almost certain that it was located on the northern side of the Abbey itself, where the cemetery of the Kelso Parish Church is today. Although is is not a building in the strict sense the cemetery, like the cauld, is the work of the monks and as such it is another vestige of mediaeval Kelso that remains visible.

So, during the reigns of the Abbots John and Osbert some aspects of Kelso itself, as opposed to simply the Abbey, begin to emerge. First there is the likelihood that the parish of Kelso followed the same boundaries (north of the Tweed) in the twelfth century as it does today. That sets a parameter for this history in that what lies within that parish should properly be included in an account of the development of the town of Kelso. In addition, the Abbey Mill and its cauld come into the picture as does the cemetery of the Abbey. Later evidence will show that the shape of modern Kelso, if not the buildings themselves, owes much to the Middle Ages.

18 Pope Innocent III writes to Kelso

Abbot Osbert died in 1203 and the monks named his prior, Geoffrey, as their new abbot. Although his reign was brief (1203 to 1206) Geoffrey became involved in a significant correspondence with the Vatican. Innocent III, one of the great mediaeval politicians, was Pope during this period and he was determined to re-establish papal authority over his church in every part of Europe. Innocent III wanted to reform the church by rooting out abuses where they had grown up. Reports must have reached the Vatican that the Abbey of Kelso's lands were not being properly administered because Innocent III wrote to the abbot on this subject:

> Innocent bishop, servant of the servants of God, sends greetings and the Apostolic benediction to our dear sons at the Abbey and Convent of Kelso in

Scotland, in the Order of St Benedict, and which belongs directly to the
Church of Rome. Regarding yourselves, it was reported in our presence
that several priests and laymen, who possess lands, houses and other things
held of your monastery in feudal tenure of by annual tax or rental, are
selling them without your permission, or giving them to priests or others,
or are imposing new taxes or services on the same possessions.

Duing the same period Innocent issued two more letters concerning Kelso.
Written in an elegant Latin, they deal with the practice of mortgaging
lands that belong to the Abbey, encroachment on the monks' lands, and
the confirmation of privileges granted by the Papacy to Kelso but never
used.

It is clear that Innocent III's civil service had a very detailed knowledge
of Kelso's domestic affairs, and that at an immense distance, even in
modern terms. At the beginning of the thirteenth century several papal
legates visited Britain and doubtless they sent back reports of abuses they
either observed or heard about. In addition the Pope employed agents to
act for him abroad and the major prelates of every European country
occasionally went to Rome themselves. Communication with Italy must
also have been helped by the regular trading in raw wool between the
Border country and the cloth-makers of Tuscany, an area sometimes under
the direct control of the Bishop of Rome.

What was also evident from the Papal letters was the lack of control
Kelso Abbey had over its lands and the people who held those lands of the
Abbey. In the seventy years since the monks moved downriver from
Selkirk they had been given regular and valuable gifts of land. By the time
of Abbot Geoffrey, Kelso was, by mediaeval standards, fabulously wealthy
by virtue of being a landlord on a huge scale. Obviously the Abbey could
not possess and cultivate these lands by its own efforts; many of the pieces
of land (and the parish churches they also owned) were too far from Kelso
to be directly controlled, and even if their estates had all been concentrated
locally the monks did not have, nor did they wish to have, the manpower to
run them directly. All over Western Europe great landowners (kings and
barons) had developed a habit of leasing parts of their estates to others in
return for certain services, food-rents or cash. It was always understood,
although by no mean always observed, that these lands never actually
passed out of the ownership of the original owner; be he king or baron. And
it was definitely the case that overlords did not allow their feudal subjects to
sell the land they held of them, or to give it away to other people without
permission.

Nevertheless this was precisely what was happening at Kelso. As a great landowner, the Abbey had given most of its estate to others in return for rents or services in the usual way. But evidently some of their feudal subjects had begun to behave as though they owned the land Kelso had leased to them. This ran counter to the motives of those people who gave the land to the Abbey in the first place. As we have seen these were usually spiritual motives, like the wish of Thomas de Gordon to be buried in the monks' cemetery or the request of David I himself who founded the Abbey for the salvation of his soul and those of his family. Donors also gave land so that Kelso could maintain itself as a thriving religious community and if its land were being sold off to others or given away, then that was clearly to the long-term detriment of the Abbey.

Innocent III's letter mentions that priests as well as laymen were guilty of these practices and this suggests that some of Kelso's parishes may have been passed on by priests to their families or even to their sons (sometimes euphemistically termed nephews). Mediaeval priests were by no means always celibate and nor was the ownership of land foreign to them. In the 1150s and 1160s there are records of Peter, the priest of Stobo, passing on his lands to his son. And later in the Kelso cartulary there is a document recording the settlement of a dispute between 'J, rector of the church of Lilliesleaf, concerning certain lands in Roxburgh, Kelso and Bowden, which he claimed by hereditary right . . . for his own church at Lilliesleaf', and the Abbot of Kelso.

In a second letter to the abbot, Innocent III complains that the lands of Kelso are being mortgaged by their incumbents, and further, that some of the land is being whittled away by encroaching outsiders. Since he addresses this to the Abbots of Jedburgh and Dryburgh, and the Prior of Coldingham, it seems likely that the Pope considered the administration of Kelso to be weak, and that some of the wrongs would be more easily righted by its neighbours. No doubt Jedburgh, Dryburgh and Coldingham could also help to identify some of the encroachers.

Innocent's last letter is about privileges that Kelso had but did not exercise. This falls into line with the Pope's policy of strengthening the independence of the church from secular forces. Coupled with the crackdown on abuses of church lands, Innocent III took the view that in order to be effective, religious institutions ought to return to first principles. That is, institutions like Kelso Abbey should remember that they existed to serve God and those who worshipped him. As such they were different from the great secular landowners and they had to set an example in the conduct of their affairs. And for purely political reasons, Innocent III wanted a strong church in each European country that would respond to papal control.

In 1206 Abbot Geoffrey died after a short reign of only three years. His successor was Richard de Cane who in turn only reigned for two years.

It may be that during this period the monks tended to elect old men to be their abbots, much in the way that the Curia of Cardinals elected ageing Popes just in case they turned out badly. At all events the next abbot, Henry, must have been slightly healthier than his immediate predecesors: he became Abbot in 1208 and lasted ten years until he died on 5 October 1218.

Henry's reign was also marked by close involvement in Papal politics. Innocent III summoned a general council in Rome in November 1215. this was to be attended by all major prelates in Europe, including the Abbot of Kelso. The council was known as the Fourth Lateran (the papal church in Rome was at that time St John Lateran) and it debated the state of the church and in particular what was to be done about the Albigensian heresy in southern France. Henry stayed in Rome for the duration of the council before travelling back to Scotland at the end of 1215. The following year, King John of England invaded the Border country and burned Roxburgh, but seems to have left the abbey alone. Just before Abbot Henry died in 1218 the new Pope, Honorius III, lifted the sentence of interdict that Innocent III had imposed on Scotland in a dispute with King William. He also lifted the excommunication of the Scottish prelates, as a further concession. All of this was a tremendous relief for the church in Scotland; interdict meant that the church was forbidden to carry out all sacraments (including baptism, marriage and burial) except communion.

In 1218 Henry's prior succeeded him. His name was Richard and like his recent namesake he did not preside over the affairs of Kelso Abbey long, dying in 1221 after a three year reign. Out of the last four abbots, three had been priors of the monastery and the fourth, John, had become Bishop of Aberdeen. Obviously prior was an important office and one that was seen as a stepping-stone to the abbacy. The prior often deputised for the abbot during his absence (for example while Henry was at the Fourth Lateran Council, Richard would have taken temporary charge of the Abbey) and he was generally responsible for the day to day running of the monastery's affairs.

19 Herbert Maunsel gives up his Office

Herbert Maunsel took over as Abbot in 1221 and he is the first man since John died in 1180 who gives any indication of character. More than just another name in the list of Kelso's abbots, Herbert came from an identifiable social background. The family of Maunsel was probably

Norman in origin and certainly town-dwellers by inclination. Simon Maunsel was a witness to many charters given at Roxburgh. And we have already seen that he gave the land on the Roxburgh side of the Tweed so that the monks could build their cauld for the Abbey Mill. Andrew's son Walter is a witness in one charter while one Gervase Maunsel is mentioned in a document of 1235. It seems possible that the new Abbot of Kelso, Herbert Maunsel, came from the family of wealthy Roxburgh burgesses.

Whatever his social background, Herbert was not an enthusiastic abbot. He probably came to the monastery to lead the religious life and to escape the cares of the temporal world. Laying up crozier and mitre on the high altar of the Abbey Kirk, he decided that he had had enough of the job his monks had given him for life. Apparently this met with approval, or at least acquiescence, because the monks elected Hugh as the new Abbot. In 1239 Cardinal Otho, the papal legate, was staying at Melrose Abbey. When he heard of Herbert Maunsel's resignation he instructed him to take up office again and Abbot Hugh was said to have willingly returned to the ranks. However documents state that Hugh was still exercising the powers of abbot in 1240 and 1241, and it seems likely that Maunsel succeeded in retiring a second time and that Hugh carried on until his death in 1248.

20 More Mediaeval Kelsonians

Immediately after he took over as abbot, Hugh received on behalf of his monks a humble gift from a tradesman living and working in Kelso. His name was Andrew, son of William, and his trade was the dying of cloth. Here is the relevant document:

> Andrew, son of William the dyer of Kelso, and his wife Senegle give greetings. Let everyone know that I resign to the Lord Abbot and Convent of Kelso all claim to that land in the burgh of Kelso which once belonged to my father and mother, and which I used to claim that I held it of them by hereditary right, and for which I used to receive two marks of silver from the Lord Abbot and the Convent. Renouncing all title and benefit by both common law and private law [and in case of any objection it is agreed by common law and custom and practice of both canon law and civil law], I wish that the aforesaid Abbot and Convent should possess that land forever under their own peaceful control, and that they should freely make a profit from it without any challenge. If any of my successors wishes to claim that land by hereditary right let him be answerable for [a penalty of] seven marks in favour of the owners of the resignation of this land . . . in the year of Grace 1237 . . . I do not have a seal of my own to witness this matter, and at my request Master Adam de Baggat then Sheriff of Roxburgh and Lord Peter de Halech provost of Roxburgh have set their seals on this document. Witnessed by Robert the Dyer, Humphrey

and Mobbe, Adam Tunnock, Richard the dyer, and the burgesses of Kelso
and many others.

Taken together with the gift to the monks of Arnald of Kelso in 1200, this
document evidences the rise of a cloth-finishing trade in Kelso during this
period. Andrew's charter was witnessed by a man called William Mercer
(who also incidentally witnessed the gift of part of the Halech to the
Abbey) who is likely to have lived in Kelso and not Roxburgh. 'Mercer'
means dealer in cloth. Counting Andrew himself, there are three dyers of
cloth mentioned in the above, and without labouring the point too heavily,
it seems that the manufacture of cloth for domestic markets was well
established at Kelso very early in its history.

As we shall see later, Kelso was split into two settlements: Easter and
Wester Kelso. Since the Abbey owned all of Easter Kelso (the village that
clustered around the church itself) it is probable that the above gift (and
Arnold's) was of land that lay in Wester Kelso.

The language of the document is sometimes obscure but the sentiment
is clear. Andrew is worried about the security of his gift and the clerks have
tried to make sure — through quoting civil law, canon law, common law,
private law, every law they could think of — that there could be no future
dispute about the new ownership. They even went to the lengths of
introducing a penalty clause to discourage claims from any of Andrew's
relatives. Perhaps these measures should be seen against the background of
the papal letters showing concern that Kelso might be suffering some loss
of land through its alienation by people not connected with the Abbey.

The final characteristic that Andrew's gift shares with that of Arnold 37
years previously is its borrowing of seals. In order to legitimise his gift,
Arnold (or more likely the monks) asked two men further up the social
scale than himself, Bernard de Hadden and Philip de Lundinus, to append
their seals on the bottom of the charter. In the same way the Sheriff of
Roxburgh, Adam de Baggat, and the Provost of Roxburgh, Peter de
Halech, witnessed Andrew's generosity to the Abbey. Not only do these
two gifts shed a little more light on the development of mediaeval Kelso,
they also show how relatively humble people enriched the monks'
holdings.

21 Kelso Abbey is Dedicated by David de Bernham

In 1243 Kelso Abbey Kirk was formally dedicated by the Bishop of St
Andrews, David de Bernham. Some historians have taken that to mean
that Kelso took 135 years to build, but while it is true that the construction

of large mediaeval churches was an especially drawn-out affair, the evidence points to a much earlier end to the building of Kelso Abbey than 1243. Compared with other churches known to be of that period, it looks as though most of the work on Kelso was done between 1175 and 1200. From the remains of the west end of the church, one can see that there was no stylistic change in the architecture. Unlike St Andrews Cathedral church, which was tremendously long (392 feet) and which took a very long time to complete, there is no switch from a style that was fashionable at the start of the project to one that was in vogue at the end. Including the porch, the west end of Kelso is executed in a consistent style which strongly suggests that the work was done over a relatively short period of time.

David de Bernham, the man who dedicated the church, came from Berwick and would have known Kelso as a young man. When he became Bishop of St Andrews, he renounced the office of Chancellor of Scotland and devoted all his energy to the church. He was a zealous reformer and issued many statutes on how the religious life should be lived. Bishop David was extremely energetic in the business of formally consecrating the churches in his diocese of St Andrews. Out of a total of 300, he consecrated 140 while he was bishop. Now this does not mean that 140 new churches were built at that time, it means that their bishop was zealous in seeing to the formal business of their dedication. It is likely that the same is true of Kelso.

When he died in 1253 David de Bernham chose to be buried at Kelso Abbey rather than at St Andrews. This was probably as a result of disagreements between the Cathedral chapter and their reforming bishop but it was also perhaps because of sentiment. David was the first native Scot to hold the see of St Andrews for 150 years and it is possible that he wished to be buried near his place of birth.

22 Local Men become Abbots

Judging by his name, another native Scot took high ecclesiastical office when Robert de Smalhame was elected Abbot of Kelso in 1248. Following Herbert Maunsel of Roxburgh and now Robert of Smailholm, the middle of the thirteenth century saw the beginning of a tradition of Borderers as Abbots of Kelso. Robert's reign was marked by the comings and goings of national politics around Kelso and Roxburgh. After the death of Alexander II in 1249, the new king, Alexander III, was only eight years old. This gave rise to faction in Scotland between a party committed to the furtherance of English influence on the young king, and a party who wished to exclude the English from Scottish affairs. In 1255 Alan Doorward, the leader of the pro-English faction, abducted Alexander III and imprisoned him in Roxburgh Castle. Henry III of England arrived with his court in September of the same year and was entertained at Roxburgh. In 1256 the young king and queen took part in a royal procession (a state occasion of some kind) from Roxburgh to Kelso Abbey where they were received by Abbot Robert. The next year saw the defeat of the English faction in Scotland and the relief of tension over the border.

Although Scotland under the rule of Alexander III entered a period of peace in the last quarter of the thirteenth century, it is difficult to tell much about how Kelso fared in this king's reign. Around the year 1266 the Melrose Chronicle seems to have petered out, and since it was the main source for the continuous history of the Border Abbeys, the picture tends to become confused. After 1266, the succession of abbots becomes unclear in the absence of the Melrose Chronicle's precise dating of their reigns. The only source for this and other information is the collection of Kelso charters itself.

When Robert de Smalhame died in 1258 the monks elected Patrick as their new abbot in the normal way. But the result did not satisfy the Treasurer of the Abbey, Henry de Lambden. He may have been an unsuccessful candidate in the election and it seems likely that he took himself off to the papal court in Rome soon after 1258. Through a mixture of intrigue and bribery, Henry persuaded Pope Alexander IV to overturn the election of Patrick and nominate himself as the new abbot. He returned to Kelso in 1260 bearing a letter from the Pope addressed to Abbot Patrick by which he was commanded to resign his office immediately into the hands of the bearer. Kelso Abbey was a rich prize, with its vast wealth and considerable influence, and it is not surprising that ambitious men like Henry de Lambden went to great lengths to acquire it.

23 Schools and Slaves

One of the most intensively cultivated parts of Kelso's huge estates was the Bowmont Valley in the Cheviot Hills, known in the Middle Ages as Molle. Gifts from the two major landowners in Molle (the family of Anselm and the de Veschy family) had allowed the Abbey to develop huge sheep-pastures, along with the income from the church at Molle and various holdings of arable land. Matilda of Molle added to the monks' wealth by giving, in 1260, her dowry (taken from lands belonging to her former husband, Richard de Lincoln) to the Abbey. It was not an unconditional gift and Matilda specified what she wanted in return — she was practised at dealing with the monks over the question of land since some years previously she and Richard de Lincoln had been in serious dispute with Kelso over grazing rights for their sheep. They had to insist that their use of her timber to build sheep-folds had to be supervised, since the monks were running down the woodland stock very quickly. Matilda requested that:

> The Abbot and Convent maintain my son William in food and drink with the better and more worthy scholars who eat in the Poor House, so long as they [the monks] hold the land [I gave them].

Schools have already been mentioned as existing at Roxburgh at an earlier date than 1260 but it sounds as though this group of scholars are living at Kelso. The 'Poor House' was probably incorporated in the complex of Abbey buildings — it is unlikely that children would go to school in Roxburgh across the river to be taught by the monks and return (presumably with the monks) to eat at Kelso. William would be taught Latin: how to read it and perhaps how to write and understand it. Latin was the language of religion, government and education in 1260. It may be that William was intended to become one of Kelso's monks and that his mother was providing for his preparatory education through the condition of her gift.

Henry de Lambden's reign cannot have been noted for his popularity because when he died in 1275, his monks refused to keep vigil over his body and buried him on the same day. It is further recorded that he died of apoplexy while eating.

Because of the lack of information in the Melrose Chronicle it is not clear who succeeded Henry but the Kelso Cartulary does mention that Richard was Abbot in 1285 when he held a court at Redden near Sprouston. He may also have been Abbot five years before that when Andrew Fraser of Gordon made a gift of some land to Kelso. The gift is unremarkable except in one respect. It shows that the Abbey did not only own huge tracts of land, it also owned people. After a long geographical description of the land he is giving, he adds:

> three acres of pasture in the lordship of Gordon, with [including] Adam, son of Henry del Hoga, my neyf and all his issue. And with pasture in the same lordship or 400 sheep and all their issue.

Neyf or *Nativus* is the mediaeval term for a slave and it is understood from this document that Adam del Hoga and his family are part of Fraser's gift to the monks. Adam and his children are noted down in just the same way as the sheep. There are records of other similar gifts to religious houses (especially to Coldingham) and it is likely that Kelso Abbey owned more than one family of slaves. Incidentally the abusive slang word 'nyaff' seems to be related to 'nyef'.

24 Kelso and the Wars of Independence

When King Alexander III died in 1286 it was the signal for a long period of destructive uncertainty for Scotland and for the Border country in particular. The Wars of Independence were in the short term a victory for Scotland but they were a disaster for the town of Roxburgh and the Abbey of Kelso.

For the period immediately following Alexander III's death, Scotland was ruled by guardians who looked after the kingdom in the name of Margaret, the Maid of Norway. As the heir to the throne, Margaret's future was the concern of the Scottish barons and clergy who met with the English King, Edward I, at the village of Birgham near Kelso. Richard, Abbot of Kelso, was a party to the Treaty of Birgham which was sealed in 1290. The Scots agreed to the marriage of Margaret to Edward I's son and heir, later to become Edward II. Although that union meant that Edward II would be king of both Scotland and England, the Scottish barons and clergy received assurances that their country would retain its separate identity in every other way. Before the terms of the Treaty of Birgham could be fulfilled, Margaret died, leaving Scotland without an obvious heir to the throne. As a prominent churchman, Richard of Kelso figured in the controversy that was to follow.

Edward I elected himself as supreme judge in the successor to the Scottish Crown, and so that his verdict would be accepted without question he occupied Scotland's major castles, including Roxburgh. That meant he could withhold them from a candidate he did not favour or award them to his man. In the event, he allowed John Balliol to be elected King of Scots and it is interesting to note that the Abbot of Kelso was one of King John's supporters. Doubtless, Richard was looking after the interests of his monks in choosing to back Balliol. Roxburgh Castle had been in English hands since 1292 and the Abbey stood very near the frontier, making it vulnerable to attack. Since he was the choice of the English king, it was politic for Kelso to support the cause of John Balliol.

After his refusal, in 1296, to give in to English abuse of his kingship, Balliol found himself at war with Edward I. On 2 September of that year, Edward was at Berwick and it is recorded that 'he restored the lands of the Abbot of Kelso'. This probably meant that Richard and his abbey were permitted to keep their lands on condition that he swore obedience to the

71

English king rather than to John Balliol. Three years later Richard apparently returned to the Scottish cause because the English accused him of being 'a rebel and an enemy' and of deserting his abbey.

There is no doubt that both Kelso and Roxburgh suffered a great deal during this period. The English used Roxburgh as a convenient place to muster their armies in both 1298 and 1303 and the castle was under their control for 22 years between 1292 and 1314. The occupying army probably behaved as occupying armies do, with little respect for the property of the natives.

The militarisation of the border with England after 1296 lasted intermittently for the rest of the mediaeval history of Kelso. This in turn caused the gradual run-down of Roxburgh as a mercantile burgh with neither the Scots nor the English wishing it to become too important to their economies in case they lost possession of it. Kelso Abbey also fared badly and it never really resumed its place at the centre of Scottish politics after the Wars of Independence.

25 The Rent Roll of the Abbey

Around the year 1300 the monks at Kelso compiled a rent-roll for the Abbey. It was a long and detailed list of their landed wealth with a note of how much rent each place owed. It was probably done to confirm a growing practice of commuting food and service-rents for money. Rather than deal with large quantities of produce or try to use services which were declining in their usefulness, the abbots began to accept their rents in cash. Not only does it show how relatively sophisticated the local economy had become by 1300, but the rent-roll is the last complete picture of the great abbey before its decline.

At the end of the list of the monks' possessions, it is stated that:

> They had an annual rent of £9.16 shillings and 9½ pence from the vill and burgh of Wester Kelso. They have all of the rents of Easter Kelso for their own use . . . and they have there land which is cultivated with seven ploughs and they also have pasture there. they have mills there which are usually worth twenty pounds a year. And they have a fishing of the Tweed from the tenement of Brokesmouth right up to the Water of Eden.

This is the first time that an explicit distinction is made between the two settlements of Wester and Easter Kelso. It is clear from the terms used for each place; burgh for Wester and village for Easter, that Wester Kelso was probably the larger of the two. Easter Kelso was completely under the control of the abbot as was the farmland that lay to the east and north-east.

Seven ploughgates may have amounted to as much as 700 or 800 acres of arable land and an unspecified area of pasture is mentioned. Unless the reference to 'mills' is a mistake, it would seem that the monks had more than one under their control.

During the Wars of Independence Kelso Abbey must have suffered severely at the hands of both sides and there is a tradition that the monks abandoned their church altogether and sought safety at other religious houses in Scotland. Two charters dated 1307 and 1311 name Walran as the Abbot of Kelso. He probably succeeded Abbot Richard but almost nothing seems to be known about him. Between 1311 and 1314/15 Thomas de Durham ruled the monastery and he was also Prior of Lesmahagow at the same time. He sounds like an Englishman and he may have owed his position at Kelso, dominated as it was by Roxburgh's garrison, to Edward II rather than any Scots king or magnate.

If names are anything to go by (they are often all there is to go by) Thomas de Durham's successor was a Scot and probably a Borderer. He carried the name of a local village and thereby added to the tradition of Borderers as Kelso Abbot, following Henry de Lambden, Richard de Smailholm and Herbert Maunsel. William de Ancrum probably became the new abbot in 1315 because a year later he is quoted in an agreement made between Kelso and the Bishop of St Andrews. William exchanged the parish church of Cranston, in Mid-Lothian, for the church of Nenthorn and the chapel of Little Newton.

26 Wester Kelso

In 1323 Wester Kelso is again mentioned in the Abbey records and this time in some detail. Here is a part of the charter:

> A court of the Lord Abbot was held in the burgh of Wester Kelso after the feast of St Thomas the Martyr in the year of our lord 1323. On that day all the burgesses of the village of Wester Kelso came to answer and make a statement to their Lord Abbot concerning a complaint which he had made against them. Namely that they had made new burgesses, licensed brewers and stall-holders and done other similar things which by law belong to the liberties of the Lord Abbot.

The document goes on to relate that the burgesses' spokesman, Hugh of Chirnside (a clerk, and probably a priest) admitted that the burgesses had no right to act as they had. He made an apology on their behalf and asserted that Wester Kelso had no intention of causing offence to its Lord, the abbot.

It is important to see this incident as another stage in Wester Kelso's development. Although the name Wester Kelso is not used until the rent roll of 1300, it seems likely that the first reference to Kelso's market in 1165/71 was more accurately a reference to Wester Kelso. Again in 1237 the cloth-finishers who gave land to the Abbey probably came from Wester Kelso —incidentally this industry was one that was usually reserved exclusively for royal burghs. And here in 1323 the burgesses of Wester Kelso are being hauled up in front of the abbot because they have been exceeding themselves. It is clear that Wester Kelso was allowed to develop as a non-royal burgh only because it enjoyed the protection of the powerful Abbots of Kelso. Perhaps the incident of 1323 came about after a period of laxity of abbatial authority that was due to the Wars of Independence.

In 1237 the word 'Burgess' had been used by the people of Wester Kelso even though it was not legally a burgh. In this dispute with the abbot it seems likely that the town had developed to the extent that the burgesses had combined as some kind of corporate entity that could, albeit illegally, create new burgesses, license brewers and stall-holders at their market. They were, in effect, taking upon themselves the powers enjoyed by royal burghs without actually being one.

27 English Occupation

William de Ancrum's name occurs in a charter dated 1326 but nothing more is heard about him after that date. When David Brus succeeded his father Robert to become David II of Scotland, his tutor, William of Dalgernock was elected Abbot of Kelso. William can have had only two or three years in which to make an impression at his new Abbey since in 1332 Edward Balliol, a man with a strong claim to David II's throne, established his political and military base at Roxburgh. As the son of King John Balliol, Edward was supported in his efforts to become King of Scotland by Edward III of England. When the Scots were decisively defeated by an English army at Halidon Hill in 1333 just outside Berwick, Balliol had himself crowned at Scone. In exchange for English support, Edward agreed to hand over to his royal namesake most of southern Scotland, including Roxburgh and Kelso, and although the Scots held Roxburgh Castle briefly in the 1340s, both abbey and castle were in English hands for more than 100 years until 1460. The English maintained a garrison at Roxburgh more less continuously during that period and that in turn meant that Kelso was effectively no longer part of Scotland. The influence on Scottish politics that its abbots had exercised virtually ceased, since their appointment must have been in the gift of the English King.

The Abbey certainly needed the protection of Edward III and there are several references to Kelso during his reign. In 1333/34 he restored the Abbey's property in Berwick and confirmed it again in 1356/56, ordering all his subjects to observe this ruling — the implication being that Kelso was having problems asserting its rights. In 1368 Edward gives the monks permission to buy food and drink in Northern England since their own farmlands had been devastated in war, and five years later he again insists that Kelso's rights should be protected. Richard II of England warned the Percys and Douglases to stop plundering the Abbey's lands and twice more during his reign he published documents about Kelso's security.

Abbot William of Dalgernock left Scotland with the young king, David II in 1334 to take refuge in the Chateau Gaillard in Normandy. In his absence Thomas de Hassynden, who must have had the support of Edward Balliol and the English, ran the affairs of Kelso Abbey and it is significant that he called himself not Abbot, but Warden of Kelso. When David II returned in 1341 the English hold on Southern Scotland receded. The following year Roxburgh Castle fell to the Scots and it is possible that Dalgernock was re-instated as abbot. In the Border warfare of the next two years Kelso Abbey must have suffered a great deal since in 1344 David II granted the monks permission to cut wood in his forests of Selkirk and Jedburgh for the repair of their buildings.

28 The Wool Trade and The Black Death

Turning aside from the effects of international politics on Kelso, there are two bits of information concerning mid-fourteenth century life in the Borders that have come to light. The first was written by an Italian wool-merchant called Pegolotti. He was a buyer who travelled around Scotland inspecting the wool crop and assessing its value. Around 1340 he compiled a list of Scottish abbeys that produced wool and Kelso (written as Ghelzo) is mentioned on it. As far as Pegolotti was concerned Kelso was not a particularly important producer and that observation may show how disorganised life had become at the Abbey — in view of the great number of sheep Kelso is known to have owned as recently as the rent-roll of 1300.

The second piece of information concerns a cataclysmic event that enveloped mediaeval Europe in the middle of the fourteenth century. The Black Death spread from the east like a tidal wave and in 1348/49 it reached Scotland. Although the comparative reticence of Scottish chroniclers on the subject may mean that the plague was less severely felt than it was in England, its arrival must nevertheless have decimated the population. At the back of the Kelso cartulary there is evidence that the monks of Kelso tried to defend their community against the Black Death. Written in Scots, there is 'A Noble Treatise Against the Pestilence' by a man called John of Burdouse (Bordeaux?) or rather there is a summary of the treatise's main points evidently done by one of the monks. Its date seems to be around the beginning of the fifteenth century but the event it was referring to happened much earlier. Here is the opening paragraph:

> Here begins a noble treatise made by a good physician, John of Burdouse, for medecine against the pestilence illness. And it is departed [set down] in 4 parts; the first part tells how a man shall keep himself in time of Pestilence so that he shall not become ill, the second chapter tells how his sickness comes, the third chapter tells of medicine against his illness, the fourth tells how he shall be kept.

The advice given is fairly lengthy but what follows are several excerpts that give some idea of how people were affected by the Black Death and how they coped, prevention is dealt with first:

> This clerk says in the first chapter that for default of good ruling [self-control] and dieting in meat and drink, men fall often fall into sickness. For when the pestilence reigns in the country men that will be kept from the illness need to keep from all outrage and excess in meat and drink, and not take baths or sweat very much for these open the pores of the body and allows the venomous air to enter and destroy the lively spirit and enfeeble the body.

Then the symptoms are described in relation to the parts of the body that are affected by the plague:

> In man are three principal parts and members; the heart, the groin and the head, and each of these has its cleaning place where the surpluses may be let out . . . the heart has its cleaning place under the arms, that is in the hole of the oxters, the cleaning place of the groin is the [rectum and urinary tract]. Both the cleaning places of the head are under the ear or under the throat.

The plague was thought to stop up the natural outflow through these cleaning places with the result that:

> it causes a man to be in pain and makes a boil or a bulge in some part of the three cleaning places mentioned above, or else near them.

And now the cure:

> The third chapter tells of help against this illness, and that it may be well helped by the letting of blood.

And this is followed by much detail about where blood should be let from and what the best time to do it are. Various foods (potage of almonds!) and drinks (small ale and diluted vinegar) are recommended as are several herbal powders. Finally John of Burdouse writes:

> [If a man pays attention to] the teaching of this treatise, through sickness he shall be hale and through the grace of God, it he will keep himself in the manner aforementioned, he shall not dread any pestilence of swellings or pains.

Unfortunately for the people who caught the Black Death, John's detailed advice was rarely of any value — except for the last reference to God's grace. Prayer was very likely the only comfort sufferers actually had through their fatal illness. The Black Death returned to Scotland many times after 1348/49 with severe outbreaks in 1362, 1379, and 1417.

29 A Confused Succession of Abbots

William of Dalgernock was probably still Abbot of Kelso in 1354 when 'William' is styled as such in a charter. Kelso must still have been under the domination of the English garrison at Roxburgh Castle and it is a measure of Edward III's control of the area around it that in 1361 he gave the Chapel of St Thomas in Wooden away to one of his subjects. The Chapel had belonged to Kelso but Edward had no compunction about giving to an Englishman and no doubt that the new owner could hold on to it even though it was technically in Scotland.

Documents dated 1370 and 1372 show that William de Bowden, a man who evidently came from a village that was one of the Abbey's richest possessions, was abbot. He sought the protection of the English king, Richard II, rather than that of Robert II of Scotland, presumably because the English were better able to control affairs in that part of Scotland.

By 1398 Patrick had become abbot and in an interesting document dated the same year he granted permission to one of his monks to go to university at either Oxford or Cambridge to study liberal arts and sciences. Only the initials of the monk are given, R de R, but it is possible that he was a man called Robert de Roxburgh. If R de R had chosen to attend Oxford University in 1398 he would have come into contact with the heretical teachings of John Wyclif. These teachings were the subject of a letter, dated 1402, from Walter Skirlaw, Bishop of Durham, to Patrick, Abbot of Kelso. Apparently two priests, Robert de Roxburgh and James

Nottingham were spreading the heretical teachings of Wyclif in the diocese of Durham. The probable reason for Skirlaw writing to Kelso was that the priests had taken refuge in Scotland and it may be that R de R had returned to his abbey to escape the wrath of the English bishop.

There exist several documents dated in Patrick's reign that concern the attendance of procurators acting for the Abbey of Kelso at Scottish parliaments. Robert III is termed 'our lord the King' and it is clear that Kelso was at that time thought of as a participating entity in the government of Scotland even though the Abbey sought the help of English kings and certainly came under English military domination from Roxburgh. Of course the Abbey owned much land all over Scotland which fell outside foreign influence, and it is possibly in this capacity that Kelso was seen as retaining some of its earlier importance in the government of Scotland.

William was abbot in 1428 when he wrote to the Pope Martin V about St James' Church in Roxburgh. Roughly 100 years previously Roger de Auldton had founded a chantry in perpetuity at St James' for the celebration of mass at certain times of the year. This had been recently discontinued because of the destruction of St James' and its property in the sporadic warfare that was taking place over the Border during that period. Abbot William arranged for the chantry to be transferred to Kelso until repairs could be made to St James'. It is a measure of the gradual decline of the town of Roxburgh that its parish church should suffer in this way, and that repairs should take such a lengthy period.

When the Bishop of St Andrews asked Abbot Thomas of Dryburgh to ensure that the above business was properly carried out, in 1434, William was mentioned as the late Abbot of Kelso. Another man called William succeeded him and was still Abbot in 1444.

30 The Coronation of James III

In the summer of 1460 James II of Scotland gathered a great army and marched south to Roxburgh. The castle had been in English hands for more than a hundred years and James was determined to remove the foreign garrison. Part of his army camped on the north side of the Tweed near to Wester Kelso, and there the Scottish artillery had been set up. On Sunday 3 August James II and his Queen, Mary of Guelders, went to inspect the canon. The gunners let off a fusillade at Roxburgh Castle to impress the royal couple, but according to a contemporary account, written in Scots:

bot the peice appeiringle, with ouer sair a chairge, flies in flinderis, with a part
of quilk, strukne in the hentch [thigh] or he was war, quhairof [allace] he dies.

James II probably bled to death through the injury to his thigh. At all
events Mary of Guelder brought her eldest son James, who was only eight
years old, to Kelso Abbey and on 10 August he was crowned at the high
altar. There are two versions of the ceremony. One states that Bishop
Kennedy of St Andrews performed the crowning as the first bishop of
Scotland traditionally did. The second version relates that the Earl of
Douglas grew impatient with the long and stately ritual. He rushed up to
the altar, took the crown and put it on the little boy's head saying, 'Now it
is on your majesty's head by my own setting, let us see who will be bold
enough to take it off again'.

James III's coronation was the last great state occasion held at Kelso
Abbey. The fateful seige of 1460 fulfilled an old prophesy that a dead man
would win Roxburgh Castle but it also meant the end of Roxburgh as a
royal castle and royal burgh. The Scots destroyed the castle to prevent it
falling once again into English hands, and by 1460 the town had virtually
disappeared as a result of the continual Border warfare. The seige and
coronation mark an emphatic end to the connection that David I had
created in 1128 between his own royal burgh and his favourite abbey. The
town of Wester Kelso had gradually been taking over the functions of
Roxburgh since the Wars of Independence but it could not attain anything
more than local importance as an economic centre.

31 Kelso in disarray

The year after the coronation the realities of life at Kelso Abbey are
highlighted in the appointment of a special procurator to sort out its
financial affairs. The Bishop of St Andrews asked the Pope for the right of
visitation to the Abbey — the papacy had exempted Kelso from this in her
heyday. And it seems that from 1460 onwards the health of the monastery
declined greatly.

A man called Alan was cited as abbot between 1464 and 1466 and in 1473
Abbot Robert was commissioned by James III to look into breaches of the
Border truce. Robert and others negotiated with English commissioners
over the naming and punishment of individuals who had broken the
conditions of the temporary peace between the two countries. An Abbot
George was a witness to a royal charter concerning the church of Glasgow
in 1473.

Two years after the accession of James IV in 1488 Kelso Abbey again sought the protection of the English king in preference to the King of Scotland. Accordingly Henry VII granted a writ confirming the right of the Abbey to the town of Kelso, to Redden, Sprouston, Wester Softlaw (acquired recently), the barony of Bowden and many other possessions. Henry also allowed the monks of Kelso to travel into England to buy lead, wax and wine and any other commodities they wished. Perhaps this was necessary from time to time when the intermittent Border warfare had cut off local supplies. The English king also permitted the monks to pursue anyone who had stolen from them into England. This looked like an early example of 'Hot Trod', a practice in the Borders whereby people might ignore national boundaries in pursuit of reivers who had stolen their cattle, or any other property.

Robert was Abbot of Kelso in 1493 when he was appointed by the Scottish Parliament to be one of the three auditors of causes and complaints. His name occurs in charters dated 1495 and 1505. Robert was probably the last Abbot of Kelso to be elected by the monks who lived there. Andrew Stuart, the bishop of Caithness, was given the Abbey 'in commendam', that is, King James IV gave him the revenues of Kelso but did not actually make him Abbot since he was not a monk. Stewart paid for the upkeep of the brethren living at Kelso but it is doubtful if he did more than make an occasional visit. Doubtless he appointed a sort of manager to look after his interests at the Abbey.

The reign of Stewart's manager came to an abrupt end the night after the disastrous battle at Flodden in 1513. Andrew Ker of Ferniehurst, known as Dand Ker, broke into the Abbey and literally threw out Stewart's man. He then installed his brother, Tam, as the 30th Abbot of Kelso. It is a sad measure of the decline of Kelso that the 30th successor of great men like Herbert and John should be a local bandit by the name of Tam Ker. Apparently Andrew Stewart continued to style himself Abbot of Kelso until his death in 1518.

32 The Dacre Raid and Others

The peace negotiations after Flodden never reached a satisfactory conclusion and war broke out again between England and Scotland in 1522 with disastrous consequences for the town of Wester Kelso, and the Abbey. The English sent an expeditionary force to plunder and pillage the Border country. It was commanded by the Earl of Shrewsbury who in turn ordered two of his lieutenants, Lords Ross and Dacre, to take Wester Kelso. They duly burned the town, but seem to have left the Abbey alone. On 22 October the Earl of Northumberland was concerned that the job had only been half done and he wrote to King Henry VIII:

> I, by the advice of my brother Clyfforthe, have devised that, within these three nights, God willing, Kelso shall be burned, with all the corn in the said town, and then they (the Scots) shall have no place to lie any garrison near to the Border. And this burning of Kelso is devised to be done secretly, by Tynedale and Redesdale.

Fortunately for Kelso, the Earl of Northumberland did not carry out his plans and the town and abbey were spared, but only for a year.

The Abbot of Kelso feared another invasion in 1523 and he wrote to the Queen Dowager of England, Margaret, the sister of Henry VIII. She was the widow of James IV and the Scots had hopes that she might deflect her brother from harrying the south of Scotland. She wrote to King Henry on 6 January 1523:

> Also my Lord, the Abbot of Kelso has prayed me to write to you to be his good lord, and for my safe you will not let any evil be done to that place, which I will pray you to do.

Margaret's efforts were in vain. Lord Dacre invaded and:

> In the morning of the day which was yesterday, we set forward and we went to Kelso where we not only burned and destroyed the whole town that would burn by any labour but also cast down the Gatehouse of the Abbey.

Dacre's men did more than he recorded. They demolished and burned the Abbot's House and the buildings around it, and the Chapel of the Blessed Virgin which was said to contain wooden stalls of beautiful workmanship. They also burned the monks' dormitory and removed all the roofing of the Abbey. This was mainly made of lead and may have been of particular value to the English as canon shot.

Tam Ker was involved in the details of peace-making after this invasion, according to a letter sent from Berwick to Archbishop Wolsey, Henry VIII's chancellor:

> The confirmation of the peace on the part of the Scots was brought hither by the Abbot of Kelso, the Headsman of the Kers of Teviotdale, well accompanied by honest men to the number of 60 persons to whom I made such cheer as I could that day at dinner. And forthwith we examined our commissions and made collation of the other of our greater writings. And so, at night we departed and kept our lodgings. And because the companions with the said Abbot were Borderers, I bid them to be well accompanied and good cheer to be made unto them. The said Abbot being a right sad and wise man,

brother to Dand Ker of Ferniehurst.

Well might Tam Ker be sad, he had presided over the sacking of the Abbey of Kelso, which, although it had needed repair often in the past, had never suffered as it did in 1523. Tam was still Abbot in 1528. An illegitimate son of James V, James Stewart, was officially named as Commendator of Kelso in 1541, a year before the storm of war burst again on the Abbey. The same man who commanded the 1523 expedition, the Earl of Surrey lately created Duke of Norfolk, turned his artillery on Kelso but it is not recorded how much damage was done.

Nevertheless the town must have recovered sufficiently for it to seem an attractive target to the combined garrisons of Wark, Cornhill, Ford, Bamburgh and Fenton. In June 1544 they took Kelso by surprise, killed forty townspeople and took some prisoners. In characteristic reiver-fashion they also helped themselves to 100 oxen, 50 horses and quantities of malt and corn.

33 The Hertford Raid. Kelso Abbey Destroyed

Compared with what was to come later in 1545 these raids were insignificant. In September, the Earl of Hertford landed at Coldingham with 12,000 men. In an attempt to force the Scots to agree to a marriage between Mary Queen of Scots and Edward, son of Henry VIII, the English King had sent Hertford on a punitive expedition to the Border country. Here is the report he sent back to London:

> From the camp at Kelso, 11th September 1545, at night. Please it your Royal Majesty to understand that upon Wednesday at 2 o'clock in the afternoon, I, Earl of Hertford, with your majesty's army did arrive here afore Kelso... and immediately upon arrival a certain number of Spaniards, without my appointment [approval], gave of their own courage an assault with their harquebuces to the Abbey but when I perceived the same to be to little purpose for the winning of it I caused them to retire and thought best to summon the House [which I did forthwith . . . and such as were within the same being in number one hundred Scots persons whereof 12 were monks] persuaded with their own folly and wilfullness to keep it which no man of consideration of the danger they were in, [the thing not being tenable], would have done, did refuse to render and deliver it. Whereupon I caused the same to be approached out of hand with ordinance and within an hour a great breach was made . . . the Scots bye and bye driven into the Steeple but the way being so dangerous and of good strength and night being at hand, I decided to leave the assault till morning, setting good watch at night about the House. Which was not well kept what a dozen of the Scots in the dark of night escaped by ropes out of back windows and corners with no little danger

to their lives. When the day was come the Steeple was soon assaulted. It was
immediately won and as many Scots as were within slain.

Dismissing an idea that the Abbey might be used as a fortress, Hertford
ordered it to be destroyed sufficiently 'so that the enemy may have little
use for it'. Lead was again taken from the roofs and sent back to Wark.
Except for the West End of the Abbey Kirk most of the buildings were
completely destroyed either by fire or by undermining them so that they
collapsed. After spending five days encamped at Kelso Hertford's army
moved off to attack and destroy Jedburgh.

In all the English attacked 287 villages, farmsteads and churches but it
seems that the heroic defence of Kelso Abbey was the only substantial
resistance they ran into. Kelso was left in such a poor state that the market
had to be moved, temporarily, to Hume.

Hertford evidently did not succeed in his main intention of rendering
the Abbey completely useless for military purposes. In 1546 Lord Eure,
English Warden of the Eastern Borders, reported that his soldiers had again
taken, 'the church of Kelso, wherein was 31 footmen'.

In 1558 the Commendator James Stewart died and the Abbey passed into
the hands of Cardinal Guise, the brother of the Queen Regent, Mary of
Lorraine. The reformation had begun to affect Scotland at this time and
there is a tradition that Kelso, and Lesmahagow, suffered at the hands of
the iconoclasts or image-breakers. The Protestant rulers of Scotland, the
Lords of the Congregation, claimed the Abbey for the crown in 1559.
Doubtless the population of Kelso also made claims on the fabric of the
building during this period. They must have stood in sore need of sound
building materials in the wake of such destruction by the English.

34 The Remnants of Kelso's Property described

The office of Abbot of Kelso virtually ceased to exist in any real sense but
there are instances when people continued to use it. One of the ubiquitous
Kers of Cesford styled himself Abbot, since he was a relative of Tam Ker. It
is possible that this man took responsibility for the remnant of the
monastery who had survived the Hertford raid and the subsequent
depradations. In 1567 the Kers and others asked the monks to draw up a list
of what the Abbey still owned, both in churches and lands. While much of
this must have been theoretical, there is a good deal of information in the
Rent-Roll to show that, compared with the listings of 1300, Kelso had not
officially lost a great deal of its property. There is also much information on
the town of Kelso and its immediate vicinity in 1567. It is written in Scots

and divided into sections that deal with each property in turn. Here is the first section:

Kelso Towne.	
Item the greit maill of the said towne	ixvj lib. xiij s. iiij d.
Item the small maillis of the cottaris thereof by the discedentis	liij lib.
Item the fishing of tued	lxvj lib. xiij s. iij d.
Item the mylnis of Kelso	lxxx lib
Item the duis and customes of Kelso and the borderflat	x lib.
Item the cowbill at roxburgh	xx lib.
Item the blak bak croft in Kelso	vj s. viij d.
Item the cowbill at maxwell	x lib.
Item the gersume callit tolsyluir	xiij lib v..
Item the cunniggers	xvj s. viij d.
item the brumebank and the hot	xiij s. iij d.
Item the westercroftis	xl s.
Item the angrieflat	xx s.
Item the brumecroft	xij s.
Item the towne croft	x s.

The rest of the rent roll is organised by parish boundary and there is no reason to think that the above entry for Kelso should refer to anything other than the land inside the old parish boundary north of the river. The first two items on the list are the maillis or rents of the town, that is the total amounts of cash owed to the Abbey by both large and small tenants. There is more detail about these later in the rent roll. The next item is the fishing of the Tweed; the monks owned the rights to fish from Brokesmouth (near Stodrig Farm) right down to the mouth of the river Eden. Evidently this was an important source of revenue since the amount of cash it brought to the abbey is the same as that for the large rents of the town. 'Mylnis', meaning mills, is in the plural and that is surprising because the monks were careful in earlier chapters to protect the monopoly of their mill and there is no mention of another one, or more. Nevertheless if the volume of business was too great for one to cope with it is always possible that they built another and enjoyed the revenue from it.

The dues and customs refer to tolls exacted from people entering the town, possibly to go to market or transact business of some kind. There were other payments associated with markets and in one as old as Kelso's these would be well-established. The name 'Borderflat' has passed out of use but it would suggest that that area lay near the parish boundary; the term 'flat' refers to a level piece of ground. The Black Back croft is another lost name but its rental value, only 6 shilling and 8 pence, is the lowest in the list and that would suggest two things; that it was a small parcel of land and that it was perhaps less fertile. Even its name implies that it was ill-considered in sixteenth century Kelso.

The word 'cowbill' is mentioned twice, at Roxburgh and at Maxwell. These are place-names lying outside the parish, opposite the western and southern banks of the Tweed. 'Cowbill' does not appear in any dictionary but there is a clue to its meaning on the western bank of the Tweed at Kelso. The riverside walk there is known as Cobby Walk and part of the river itself, just below the northern end of Roxburgh Street, is called 'The Coble Hole'. Now if 'cowbill' is said quickly it begins to sound like 'coble' and that is a word which appears in even the shortest dictionary. It means a flat-bottomed type of boat commonly used as a ferry. It seems likely that the Coble Hole marks the departure quay for the ancient ferry that took passengers and livestock from Kelso to Roxburgh. Traffic over to the old burgh must have been heavier than that using the ferry to Maxwell since the revenue, even as late as 1567, is twice as large.

'Gersume' is a kind of payment like a toll or more like a special impost and easily levied on a particular traffic or activity — 'tolsyluir' is toll-silver or toll revenues. 'Cunningers' is straightforward: it is an old Scots word for a rabbit warren. Rabbits still burrow all along the steep bank that runs from Sharpitlaw House westwards to the Edinburgh road and this property might have been all or more likely part of that geographical feature. 'Broombank' may also refer to that same bank or part of it and modern Broomlands estate ran from Queen's House to Hendersyde. West Broomlands was the former name of what is now a residential built-up area stretching from Abbotseat (a name, incidental which seems to have no connection with the Abbey) almost to the Edinburgh road. 'Broomcroft' may refer to the flat area at the top of the bank, either side of the road to Ednam.

'Westercroft' is difficult to place but if one assumes that it was to the west of Wester Kelso it could be that piece of land is now lying inside the walls of Floors estate called the Wester Anna. The 'Angrieflat' is one name that has come down to us intact: the wood above Croft Park on the other side of the road leading to Kelso Race Course and to the right of the Edinburgh road is still known by Kelsonians as Angryflat Plantation. There are the remains of ancient cultivation terraces there, but these might have been the creation of a much earlier agricultural community. Finally the 'Town Croft' was probably an early name for what became Croft Farm. A map of 1823 shows it lying on the flat ground below Angryflat, between it and Inch Road to the south, with its western limit the Edinburgh road and its eastern, the Ednam road.

Later on in the rent roll there is a list of other locations inside Kelso Parish. Beside them are the amounts in kind that are owed to Kelso Kirk — the Abbey. The list comprises Kelso Towne, Bokislaw, The Fluris, The Gallowlaw, Eister Meirdene and opposite each place is written the amount of corn and beer due to the monks. Apart from Kelso these seem to be hamlets or farm-touns treated as units by the writers of the roll. Bokislaw is obscure but the others are now farms. Incidentally this is the first mention of Floors and it is clear that the modern spelling of Galalaw now hides the rather more grim origins of the place-name.

Maxwell Kirk is also accounted for and this entry must refer to St Michael's Church which lay in what is now the Border Union Showground. The Ordnance Survey maps show its site as being near the main grandstand. Most of the names have survived in Maxwell's list of places owing corn and beer; 'The Towne of Maxveill, with the Manis of Wester Wooden and Howden, Pendicill Hill, Easter Wooden, Wester Wooden and Wester Softlaw'. A 'pendicle' is a Scots word for a small bit of land, some times attached to a larger, or it can simply mean a small farm.

It is strange that there is no mention of Roxburgh or St James' Church in all of these lists of Kelso's property. In 1649, almost a century after this point, St James' is said to be still in existence —although only just, for it had six communicants. The 1567 list of churches is detailed and even if only a remnant of St James' and its parish had remained, it would have rated a mention.

The painstaking nature of the rent roll is exmplified later on in the long sections which deal with the people who rented their lands from Kelso Abbey. The renters are actually named and they are divided into three types; the small maillis (rents), the greit maillis and the almarie lands. In all 251 people are listed as holding land in Kelso and owing rent for it to the Abbey. This is the first historical record of the mass of ordinary citizens of the town and one of the remarkable things about it is how the names (all of the men and women her have by this period acquired surnames) have survived. There are Hoggs, Middlemasses, Hoods, Lillies, Achesons, Gladstones and Pearsons living in Kelso now and they may be the lineal descendents of those bearing the same names in the 1567 rent roll.

If the Abbey was the owner of all the land in Kelso, the 251 names might provide the basis for an estimate of the town's population in the mid sixteenth century. Assuming that the Abbey only listed the householders as liable to pay rent —although some women are mentioned, but they may simply be the heritors of family property — that would suggest a total of

251 families. In 1751 the average size of a Kelso family is recorded as being four. Since medicine and the conditions of life did not improve much in the 190 years between the two dates, it is possible that a family size of four would be about right for Kelso in 1567. That makes a population of around a thousand souls at that period.

Occasionally in the listings a man's craft is noted down. One Willie Browne was a 'cordener'; that is a Scots spelling for cordwainer which is an old name for a shoemaker. Robert Davidsoun the 'fleichour' or butcher is mentioned and that is an instance of a peculiar Scots word for a butcher that is still in use. The Kelso Co-op does not have a butcher's shop, it has a fleshing department, a term unknown in England. Willie ker (surnames are not always given a capital letter) was a fyscher and later in the list three men, Johne hog, George alene and Thomas dowglas pay extra rent for their 'kill' or kilns.

The three divisions, small maillis, greit maillis and the almarie landis, are made between types of rent paid, not the places where the rent is due. Or so it seems, because the origin of the word 'almarie' is not clear. It may be a reference to the patron saint of the Abbey St Mary but more likely it is a corruption of the latin *eleemosina* or free gift. These lands are rented for standard amounts; most of them for five or ten shillings and two chickens. At the beginning of the list, David Leirmont is called a 'bailze' or a baillie. That is a Scots term for a farm steward or foreman and it seems likely that the 'almarie' lands formed a group of abbey possessions under the direction of a man who acted as agent for the monks. At all events the name has not survived in any geographical sense and there are no present-day citizens of Kelso holding land by 'almarie' tenure.

In the sections of the rent roll dealing with 'small maillis' and 'almarie landis' there is no indication of where people's possessions were. But at the very end of the list some names are attached to places. Mostly these are locations already discussed:

> Adame pamer for the west croftis in mail xl s.
> Thomas ker for the middilmest landis in maill xij s.
> Johne pamer for the angrie flat in maill xx s.
> Robert mow for the brum banke and hott xiij s. iij d.
> Johne ker for the cunnigers in maill xxj s. viij d.
> Johne ker for the eist . . . viij bollis aittis and ij fudder of turris.
> Johne ker for the bankheid scheill vi bollis of strakit meill.
> Willie browne for the blak bak in maill vi s, viij d.
> Johne pamer for the ferrie cowbill at maxveill x li.
> The mailleris croftis x s. viiij d.
> The keping of the brumes and the vester mido in the Placis handis Sir Walter of

ceffurd knycht for the fysching of the ewer vater and ferrie cowbill. Summa xx li.

Gilbert ker of the greinheid for the maillis summa lxxx pundis.

Item for the fysching of the nether vater and ferrie cowbill at sprouston. Summa Lxvi li. xiij s. iij d.

Item to the place to have salmount for ij s the peis.

Item the gilsis viij d and trowtis iiij d.

Daud Leirmount for the duis and customis and border flat x li.

The first six properties listed seem to run from west to east, starting with Adame pamer's Westcrofts and then leading to a known location at Angrie Flat and thence to Brum banke, which may be the origin of the name Broomlands, ending at Johne ker's property — Johne ker was bound to deliver 2 cartloads of peats to the Abbey and the peat bog lay in the east. Three new place-names occur in the above; the 'Middlemest landis', the 'Bank heid Scheill' and the 'Wester Mido (meadow)'. The first is obscure but if the order of the first six properties is correct then the 'Middelmest landis' might have been that piece of woodland that is now known as Kelso Bank Plantation. A 'scheill' is a Scots word for a hut used as temporary accommodation by shepherds, but it has another meaning that might fit better in this context. 'Bankheid Scheill' suggests that the scheill is up on a height and the word can mean 'a winnowing hill' or a place where it was windy enough to separate grain from its husks. That contention is supported by the fact that Johne ker had to give for his land 6 measures of properly winnowed grain. The Wester Meadow was probably common grazing land but there is no clue to its location other than it lay in the west.

The Pamers and the Kers predominate in the above list but right at the end there is a note that Daud Leirmount owned the right to collect the dues and customes for Kelso and the Border Flat. If Leirmount's title of Baillie also had its other, related meaning of magistrate this would suit his role as collecter of local taxes. Like Ralph, the burgess of Kelso in 1200, Daud or David Leirmount could be seen as an early Provost of Kelso. If he was Baillie of Kelso, he would sit as the magistrate of the Baron Court. In the past the Abbots of Kelso, as the feudal superior of the community, would have occupied this position but since the Abbey had been mainly in the hands of absentee commendators since 1511, it is not surprising to see a local man fulfilling this role.

Most of the rents were computed in shillings and pounds, and occasionally pence. But here there is a mixture of money and kind. Johne ker owed the monks properly winnowed meal for the bankheid scheill. He also owed 8 measures of 'aittis' or oats and 2 'fudder of turris' for land he held in the eastern part of Kelso parish. A 'fudder' is a cartload and 'turris' is a mis-spelling of turfis or peats. The nearest peat-bog to Kelso Abbey did indeed lie to the eastern side of the parish and that was up on Ferneyhill, beside the modern road to Ednam. It was probably a useful rent for the monks to retain in kind since their abbey buildings would require much peat to keep them warm in the damp and cold of the winter months.

The fishings of Tweed were lucrative and they are dealt with in some detail in this last part of the rent roll. Sir Walter Ker of Cesford Castle owned the fishing of the Tweed above Kelso, and the revenues of the ferry to Roxburgh. His kinsman, Sir Gilbert Ker, was the owner of the rents of Kelso — in fact it seems likely that both these men inherited what were the rights of the Abbot of Kelso from their recent ancestor, Tam Ker, who had been Abbot in the earlier part of the sixteenth century. The fishing of the nether water, or the Tweed downstream from Kelso, and the revenues of the ferry at Sprouston are linked although it is not stated who owned them. It is interesting to note that the Sprouston Ferry was the last of Kelso's three ferries to go out of service, surviving until the mid 1960s. Finally in the rent roll of 1567, there are two entries concerning the fishing of Tweed. The abbots evidently had the right to buy salmon for 2 shillings the peice, young salmon (gilsis) at fourpence and trout at fourpence. Since fish was the main source of protein in the monks' diet it was essential to arrange for the purchase of fish at a fixed price.

The Abbey and its possessions were passed around various people in the 1560s and 70s until in 1587 an act of the Scottish Parliament records that:

> Forasmeikle as the haill monkis of the abbay of Kelso ar decessit, sua that
> presentlie there is na convent thairof, quhairby the tennents and taksmen of
> the said abbey ar uncertaine in quhat manner thai sall provide thair securities
> anent thair takkis, fewis, and rentalis, quhilk thai have tane, or may tak
> heirafter, of the said place and abbay of Kelso: Thairfor Sir Johne Maitland of
> Thirlestane . . .[is] to haif full rucht . . . of setting all fewis, takkis and rentalis

In 1540 there were 21 monks at Kelso, a surprisingly large number. But by 1576 only two remained; James Ancrame and Thomas Symsone.

Maitland did not enjoy the revenues for Kelso for long and they passed to the Bothwell family who in turn lost them when they were convicted of treason in 1594. Sir Robert Ker of Cesford was created Lord Roxburghe in 1599 and 3 years later he was granted the town of Kelso and the estates of the Abbey. The churches previously controlled by the Abbot reverted to the Crown in 1639. The Kers only formally received in 1602 what they seemed, at least partly, to own in 1567. The estates of the present Dukes of Roxburghe are extensive and historically owe much to the initiative of Dand Ker in 1513, in the aftermath of Flodden when he made his brother Tam the Abbot of Kelso.

Part Four

THE ABBEY KIRK AND THE BUILDINGS AROUND IT

OF THE FOUR Border abbeys, history has been the least kind to Kelso. It is comparatively easy to imagine what Melrose, Jedburgh and Dryburgh actually looked like in their former architectural glory, but so little now remains of Kelso that until recently historians were quite wrong about the original layout of the Abbey Kirk. The surviving fragment of the church was the West End and it was thought, perhaps because it was such a massive structure, that this represented the crossing and that the entrance porch was the nave. In fact the design of Kelso was unique in Scotland in that it had two crossings at both east and west ends with a tower over each one. This reconstruction is supported by archaeological and documentary evidence.

1 Duncan's Description

The latter comes from the Vatican archives in Rome in the shape of a description of what Kelso looked like in 1517 before it had suffered at the hands of Dacre and Hertford. A priest from the diocese of Glasgow, John Duncan, gave his account of the Abbey to a papal notary who copied it down for his records. Here is what he wrote:

> The church or monastery of Calco took its name from the small town of that name by which it stands. Its dedication is to St Mary . . . It is in the diocese of St Andrews, but is wholly exempt from any jurisdication of the archbishop and is certainly subject to the Apostolic See . . . It lies on the bank of a certain stream which is called in their language the Tweed [*Tuid sive Tueda*] and which today divides Scotland from the English . . .
>
> The monastery itself is double, for not only is it conventual, having a

convent of monks, but it is also a ministry; for it possesses a wide parish with the accompanying cure of souls which the Abbot is accustomed to exercise through a secular presbyter-vicar, removable at his pleasure. The Abbot exercises episcopal jurisdication over his parishioners himself.

The church, in size and shape, resembles that of St Augustine de Urbe, except that at each end it has two high chapels on each side, like wings, which give the church the likeness of a double cross. Its fabric is of squared grey stone, and it is very old indeed. It has three doorways, one towards the west, in the fore-part and the other two at the sides. It is divided into three naves by a double row of columns. The entire roof of the church is wooden, and its outer covering is of leaden sheets. The ground within is partly paved with stone and partly floored with bare earth. It has two towers, one at the fist entrance to the church, the other in the inner part like the tower of the Basilica of St Peter. The first contains many sweet-sounding bells, the other, at the choir, is empty on account of decay and age. The church is divided by a transverse wall into two parts; the outer part is open to all, especially parishioners both women and men, who there hear masses and receive all sacraments from their parochial vicar. The other part, the back of the church, takes only monks who chant and celebrate the Divine Office. Laymen do not go in except at the time of Divine Service, and then only men; but on some of the more solemn festivals of the year women are also admitted. In this furthest-back part, at the head of the church, there is an old wooden choir.

The high altar is at the head of the choir, facing east, and on this several choral masses are celebrated daily, one for the founder and the other according to the current feast or holiday. There are besides, in the whole church, twelve or thirteen altars on which several masses are said daily, both by monks and by secular chaplains. In the middle of the church, on the wall which divides the monks from the parishioners, there is a platform of wood; here stands the altar of the Holy Rood, on which the Body of Christ is reserved and assiduously worshipped, and there is the great worship and devotion of the parishioners. On the same platform there is also an organ of tin. The sacristy is on the righthand side of the choir; in it are kept a silver cross, many chalices and vessels of silver, and other sufficiently precious ornaments belonging to the altar and the priests, as well as the mitre and pastoral staff.

The cemetery is on the north, large and square, and enclosed with a low wall to keep out beasts. It is joined to the church. The cloister, or home of the monks, is on the south and is also joined to the church; it is spacious and square in shape, and it partly covered with lead and partly unroofed through the fury and impiety of enemies. In the cloister there is, on the one side, the chapter-house and the dormitory and on the other two refectories, a greater and lesser. The cloister has a wide court round which are many houses and lodgings; there also are guest-quarters common to both English and Scots.

There are granaries and other places where merchants and the neighbours store their corn, wares and goods and keep them safe from enemies. There is also an orchard and a beautiful garden.

In the cloister there is usually the Abbot, the Prior, and the Superior; and in time of peace thirty six or forty professed monks reside there. The town by which the monastery stands is called Calco, as has been said, or rather, in their common tongue, Chelso; it contains not more than sixty dwellings and is subject to the Abbot in respect of both temporal and spiritual jurisdiction. Nearly all the inhabitants are husbandmen and cultivators of the fields of the monastery, and none of them pays tithe or dues; on the contrary they receive payment from the Abbot, that they may be able to withstand and repel from the monastery the continual attacks of enemies.

The Abbey has, in addition, three or four other hamlets under it from which it receives tithes. It also holds the patronage of many parish churches from the vicars of which it receives part of the fruits. The Abbot's house is separate from that of the monks, but their table is in common.

Its value is somewhat uncertain because of the continual raids and pillaging of enemies and robbers, but by common opinion it is estimated at 1,500 ducats or thereabouts: and its fruits consist in church dues, tithes, provisions and rentals.

John Duncan's description of Kelso Abbey is not a complete one nor is it a picture of one of Scotland's greatest monastic foundations in its prime. By the time Duncan saw the Abbey in 1517 it had suffered from two hundred years of intermittent warfare since the militarisation of the Border country after the Wars of Independence. Nevertheless it is fortunate that someone took the trouble to record a description of Kelso before Dacre and Hertford obliterated all but the west end of the Kirk. Without it any attempt at a reconstruction of David I's favourite abbey would have to depend almost exclusively on conjecture.

2 Kelso Built on a Grand Scale

The very first gifts of lands and revenues to the Abbey, detailed so carefully in the foundation charter, show that King David wanted his foundation to be on a grand scale. The building of a great mediaeval church was a massive undertaking. Skilled masons, carpenters, window-makers and all the other craftsmen needed to begin work on the kirk and its monastery would have been both resident and passing through the developing burgh of Roxburgh. In addition, the amount of good quality stone the masons needed was certainly to be found around Kelso and Roxburgh. There were quarries at Broombank on the north side of the Tweed while on the southern shore at Sprouston there is evidence that mediaeval workmen hewed blocks of stone out of open pits. Log rafts would have been used to move the stones across and up the river to the building site at Kelso.

The men who surveyed likely locations for the new abbey must have been impressed with the virtues of the site that was eventually chosen; it lay near enough the river for it to be used in transporting building materials, it was not susceptible to flooding since it was protected by Kelso's chalk-heugh on the west, and the loop in the river made it partially defensible. In addition the pre-existence of the church of St Mary and the small hamlet around it provided temporary accommodation and a means of support for the transplanted colony while the Abbey was under construction.

3 Recent Archaeological Discoveries

Evidence from English sources shows that in the twelfth century the building trade was in the hands of laymen. Although the Tironians were noted for their skills in handicrafts, it is likely that their masons were not monks but men who worked for payment, either in kind or in cash or both. The church of St James at Roxburgh was being built at the same time as Kelso Abbey — it was consecrated in 1136, only eight years after the monks arrived in the area — and doubtless work was also being done at Roxburgh Castle and other sites in the burgh. Recent archaeological excavations in the garden of Kelso's parish church manse have revealed the location of the builders' yard for the Abbey Kirk, and something about the methods of carrying out the work.

Under the floors and walls of a later monastic building, traces were found of small dumps of unused mortar lying on the natural river-gravel. Nearby a large pit was discovered that contained one of the ingredients used by the masons in mixing their mortar, pea gravel. In the same small area a lead-smelting pit was found. Lead-ore was placed in the pit along with wood or charcoal and the resultant purified and molten lead ran into a crucible that had been set at the bottom of the pit. Before the lead cooled it was then taken to a stone hearth nearby where it was cast. The main use of lead was for roofing the kirk and casting into window cames. While work was going on in this builder's yard, the masons, and possibly the monks as well, lived in temporary wooden huts erected at the site. The huts were supported by several stone-packed post-holes and these came to light during the course of the excavations.

Turning to the Abbey Kirk itself the archaeologists were able to ascertain in a dig carried out in 1971 where the east end of the Kirk was, what the southern limit of the building was, and how many bays the nave had. They did this by digging five pits around the nineteenth century Abbey School. Two of the pits lay too far to the east to hold any remains of the Kirk at all, but the three on the western side of the school were more informative. These showed where the foundation trench of the east to west arcading ran and where another trench going from north to south

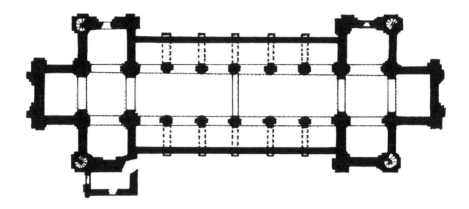

GROUND PLAN OF KELSO ABBEY SHOWING 'GALILEE PORCHES'
FAVOURED BY THE TIRONENSIAN SECT OF BENEDICTINES

Plan of Kelso Abbey

intersected with it. This was the site of one of the southern pillars supporting the eastern crossing of the Kirk, echoing the remaining one in the west. In turn that allowed the archaeologists to state that the nave of the abbey had only six bays in all, including the southern two that survive.

All the excavations at the east end of the Abbey Kirk showed how complete the destruction of 1545 was. Hertford seems to have razed the east end of the Kirk to the ground and he gives his reason in the reports quoted earlier. He destroyed the purely monastic part of the church and deliberately left intact the west end where the lay congregation worshipped. Duncan is clear in his description that the Kirk was split into two sections; the east end for the monks and the west end for the townspeople. It is likely that Hertford also destroyed all the conventual buildings around the Abbeys since most of them existed only for the use of the monks. Doubtless the task of destruction was assisted by the attentions of local stone-robbers and even a cursory glance at some of the buildings in Kelso today will reveal the ultimate fate of much of the fabric of the Abbey.

4 Architectural Style

The architectural style of Kelso Abbey is romanesque and it is easy to observe the most common characteristic of that style in the numerous round-headed windows in the west end. Since it was a comparatively early building in mediaeval Scotland and certainly one of the most impressive, Kelso was imitated elsewhere. The other Tironian abbeys at Arbroath, Kilwinning, and Lindores have similarities with Kelso and each other, and their common simplicity of decoration coupled with a largeness and solidity of scale might be called a Tironian style. When colonies of monks went out from Kelso, it would be natural for them to ask their masons to incorporate features from the mother house in the designs for the new abbeys.

It was in this way that particular architectural styles spread throughout Western Europe, and it is possible tht David I suggested the original shape that Kelso Abbey was to take. The form of a double crossing at Kelso is a rare one and without doubt the first in Scotland. In England there are few churches of this design but two of them were probably known to David as a young man. He was Earl of Huntingdon and not far from his estates was the Abbey of Ely. Like Kelso it has a double cross and a large west door, known in both buildings as a Galilee Porch. To the south of Huntingdon lay the Abbey of Bury St Edmunds, between David's estates and London. Much of Bury St Edmunds' Abbey has now disappeared but the western tower that survives has strong similarities to Kelso in the handling of the windows and doorways. As a member of Henry I's court, David would have travelled around England with it and it is known that the English court stayed for lengthy periods at both these abbeys. It may be that when considering his first great monastic foundation at Kelso, the young prince elected to have a partial copy of churches he had seen in England.

Outside of the Tironian order, Kelso was influential in two older Scottish churches. The Abbot Arnold became Bishop of St Andrews in 1160 when the building of the massive cathedral was just beginning and it is possible to detect links with Kelso in earlier part of the remains. And on a much smaller, but more complete scale the Priory church of Coldingham's architecture —especially in the design of its small nave — owes something to the work of the master masons at Kelso.

5 The Buildings Around the Abbey Kirk

Because almost all of Kelso's conventual buildings have perished, leaving only the small Outer Parlour immediately south of the south transept of the west end and a door set into the modern burial cloister which was probably the doorway of the Chapter House, it is difficult to reconstruct the layout of the Abbey. In a series of excavations done in 1976 in the garden of the parish church manse, the remains of the Abbey Infirmary and its Kitchen were found. This was the hospital that housed the elderly and infirm monks and it seems to have been a relatively large building, in excess of 23 metres long and 16.5 metres wide. That in itself reflects a large community of monks. The building had been badly disturbed by stone-robbers but enough evidence was found to show that the Infirmary had been a vaulted structure with two side-aisles flanking a central corridor, rather like modern hospital wards. To the west of the Infirmary lay the remains of a smaller building, the kitchen used for the preparation of food for the sick and the elderly. The food they ate was different from the monks' ordinary fare in that it was high in protein, which was usually derived from the fish caught in the Tweed.

Other discoveries included the Abbey's drainage system which ran under the floor of the kitchen. The south wall of that building had been shored up at some point in the early thirteenth century because of subsidence. This was caused by one of the gravel pits used by the masons who built the Abbey, and the monks' solution was to fill the pit with all the debris that was lying around. They probably did this in a matter of days and a large part of what they packed into the pit was pottery, mostly old and broken. Nevertheless their emergency action has allowed the discovery of one of the most significant pottery finds in Scotland. Moreover, the pots are all of the same period, rather than the usual randomly dated finds made on mediaeval sites, and they are the best find of mediaeval cooking ware to be made in Scotland.

The monks' interest in crafts extended further than pottery and they were noted bell-founders. The north transept of the west end of the Abbey Kirk has a structure with three arches on top. This is the place where the monks hung their bells that were used to call the congregation, lay and monastic, to prayer. As recently as 1823 bells were being rung from the north transept, and for a while in the early nineteenth century the town clock resided there.

The monks of Kelso were skilled at many other things, not least of which was writing or to give it its more priestly term, clerking. The Abbey had a scriptorium or writing room where scribes toiled over the important business of copying documents and writing new charters. The seals that the Abbots of Kelso appended to their charters were beautiful examples of the craft of metalwork, but perhaps the most impressive pictorial or graphic art to come out of Kelso scriptorium is something that takes the story of the abbey and the town right back to its beginnings in the twelfth century Scotland. When Malcolm IV gave the Abbey a charter confirming all the original grants made by David I, the scribes decorated the capital

Reconstruction of Kelso Abbey

'M' for 'Malocolmus' at the start of the document. In the twin loops of the letter they painted two crowned figures; one was Malcolm IV and the other his grandfather, David I, the man who had the vision to bring 13 monks to his forest of Selkirk and then down to the small hamlet of Kelso.

Part Five

THE SEVENTEENTH CENTURY

MEDIAEVAL KELSO was essentially monastic Kelso. The history of the settlement from 1128 to the end of the sixteenth century has come down to us in the five hundred and sixty or so documents that the monks left after them. Sometimes their Latin is precise, sometimes infuriatingly vague but their land grants, deeds of gift, descriptions of places do form a coherent testimony to four hundred and fifty years of experience in one place.

After 1587 when the Scottish Parliament recorded that 'the haill monkis of the abbay of Kelso or decessit', the documentary evidence for a history of the town becomes fragmentary and therefore hard to come by. Nonetheless it is possible to discern a number of changes in Kelso in the seventeenth century. The Ker family consolidated their ownership of the burgh during this period. By 1634 Kelso had become a burgh of barony rather than an ecclesiastical burgh as it had been under the successive Abbots of Kelso.

Religion, the Protestant sort as opposed to the Catholicism that had founded and sustained Kelso in the mediaeval period, began to be important as an agent of change. Not only the wider issues of Civil War and the National Covenant, but also the small change of parish affairs provide rare information about events in the town.

And finally education in Kelso comes into focus as the Grammar School (meaning a school which taught Latin grammar) emerges as an institution with a continuous and sometimes surprising history.

1 Property in Wester Kelso

But the first glimpse of secular life in Kelso surfaces in 1566. As usual, property and the clarification of its ownership is the issue. On 10 April the register of the Privy Council of Scotland, which was sitting in Edinburgh, records that:

> Robert Mow produced a charter . . . of all the four merk lands which he occupies, lying in the town of Kelso, between the tenement of George Johnnestoun on the east, the tenement of Richard Palmer on the west, the marcat gait to the wynd on the south, and the said Abbot and Convent's land on the north part.

Although it exists in English the style of this is very much like the Latin documents which described property ownership in the town of Roxburgh, and it can be interpreted so that it produces a number of bits of information about Kelso in 1566.

First the question of which Kelso the charter is dealing with — Wester or Easter. The location of the Johnnestoun and Palmer properties on the east and west make it fairly clear that the 'marcat gait' or market street runs along the frontage of these three tenements, that is, east/west. Early maps of Kelso show that the town had (as it has now) two market squares, the Square and Coal Market. The only other candidates as market 'streets' are Woodmarket and Horsemarket but unfortunately they have the wrong orientation running in parallel from the south west to the north east. Of Kelso's old layout, that leaves Roxburgh Street which nowadays runs from the south east to the north west. That is its present orientation, but close examination of a survey of Floors done in 1736 for the Duke of Roxburgh shows that Roxburgh Street used to be a bit longer. Where the street presently widens out and then abruptly stops at Lady's Well Lane (leading down to the Cobby) it used to continue westwards turning slightly south so that its sides enclosed the site of the market cross of Wester Kelso. That site is still marked on the Ordnance Survey map as lying just inside the walls of Floors in what used to be the old ducal garden. This end of Roxburgh Street was altered in the early nineteenth century so that the garden could be created and ultimately a grander and more imposing entrance to Floors constructed. That involved, according to one relatively reliable historian, much demolition of town property and a re-direction of the street so that it could join Bowmont Street and form the main northern exit route from the town.

Now all of this means that Robert Mow probably meant to confirm his ownership of property in Wester Kelso. Here are two more hints that as the Abbey and Easter Kelso declined towards the end of the sixteenth century, the Wester settlement was the more important. Three years after the Mow charter, on 6 April 1569 a remarkable bond was agreed to and witnessed at Kelso. The Privy Council under the Regent Murray bound the inhabitants of the sheriffdoms of Berwick, Roxburgh, Selkirk and Peebles to keep the peace and to resist lawbreakers and thieves — especially persons of the surnames of 'Armestrong, Ellot, Niksoun, Croser, Littel, Batesoun, Thomsoun, Irwing, Bell, Johnesstoun, Glendonyng, Routlaige, Henderson and Scottis'. This bond and this list, (which sounds remarkably like the Langholm first XV) were then proclaimed from the 'marcat cross' of Kelso, or Wester Kelso.

In 1582 the Bishop of Orkney complained to the Privy Council about a group of Borderers, sixteen of whom bore the surname of Leirmonth. So that he put the finger on them with precision, his complaint distinguishes between those Leirmonths from Kelso, and those from 'Faircroce'. This may be a muddled but observable distinction between two settlements by a man who did not know the area well.

2 A Tough Town

As the bond of 1569 shows, Kelso and the Borders were not peaceful during this period. The town suffered from being a political football kicked around from owner to new owner. After the Reformation it passed through several pairs of hands until it came into the possession of Francis Stewart, Earl of Bothwell. When he was attainted in 1592 for repeated acts of treason, the inhabitants of Kelso (with the named exception of one William Lauder) were accused of assisting Bothwell. The king fined them 1700 merks and forbad anyone to contact Bothwell. By 1599 Rob Ker of Cessford had been created Lord Roxburghe and was the final owner of Kelso.

It is significant that in 1569 the Regent Murray stayed in the town for a full six weeks in order to suppress petty feuding in the surrounding area. The records of the Privy Council show that Kelsonians were far from peaceful. The famous Leirmonth clan reappear in 1585. They were ordered to be removed from John Aird's (a burgess of Canongate near Edinburgh): 'kindlie rowme and stedding in Kelso.' To which the bold William Leirmonth replied that he would: 'cutt his hochis' if Aird came anywhere near the town. The Privy Council Register contains no record of action being taken against the Leirmonths. John Aird probably valued the health of his 'hochis' too highly to venture south from Canongate.

Three years later another case in Kelso comes to light. Isobel Davidson, a relatively wealthy woman, had died intestate. The Sheriff of Roxburgh tried to get sufficient information about her property from one Michael Chatto to enable him to compile an inventory. He sent John Fisher, one of his officers, to Kelso to talk to Chatto. When he arrived in the town, Chatto compelled Fisher to:

> pas with him to the baksyde of the gairdis of the toun of Kelso, quair, in ane desert and quiet place, he not onlie maist cruellie and unmercifullie straike and dang the said John, and gve him mony bauck and bla Strikis in his heid, armes, bak and divers utheris pairtis of his body, and left him lyand for deid.

Michael Chatto and his brother-in-law Johnne Davidsoun (known as 'Shorte Jok') followed this up by going up to Lauder to menace witnesses in the Sheriff's investigation. Finally the behaviour of Chatto and 'Shorte Jok' became so outrageous that the Privy Council declared them both outlaws.

In 1603, as a footnote to this series of incidents, the Privy Council notice that the Leirmonth clan (all thirteen of them) each buy a complete stand of footman's armour. Clearly Roxburgh Street was no longer as safe as it used to be when Michael Chatto and 'Shorte Jok' were abroad.

Coupled with what is known about the generally troubled state of the Border country in the late sixteenth and early seventeenth centuries, and these local disturbances, a picture of a tough and unruly town emerges. There was plague in Kelso in 1579 and travel to England was officially forbidden (presumably the disease was believed to have come from the south). Both Duns and Kelso markets were cancelled. Against this background it is easy to understand the despair felt by the laird of Makerston when he said in 1598:

> that he would make the land more profitable by sowing salt on it.

6 A Change of Religion

Just as secular conflict beset the inhabitants of Kelso at this time so the great upheaval of the Reformation must have added further confusion. In 1559 the Lords of the Congregation, the Protestant leaders of Scotland, claimed the Abbey. There is a tradition that from that date until around 1580 'Protestant intolerance of all things Catholic led to further destruction of the Abbey', but there exists no evidence to support this. In any case it seems that the monks were not driven out (as happened in England) but allowed to carry on peacefully until 1587 when the last of them died. The destruction caused by Hertford's canon probably reduced the Abbey so much that the only destruction that could take place was simple stone-robbing by locals who were anxious to improve their property.

Nonetheless there seems to have been some disruption in the religious

102

life of Kelso around 1559. There is no record of a minister being found immediately to replace the abbey priests — it would have been extraordinary if someone had simply stepped into the monks' charge. Sometime before 1569 Adam Clerk was appointed 'exhorter' of both Kelso and Nisbet parishes. Exhorters were allowed to conduct public worship but were not officially qualified to administer the sacraments of baptism and communion, nor to perform the ceremony of marriage. There was a fully qualified minister at Jedburgh, Paul Methven, and those Kelsonians wishing to have their children baptised or wishing to be married could have travelled the eleven miles to him. That is until he was put out of his living for immorality. More likely the local people carried on being baptised and married by the old monks, possibly in secret out of the sight or knowledge of Adam the Exhorter.

In 1574 Paul Knox, the nephew of John Knox the great Reformer, was appointed to be Minister of Kelso. He also had Ednam, Makerston and Nenthorn kirks in his charge. Knox managed this burden for two years before he left the parish in the care of a series of preachers whose names have not come down to us. William Balfour became Kelso's Minister in 1585. In 1589 he either moved to the kirk at Maxwellheugh or added it to his living at Kelso. At all events he is again recorded as being Kelso's Minister in 1591.

The next name to surface is another Knox in 1605. James Knox held an MA from Edinburgh University where he had also been a teacher. He was the nephew of Paul and the grand-nephew of the Reformer. He is more interesting than the others because his living conditions were written down. It appears that he used bits of the old Abbey as his manse. One room was a hall and kitchen while another served as Knox's bedroom and closet. Both seem to have been vaults 'much below the level of the ground'. James Knox was succeeded in 1633 by his eldest son Robert. He was given the use of two 'galleries' or 'to-falls', one of which he converted into a bedroom, the other a place to walk and study. This sounds like the surviving segments of the cloister walk. It lay on the southern side of the Abbey church close to where the modern reconstruction now stands. If Robert Knox converted a part of this into a bedroom he would want it to adjoin the living quarters used by his father (presumably where the young Knox was born and reared). That points to the Knox's manse being in the Outer Parlour, the dark room which lies next to the south transept of the (remaining) western crossing of the Abbey church. The fact that the cobbled floor of that room is below present-day ground level would seem to confirm that supposition.

What the early ministers of Kelso and their congregation used for a church is not recorded but it was probably some part of the abbey fabric. Perhaps the roof over the western crossing survived for a time into the early seventeenth century.

4 The Abbey School

The precincts of the abbey continued to be a focus for the community at Kelso, not only in a religious sense but in other ways also. In 1670 a new school was built near the Abbey, on the site of the present Abbey School building. The Kirk Session minute of 7 June 1672 makes reference to the 'old' school and in 1642 a Mr Johne was hired as schoolmaster in what was clearly a well-established concern at that time. Considering the emphasis that the Protestant Reformers placed on parish education, coupled with the tradition of a monastic school at Kelso, it seems likely that education went on at an Abbey School of some sort well before 1642.

5 Roxburgh Street

If there was indeed a school near the abbey at the turn of the sixteenth and seventeenth centuries it is significant that it stayed in Easter Kelso, near the church and manse. Significant because it shows that Kelso was probably two places in 1600. The market cross was in Wester Kelso. Regent Murray clearly believed it was the focal point of the community in 1569 because it was there he promulgated his important proclamation about lawlessness. Also, very obviously, a market was held there — after the gradual demise of the Abbey and its market, probably Kelso's only market. Half a mile away to the south east, the church, the manse and perhaps a school.

Although there are no buildings in it dated as early as 1600, it seems likely that Roxburgh Street formed the old link between Wester and Easter Kelso. Here is some evidence that shows the southern end of Roxburgh Street in being at that time. In a charter dated 12 March 1603 King James VI infefts John Ker, burgess of Edinburgh, and his wife Elizabeth Weir with substantial property in Kelso:

> a tenement in the town of Kelso, in the fore street [anteriori via] on the west side, between the lands of Gilbert Mow on the north, the mill street on the south, the lands of John Waugh on the west, and the 'flesche stokis' on the east, occupied by David Robieson, all of which lands formerly belonged to the Abbey of Kelso.

Now, there is a great deal in this. First this property grant by the King is of old abbey lands which had reverted to the crown. That points to a location in Easter rather than Wester Kelso, the latter being and having been a settlement independent of the Abbey. Second and more important, the name of a street in Kelso is mentioned for the first time. 'Mill Street' is Mill Wynd and that places the property emphatically in Easter Kelso. There was no mill on the Tweed at Wester Kelso, the abbot having historically controlled the milling of corn for the town and the immediate area.

The 'fore-street on the west side' must indicate the west side of the Square, which cannot have been a square at that time since the word 'street' is specifically used in the document. Also why mention the 'west side' if there is not an eastern one? What lay on the east was not another tenement or occupied town dwelling but the 'flesche stokis', owned by David Robieson. 'Flesche stokis' are stockyards, a series of enclosures for keeping animals. Is this the bit of ground which became Kelso Square? Animals were traditionally bought and sold in the Square up to modern times and the survival of the bull ring is a permanent reminder of that ancient function. Nevertheless the word 'street' is used and it may be that what is glimpsed in 1603 is a stage in the evolution of the irregular open space that gradually became Kelso Square, possibly developing from an area to the north of the Abbey's graveyard which the monks used to hold their weekly market.

The Kers' property did not extend for the whole length of Mill Wynd since the land belonging to John Waugh are said to lie to the west of it. Even so, it is clear that Easter Kelso co-existed with Wester Kelso around 1600, and that Roxburgh Street was seen as a street probably leading from the west door of the old Abbey up to the market cross half a mile to the north west. That suggests Roxburgh Street as the basis from which modern Kelso grew, rather than the Square.

6 The Earl of Roxburgh and Kelso

In 1630 the Earl of Roxburgh was confirming his ownership of the lands that had formerly belonged to the Abbey of Kelso. Like the monks, he had a long list of his possessions written down, but unlike them, he was not so precise and therefore not as informative. One reason for that is the language; the Scots of the period was nothing like as precise as the mediaeval Latin of the abbey's own charters. Here is the bit relevant to Kelso:

[The Earl of Roxburgh claims] the silver duty payed by the tacksmen of Kelso, and teynds of the lordship of Kelso, £119.

Twenty-seven fewars of the lands in the town and territory of Kelso, paye of feu-duty, £68,6s.8d, comprehending 20sh for Angreflatt.

Twenty-one fewars of Willands and crofts in Kelso, paye of few, L.2,11s.4d.

That general statement was modified a number of times but it does show a distinction between those who held lands or property in the town of Kelso, and those who held farming land ('Willands' is an unusual word whose meaning is unclear but it may have something to do with a 'vill' or village) in the parish of Kelso. It makes no distinction between Easter and Wester Kelso.

After a certain amount of bargaining — the Earl of Roxburgh had to give up twenty kirks to the crown — Kelso was created a free Burgh of Barony. The Kers were confirmed in 1634 as its superiors, in place of the Abbots of Kelso. From this date onwards the administration of the Burgh takes on a familiar shape, one that changed little until the late nineteenth century. It worked like this: ·the burgh superior was the Earl (later Duke) of Roxburgh. He basically owned the place and appointed a Baron Baillie to act for him. The Baron Baillie was assisted by fifteen stentmasters, eight of these were appointed by the superior and seven by the Incorporated Trades (or Trade Guilds as they later became) of the town. The stentmasters (a stent is a Scottish word for a tax or rate) were like a town council and did form some kind of representation for the better-off sort of Kelsonian.

7 The Guilds

That administrative structure dates from 1634 but there is evidence that the trade guilds in Kelso were even older. There is no doubt that the idea of a guild itself is a mediaeval one but not until 1619 does one surface in the burgh. The records of the Tailors' Guild went back to that date according to a reliable nineteenth century historian, but sadly they are now lost. Nonetheless the other six guilds were probably co-existent with the Tailors and they were the Merchant Company, the Skinners, the Weavers, the Shoemakers, the Fleshers and the Hammermen. The last group, the Hammermen — so-called because they were metal workers who used the hammer — were pre-eminent as a result of their skills as armourers. They led processions of the trade guilds on ceremonial occasions. Sometimes the names of the individual guilds change; for example Shoemakers could be known as Cordwainers (a Scots word) or Skinners more particularly as Glovers.

In Kelso as elsewhere the guilds were very restrictive — that was their function, to protect their members by being strict about who entered the trade. In 1656 the Tailors' Guild records fines of four shillings for non-attendance at church on the Sabbath. Their apprentices has to pay for their freedom from masters and pay a further £10 to set up on their own in the town. Incomers to Kelso had to pay double. Before they could be regarded as competent craftsmen, apprentices had to produce an 'essay'. In 1759 William Redpath submitted his 'essay' to the guild of Hammermen. He had made a wheel, a chamber box and a leaded glass window. Other 'essays' included hour and minutes hands for an eight day clock, and a pendulum, also a plough, a spoked cartwheel and a horse shoe plus nails.

In 1717 the Whipmen or farm-servants/ploughmen wanted to form a guild or secret society but there is no record of their being admitted to the Incorporated Trades. Moving back to 1631 that date sees the start of continous records for a Kelso guild. 'The Book of the Glovers' Actes in Kelso' runs from 1631 to 1745. It deals with the running of the guild, tabulates the obligations of members; compulsory church-going, length of apprenticeship, employment of non-Kelsonians, peddling, licensing of craftsmen, poor relief and the provision of mort cloths (shrouds) for deceased members. The Glovers' Book shows it acting as a trade union, as a source of help to the community and as a supporter of the status quo, especially in the matter of religious observance. And yet the Glovers complained bitterly when they met in the abbey graveyard in 1650 that they were no longer being allowed to dry their hides on the gravestones.

Aside from telling us that the abbey graveyard was probably used for burials in the mid-seventeenth century (otherwise why should there be objections to the drying of hides if they didn't come from the relatives of the recently buried?) they also mention that they had the privilege of ringing the old abbey bells at the burial of their dead. The bells, evidently, still hung in the north porch of the abbey above the doorway which faces up Abbey Row. All of this confirms the assumption that church services were carried on under the western crossing of the old Abbey even after the massive destruction of the Hertford Raids and even after the strictures of the Reformation. It is perhaps because the assumption is such an obvious one that there is no mention of it until 1649.

8 The Stent

The burgh stent (or rates) was imposed on those sufficiently well off to pay it. The money was used for poor relief, to pay for burgh officers and some of it sent to the Duke of Roxburgh. Baron courts existed at Kelso and their records begin in 1649. They were allowed to try cases of only a relatively trivial sort (up to a value of 40s fines) with anything remotely serious going to the sheriff court. A burgh of barony could hold weekly markets and was responsible for enforcing the regulations peculiar to that operation. In the early seventeenth century the market at Kelso was almost certainly held around the Market Cross at Wester Kelso.

9 Time

The burgh was also responsible for time. Clocks were very rare in the seventeenth century, especially in a poor economy like Scotland's, and although the town tolbooth which predated the present town hall (on the same site) seems to have had a clock there was a town piper and a town drummer whose job it was to march around Kelso at 6 am every weekday morning to rouse the working populace. At 8 pm they marched around again to signal the end of the working day. How it was the piper and drummer knew the time is not recorded.

10 Justice at Kelso

The Register of the Privy Council offers a few examples of justice and its workings at Kelso. In 1615 the bailies of Kelso arrested Jonett Donnaldsoan for arson. Evidently she was alleged to have burnt down a tenement at Kelso. In an age where almost all buildings were wooden in construction and often grouped closely together, this was a serious offence, too serious for the baron court at Kelso. Jonett was taken to Edinburgh where she was remanded for trial in the Tolbooth. Surprisingly the Privy Council minute notes that she is to stand trial but not be hanged.

In 1623 Kelso did see the trial of a serious case. James Hardie of Smailholm had been murdered and Robert Fala and his wife Mary Dodis were accused. Gilbert Ker of Greenhead, Andrew Ker of Roxburgh and Andrew Ker of Brummandis, bailie of Kelso were given a dispensation to try the case. Their verdict is not recorded but the affair does hold one bit of information. The prisoners were held in Kelso Tolbooth. This is the first mention of this building and although no clue is offered as to its location, it is likely to have been one of two places. The old town hall that stood in the square on the site of the present one was sometimes called the Tolbooth and part of it may have been used as a jail. In Scots the term town-hall is interchangeable, lexically, with town-jail. The other possible location for the Tolbooth is in the Butts. Wood's map of 1823 places Kelso's jail halfway along the little street, a small building standing by itself.

The Tolbooth is mentioned repeatedly in the seventeenth century, but the cases of two groups of prisoners is especially interesting. In 1627 William Wood and others complain that Andrew Ker of Maisondieu has imprisoned them unlawfully in Kelso jail for some weeks at their own cost (like most prisoners they depended on friends and relatives bringing food and drink to them). And then, they claim, Ker sold them as soldiers to one Captain Touris. A similar case nine years later explains. The bailies of Kelso were ordered to give up prisoners held in the Tolbooth for theft. They are named as Andrew Rutherford, some Kers and Mabons. The Earl of Roxburgh wants them so that 'they may be sent out of the countrie to the warres under the charge of such captans as the Earl sall think meit'.

So, prisoners were sold as mercenaries, often in Europe. The Thirty Years War used many foreign mercenaries, perhaps some Kers, Mabons or Rutherfords fought in 'High Germany' after first lining the pockets of the Earl of Roxburgh for the privilege.

A number of crimes committed in Kelso are mentioned in the records. The more exotic include several cases of witchcraft. In 1635 James Mow of Attonburn confessed that he had consulted a witch although we are not told what he consulted her (or him) about. And four years later Meg Russell of Heyhope was accused of witchcraft. All of this falls in with the Scottish seventeenth century obsession with witches and the supernatural.

So, what these records show is Kelso operating as a burgh of barony in the decades following the Reformation and the end of the life of the Abbey. The aims of the burgh administration were sensible and modest. They wanted to provide shopping facilities, in the shape of weekly markets, for country and town dwellers at no unreasonable distance from their homes. The services of the humbler sort of craftsmen were organised and made available by the guild system and rudimentary justice was dispensed by the burgh court. And finally through the burgh stent or rates, there does seem to have been a kind of poor relief, and an elementary administrative set-up was paid for.

11 The Covenanters Occupy the Town

Religion was a less settled business. In 1639 the national religion and therefore national politics once again made a mark on the history of Kelso. King Charles I re-introduced the Anglican ritual to Scotland. This prompted an immediate and contrary response in the signing of the National Covenant at the Greyfriars Kirkyard in Edinburgh. The Covenanters' general, David Leslie, marched south with 4,000 soldiers to discourage loyalist incursions from England, which was engulfed in Civil

War. Leslie decided to base himself and his army at Kelso.

The first thing Leslie did was to dig himself in. Trenchworks were thrown around Kelso and an elaborate system of keeping watch was organised. Royalist troops — a significant force of 3,000 foot and 13 troops of horse with four pieces of artillery — under the command of the Earl of Holland approached the town with a view to attacking Leslie's army. When they saw the extensive fortifications, they thought better of it (they probably were unwilling to undertake a siege of any duration with only four guns and a large force to maintain) and retreated without delay.

Two years after this the Kelso townspeople wrote to the Privy Council of Scotland to complain that they had not been paid for their trouble in billeting Leslie's soldiers at Kelso. There is no record of any payment being made nor does there seem to be any trace of the trenchwork made by the Covenanters' army, except at Kaim Knowe and Floors Home Farm where there are the remains of a very long ditch running from the south east to the north west. In Scots 'Kaim Knowe' could be read as 'fortress mound'.

12 Recognizable Names

Returning to local affairs here is a document which brings the shape of seventeenth century Kelso into sharper focus. On 12 January 1642 Robert Ker of Broomlands infefts his wife, Jonet Falsyde, with:

> the lands of Wester Broomlands, with the meadow adjacent, bounded by the common highway or loaning called the Pypwell on the east, the common highway called the Broomlone on the west, the marsh called Inchmyre on the south and . . . on the north.

Now this is clear enough. Four place-names are used which have come down to us intact, and therefore allow us to locate Jonet Falsyde's property with ease. On the Ordnance Survey West Broomlands is that area now built on by the Abbotseat estate in the 1950s and later by more housing on the west in the 1960s and 1970s. What is now called the Angraflat Road on the map is known by local people as the Broomloan and in the seventeenth century it extended all the way to join the Ednam Road — all the way, that is, along what is now a pleasant hedge-lined walk sometimes called the Green Loaning. It now cuts through Kelso's golf course and race course but in Jonet Falsyde's time it was 'the common highway'. On the east was the 'Pypwell' or the Ednam Road. Its name permits an early dating for the well whose water was conducted down the brae to an outlet in what was then and is now known as Inchmyre. Perhaps the meadow referred to is the area named as West Broomlands Plantation on the Ordnance Survey but better known in Kelso as the 'Meedies' or meadows. It used to be a natural playground for children with its shrubs, whins and gorse but now it has been stripped of much of its vegetation.

13 Kelso's Mills

Jonet Falsyde's document is the first in a number of glimpses of a recognisable Kelso in the mid-seventeenth century. In 1643 Sir Andrew Ker of Greenhead owned the mills of Kelso. The plural is important because in addition to the old Abbey Mill, the records mention a mill at a place called 'Bridge-end'. And again, later in the document, the haugh of Bridge-End is mentioned. The mill must be what is now known as Maxwellheugh Mill. It stands near the confluence of Tweed and Teviot on the right bank of the latter. Its mill lade ran between an anna in the Teviot and that bank of the river.

The location of the mill and the repitition of the name 'Bridge-End', especially with the term 'haugh' leads inevitably to the conclusion that Bridge-End is the old name for Springwood. In fact this is confirmed on the large-scale Ordnance Survey of 1860 (the earliest survey for Kelso, and Scotland) where Springwood Park is marked as 'Bridge-end' Haugh. Now, of course the name is applied only to the park at the south-western end of Kelso Bridge.

But what bridge? How did that bit of land get its name? Ker of Greenhead's document about the mills is dated 1643, well before the first bridge at Kelso in 1754 and the Teviot Bridge which was built in the early nineteenth century. The question is: did the name derive from a bridge that crossed the Teviot to service traffic to and from Roxburgh, or did it exist to link Kelso to the southern side of the Tweed? Sadly, there is no documentary evidence to answer that question, all that the name does show is the early existence of some kind of bridge.

14 Fire

In 1645 the Covenanters' army again appeared in Kelso. This time it was led by the younger David Leslie (it had been his father in 1639) and they came to the Borders to meet Montrose who aimed to reclaim Scotland for Charles I. The two armies circled each other in the neighbourhood of Kelso before fighting the decisive battle at Philiphaugh near Selkirk.

More important for the townspeople, 1645 saw a disastrous fire at Kelso. It seems to have started because of another problem. Plague had broken out once more in the town and in an attempt to contain it the house of the victims had been burned. This led to an uncontrollable fire which swept through the wooden houses of the burgh. So many people were left homeless and so much valuable property destroyed that the minister of Kelso, Robert Knox, went to the General Assembly in Edinburgh to plead for help. His colleagues agreed to ask the presbyteries of Roxburgh, Selkirk and Berwickshire, and the men with the Scottish army (under Leslie) in Newcastle to contribute cash to re-build the town. All seems to have gone well except in Jedburgh where the provost, Alexander Kirkton, was not happy. He objected to his citizens being asked to give money to Kelso and he attacked his minister, Mr William, for supporting the application for help. Unfortunately Kirkton's exact words are not recorded.

15 *Robert Knox Reports on the State of the Kirks*

What is on record is a report written in 1649 by Robert Knox. His subject is the state of the kirks in the presbytery of Kelso, and in common with the ministers of surrounding parish churches, Knox wrote it for submission to the General Assembly. Here it is:

> The paroche of Kelso, as it presently standeth, and hath since the Reformatione, containeth 1500 communicants, or thereby. It was thrie paroches of old, viz — Kelso lyeing all alongs upone the east and north of Tweid, wherein ar 1300 communicants and odds; St James his Kirk in the continent betwix Tiviot and Tweid, wherein ar 6 communicants and Maxwellheughe upon the south and east of Tweid and Tiviote, ar about 150 communicants. The kirk is vary neir the mids of the present wholl paroche, whereof not above 100 communicants will be without shout and cry from the stipleheid and the furthest distance bot ane large mylle. All thrie ar of the Erectione of Kelso whereof the King was patrone. The present provisione, as it was settled be the plot after the Erectine 1609, is eight chalder of victuall, Lothiane measure, two parts oatmeill, third part beir, ane hundred marks and the vicarage teinds estimat to ane 100 lb. The Commissione for Surrender, in anno 1635, maid no alteratione in the provisione, only setled the localite, and valued the teinds, as it standeth in the register, to the triple of that the minister recieveth. There is not ane houss of all this paroche so neir ane other Kirk as their owen.
>
> *Subscribitur, Mr Rot. Knox*

So, according to Knox, Kelso Parish has had three kirks in it since the Reformation took place around the 1560s. Apparently, they are all going concerns, just. St James, the last remnant of the old town of Roxburgh, has only six communicants. They probably came from the farm of Friars.

Owned by the Kers it stood on the site of the old Franciscan Friary of St Peter in the southern quarter of the Roxburgh peninsula. Nonetheless, for all its obvious enfeeblement, St James must still have been standing as a place where divine service could take place. Knox does not say which minister served the 6 communicants, he might have done it himself.

16 Maxwell, St Michael's and Maxwellheugh

The kirk at Maxwellheugh (as he miscalls it) was served by Robert Knox prior to his report of 1649. He was continuing a long tradition of Kelso priests who held the cure of souls at Maxwell. In 1159 the little church of St Michael was given by its owner, Herbert de Maccuswell, to the monks at Kelso. His father, Maccus, had witnessed the original charter to found the abbey at Selkirk and he was clearly an important and distinguished man in the reigns of both Alexander I and David I. David gave him the land which came to be known as Maccuswell or Maccusvill and ultimately Maxwell. This grant included the toun of Maxwell, Maxwellheugh, the Mains, Springwood Park, Pinnaclehill (or Pendiclehill), the Woodens (Easter and Wester), the Softlaws (Easter and Wester), the Chapel lands and the Kirklands.

The village of Maxwell lay in what is now called Springwood Park. The Ordnance Survey shows the site of St Michael's Church as lying between the north-eastern end of the long low warehouse used by the Border Union Show and the public toilets behind it. As late as 1873 the graveyard of the church was marked by a stand of trees enclosed by a wall.

By 1649 the village of Maxwell was in decline. Twenty two years previously the kirk of St Michael had had 233 communicants and doubtless the removal of divine service to Kelso (clearly implied in Knox's report) accelerated its decline. Now, of course, nothing is left and as at Roxburgh not even aerial photography can show any trace of the old settlement. The village at the top of the hill —Maxwellheugh — is a modern development of Kelso which came into being first as a result of the building of a safe bridge over the Tweed and then as a consequence of the arrival of the railway.

17 The Abbey as the Parish Kirk

1649 was probably the year in which some building work was carried out on the old abbey fabric. In order to convert it into a sufficiently large parish church, a wall was erected to close off the eastern end of the remaining (western) crossing. Including the Galilee Porch on the west, that would have had the effect of making the church cruciform. There was also a vestry extending eastwards into what had been the nave of the Abbey Church. This ungainly structure stood as Kelso's church until 1773 when the new parish church was completed.

Knox's reference to the 'stipleheid' probably means the top of the northern facade of the abbey; it was the place where the church bells were hung.

18 More Recognizable Names

On 7 July 1666, William, Earl of Roxburgh granted in liferent to Patrick Don, bailie of Kelso, and his heirs:

> Those three and a half merk lands of the lands of Kelso, of which three merk lands lie in those two "shotts" (divisions) of land called the Barneyairds and Longwhanges respectively, and the half merk land lies rinrig among the other lands of Kelso . . . and (much else) comprehending rigs, acres and shotts of land in the old Orchyaird, Bairneyarids, Langwhanges, Pypwellfoot, Cruickitaiker (crooked acre), Broomebanks, Pypellheid, Abbotsheid . . . and also that tenement of land with garden belonging to John Mow, bounded between the tenement of Robert Meine on the west, that of Isobelle Thomson on the east, the lands called Tofts on the north and the common way of the burgh on the south, with the liberty of accumulating dung on the whole hie street to the south side of the gutter of the same, comprehending that part of the said tenement formerly belonging to William Kennedy, and which tenement and garden belonging to the four merk lands of Robert Mow; with pasturage, grazing, moor and moss belonging to the said lands, lying near and about Spitle loch and Berrie loch, with other pertinents presently possessed by Patrick Don and his tenants, within the bounds of the town and lands of Kelso.

Patrick Don was a successful man. His family were wealthy and not only in Kelso. They owned extensive lands in the Cheviot Hills around Attonburn. The Earl of Roxburgh obviously looked on Don with favour and with the use of the term 'bailie' he probably meant to call him 'Baron Baillie'. This was the title given to the man who headed the burgh's council before Kelso's first provost was appointed in 1893.

The Don family completed a grand house at Broomlands in 1719, and these grants of land in Kelso (probably confirmations of ownership) half a century earlier form the basis of the Dons' estate. They had enough money to employ William Adam, the Master Mason to the Ordnance in Scotland, and the father of Robert Adam, one of the greatest of European architects. William Adam wrote *Vitruvius Scoticus* which was subtitled *Noblemens and gentlemens houses principally from the designs of William Adam.* This text book contained many plans, including those of Broomlands House. Clearly the Dons had not only taste but also the money to indulge it, since they were able to engage the services of Scotland's foremost architect of the day.

The Earl of Roxburgh was generous to Patrick Don. He gave him land all over Kelso and this document mentions areas for the first time. The list of 'the old Orchyaird, Bairnyairds, Langwhanges, Pypwellfoot, Cruickitaiker, Broombanks, Pypwellheid, Abbotsheid' seems to be working outwards from the centre of Kelso. The Old Orchard is probably a reference to fruit trees cultivated by the monks, near the Abbey. Although no map uses the name, it is worth noting that on a well-drawn map of 1805 there is a large, specifically tree-covered area which extends from the southern side of Simon Square all the way down to the river, and from the path leading down to the Tweed in the west over to Hermitage Lane in the east. If all of this bit of land had been taken up with fruit trees then it would have been a very large orchard indeed, but it is not too fanciful to suppose a part of it as the abbey orchard.

'Bairneyairds' or barnyards offers even fewer clues but it seems possible that this place was in the same area as the orchard. If it refers to abbey property then it is likely that barnyards where animals were kept or fed or both would be near where the monks lived. The fact that 'Hoggs Lane' is an old name for Abbotsford Grove would tend to support this. Also, on the Ordnance Survey of 1860 there is a property marked as 'The Malt Barns' near where the council houses in Mayfield now stand. It is interesting that this area has remained largely free of dense housing even though it lies very close to the centre of the town. Whatever the attitudes of owners in modern times, it may be that that openness and indeed the present garden nursery echo a centuries-old tradition of land use started by the monks at Kelso.

'Langwhanges' is much easier. This is a name used by several maps and it means present-day terms the cemetery and Woodside. 'Pypwellfoot' is a bit of land at the foot of Pipewell Brae — it might mean Eschiehaugh since the area on the other side of the road was certainly called Inchmyre then as now. 'Cruickitaiker' is obscure but in the same general area as 'Broomebanks' which is very likely what is now known as Broomlands Bank Plantation on the Ordnance Survey. 'Pypwellheid' is Abbotseat and 'Abbotsheid' is Broompark according to the map of 1805.

If that list does work outwards from the old orchard between the Abbey and the river, sweeping up in an arc to Broompark in the north, it probably deals in a group with bits of farmland. The terms 'rigs', 'acres' and 'shots' apply usually only to open farmland rather than to land associated with any particular dwelling. In the next section of the list of land given to Patrick

Don, the Earl of Roxburgh sets down town properties or tenements, as distinct from the rest of the grant.

Once again judging by the orientation of neighbouring property, it sounds as though John Mow's 'tenement of land with garden' was in Horsemarket. Although that street runs north-west to south-east, the mention of 'the Tofts' can leave little doubt. Most maps up to and including the Ordnance Survey of 1860 mark a large area behind Horsemarket and over as far as where Edenside Primary School now stands as the Tofts. A much bigger area than the street which now remembers the name. The 'common way of the burgh on the south' is so-called because it was the start of Ednam Road. As such there must have been a worthwhile amount of dung dropped by passing horse or horse-drawn traffic. The document is specific about Patrick Don's right to lift this manure which he probably uysed in his town-dwelling gardens or sold to the tenants therein.

Don also had his rights of pasture, moor and moss confirmed at Spitle Loch and Berrie Loch. The latter is clearly Berry Moss and the use of the word 'loch' implies much more standing water in this period than in the twentieth century. 'Spitle Loch' is more awkward. A 'Spitle' is a hospital which had the more general meaning of a place for travellers or a refuge in the Middle Ages. On the Ordnance Survey of 1971 there is a site marked near Ferneyhill Toll for a hospital, called St Leonards. There is no mention of this establishment in any of the Abbey charters. It may be that the Ordnance Survey cartographers have located the site in that place because of nothing more than tradition. At all events it looks like 'Spitle Loch' was named after St Leonards and lay near its site. In its turn the name for that bit of land has passed out of use.

19 9 Roxburgh Street

Patrick Don's charter not only records his name it also mentions another familiar Kelso surname, that of Robert Mow. An ancestor of his with the same name owned land, probably in Wester Kelso, exactly one hundred years earlier, as we have seen. Another Kelso surname reappears in 1666. John Chatto was the owner of number 9 Roxburgh Street and it is possible that he was related to the hooligan Michael Chatto, the associate of 'Shorte Jok' and the attacker of John Fisher, the Sheriff Officer.

John Chatto owned 9 Roxburgh Street between 1666 and 1668 when he rebuilt the property. Although the facade and the ground floor have been altered, the fabric was substantially the oldest piece of domestic building in Kelso. It was condemned as unfit for human habitation before the last war but before it was recently demolished it contained two shop units.

Chatto's house was three storeys high, excluding the cellarage and the garret, and it had an L-shaped layout. The main block faced Roxburgh Street and a wing ran north-east in line with Jamieson's Entry. Extending from the wing were a series of stables and other low outbuildings all fronting a narrow courtyard which was entered from Jamieson's Entry. In the main block on the first floor, one of the rooms had seventeenth century panelling on one wall, a contemporary door and fireplace. There were also traces of early panelling in rooms on the second floor.

Chatto sounds like a relatively wealthy man. He could rebuild his house and indulge in some sort of interior decoration. It is significant that a man of such means was living in Easter Kelso and developing his property there — it shows that Wester Kelso may have been in decline by the latter half of the seventeenth century.

20 The Ferme at Freers

Across the Tweed, Roxburgh too was gradually disappearing but there is evidence in 1669 that the site was clinging to some of its former importance. The Earl of Roxburgh made the 'Ferme at Freers' his occasional residence. It was here that he chose to entertain the King's High Commissioner, the Earl of Lauderdale, on 8 October 1669, on his progress to Edinburgh to hold the parliament on behalf of Charles II. He was attended at Freers by the noblemen and gentlemen of the Merse and according to one estimate two thousand men gathered on the site of the old friary of St Peter. On Wyeth's map of 1736 Freers is shown as a substantial place with an extensive steading a a large house. There is nothing now on the site apart from the two cottages by the roadside.

21 Education at Kelso

In 1670, as we have seen, a new school was built at Kelso. But post-mediaeval records of education at Kelso go back slightly earlier into the seventeenth century. Here is one of the few legible bits of the Kirk Session records:

> Sept 24th, 1642, quilk day there cam ane refer from the court [the baron court of the burgh] to the session concerning the school, wherein those actes following were concluded,
> 1. That all male chidreng being 7 yeares of age should come to the comon

school, and to be put to no uther school, nether within the town nor without the samin, and the contraveiners ordeined to pay during their away being to ye master quarterly 13s 4d Scots.,
2. That those who comes to the school shall pay for their schooling . . . and gif the master have caus to compleine to cum to ye officer, who is ordeined to pund their parents,' and gif they [pay] not ther pund within eight dayes, to ward themselves.'

And later in 1643 the Clerk of the Kirk Session:

is ordeined to ring the six hour bell for the convenency of ye bairnes to the school.

So, Kelso was putting into practice one of the central tenets of Reformation Scotland. It had a strictly organised common school where attendance was compulsory and which started its day at six in the morning. It is known that in Peebles the children attended six days a week with three sessions each day; they were at school from 6am to 9am, 10am to noon, 1pm to 6pm. It seems likely that the hours at Kelso were equally demanding. The other point to notice is that education at that time was for boys only.

Mr Johne is the first master or teacher at Kelso to be named. The Kirk Session records of 2 February 1646 discuss his serious illness and a number of subsequent reports imply that he died soon afterwards. Mr David succeeded in 1647 and his period at Kelso throws some light on the educational alternatives that existed. The Kirk Session ask Mr David to report on the 'by-schools' or the other schools that had grown up in the burgh. Both parents and teachers who were involved with these schools (a definite plural) were warned to desist from sending their children to them. One of the by-school teachers, John Riddell, was singled out as was his daughter. This last implies that some of the by-schools admitted girls.

Kelso School had exams. Not the written, formal qualifications that are conducted now, but a visitation of the Kirk elders. These were apparently the high-point of the academic year and they promoted rivalry amongst the pupils as they tried individually to impress the solemn men of the Kirk Session.

But they also had holidays. In 1656 the pupils asked for a break and were granted twenty days off.

22 The Kirk Session and the Book of Discipline

It seems from the records that Mr David had at least one assistant teacher and in 1659 a Mr William Scot held the post. At this early period the Rector doubled as Session Clerk, presumably because of his literacy, but certainly not because of his ability to write legibly, at least to a modern eye. Mr David's writing is very hard to decipher and it is only when George Adam takes over as Rector in 1668 that the Kirk Session records become readable — and then only intermittently.

Nonetheless the first complete entry, dated June 1668, does set the tone of the kind of information the Session records provide for both the seventeenth and eighteenth centuries. Here is the extract from the ominously named 'Book of Discipline':

> Compeared [appeared before the Kirk Session] Alexander Bell being cited. And [he] confessed fornication with Rachel Eliot, but purported that the child was not his, affirming he sinned with her only once viz, tenth day before Martinmas last.

Well, that is the small change of burgh life at the time. Much is made of Bell's 'sin' but no mention of Rachel Eliot and her bastard child. Officially stigmatised as a fornicator and not owned by any man who would support her, life must have been tough for Rachel Eliot. We shall hear more later of women like her who took drastic action to change their circumstances.

However, sin is the main subject matter of the remaining Kirk Session records over this period. Erring Kelsonians are rebuked for various sins, apart from fornication. Drunkenness and swearing on the Sabbath, and of course, non-attendance at Kirk were the most common crimes. More seriously the 1669 records list the names of all the Quakers in Kelso so that they might be proceeded against.

In 1673 Charles Ormestoun and ten other Quakers were rounded up and locked in the Kelso Tolbooth. Their crime was to hold a meeting. Later the same year they petitioned the Privy Council for their release.

The Kirk Session was clearly a very powerful organisation but it was not always repressive. Early in 1684 they gave orders for alms to be distributed to the poor and it seems likely that this was a regular practice.

Rector Adam had his school enlarged some time after he came to teach in Kelso. Either the population was expanding or the popularity of the 'by-schools' was contracting. There is also word of a 'scholars' loft' being built above the parish church that existed inside the ruins of the Abbey. Another loft apparently existed before 1668. It is called 'ye marchands' loft' and it looks like it might have been a meeting place for the Incorporated Trades of the burgh. The scholars had desks made for them in 1670 by order of the Session — before that date they had probably sat on the floor, cross-legged with their slates on their knees.

Life in the town had its lighter moments. One of them must have been 23 August 1681 when the schoolboys put on a play for the local people. It was a comedy by Terence with the dubious title of *Eunuchus*. The boys performed it in Latin, no doubt with enough acting to make it accessible to those without a classical education. After the show, the school went on a four week holiday. In order to interpret that as a reward or a merciful release, one would have to have seen the play.

The old Kelso School has long gone but one building does remain from this period, what is now called Turret House. Its address is 8 and 9 Abbey Court and it fronts onto the street which once led to Kelso's bridge, the one which predated Rennie's. Turret House has been much altered in the eighteenth and nineteenth centuries but above one lintel there is an inscription 'IMP 1678'. It seems always to have been used as a dwelling house.

23 Dragoons Are Billeted in the Town

Turning away again from the detail of domestic life in Kelso, national affairs again made an impact on the townspeople. After the restoration of Charles II in 1600 covenanting had continued in Scotland. Often field conventicles were held and a favourite place (near enough to Kelso but remote enough to discourage interference — and an easy place to keep a watch) was Gateshaw Brae where sometimes thousands attended the services. To combat these conventicles two companies of dragoons were stationed at Kelso in 1678. The soldiers, sent by central government, were to be victualled at market prices by the local suppliers. The problem was that the dragoons, already unpopular, were not being regularly paid. The following year one company was still billeted at Kelso when a Major Maines of Alnwick offered his services to the Privy Council against the Covenanters. The Council sent him to the town with the names of three men suspected of organising conventicles. They were Frank Pringle, the Bailie of Kelso, John Brown, a merchant and James Handisyd. The Council, it seems, were not able to make it stick and there is no record of either arrest or conviction.

In 1680 another Kelsonian, John Ffala, was arrested on suspicion of being a Covenanter. He was tried at Edinburgh and released when he was able to produce a convincing alibi. But in 1684 the government troops took him again to Edinburgh where he was convicted and sentenced to transportation to the West Indies to be sold into slavery. In the same year Agnes Mein of Kelso was fined a huge sum, £156, for suspected covenanting.

The issue of covenanting and its repression by the government came to a head in 1679. In that year a group of fanatical covenanters murdered Archbishop Sharp in St Andrews. The Privy Council sent James Graham of Claverhouse to enforce the law against the dissidents and he hunted down attenders at field conventicles with zeal. The covenanting army was finally destroyed on the 1 June 1679 at Bothwell Brig by a royal army supplemented with English troops. At almost the same time, probably before news of the disaster at Bothwell had reached the eastern Borders, this incident took place:

> From the Register of the Privy Council of Scotland, dated 4th July 1679:
> Upon . . . June last a considerable party of the rebels having come near to the town of Kelso and robbed and stolen several gentlemens' horses and arms with a design to have entered the town of Kelso and taken and possessed themselves of the militia arms that were within the same and plundered and abused the inhabitants, whereupon Thomas Boudone, lieutenant of the militia, Charles Robertsone, sergeant, William Young, glover and some others of the militia, being informed and apprehending the present danger, did cause the militia drummer beat drums for calling them together and giving alarm to the inhabitants to put themselves in a posture of defence, nowadays doubting but that any who did represent his Majesties authority as magistrate within the said town, their persons, goods, arms and ammunition, a prey to the enemies, insofaras that, while the militia drummer was beating, he or some other by his direction did beat the drummer and cause beat out the drum-head, and imprisoned the said Thomas Boudone and Charles Robertsone and William Young; and thereafter some of the town having got notice of the bailie's intentions for conniving with the rebels and betraying the town, they caused ring the common bell for alarming the inhabitants in and about the town for their own defence whereupon the said Frank Pringle did cause cut the bell towes of purpose to hinder the said alarm.

It is not clear from this whether or not the militia are local volunteers or the troop of dragoons known to have been stationed in the town at this time. One of the soldiers, William Young, is named as a glover and that suggests that he is a volunteer. On the other hand the document is a government record with an interest in showing Frank Pringle and his supporters as isolated rebels intent on doing harm to the townspeople. Whatever the political battle-lines within the community at Kelso, there is no doubt that June 1679 saw a tremendous commotion in the town. Perhaps the most fitting postscript to all this is the fact that Major Maines of Alnwick left an unpaid bill for £642-9s-10d for food for his troops and forage for the horses.

24 Disaster

Five years later, the politicking of Frank Pringle and the bad debts of Major

Maines would seem insignificant to the townspeople of Kelso, compared with the disaster that burst on the town.

Between the 3 and 4 o'clock in the morning on 8 August, 1684, a calamitous fire broke out in Kelso:

> It began first in a malt kill whereby some neighbouring stacks of corn were kindled and there by the violent tempestuous wind blowing over the town did in a sudden put the whole in so universal a conflagration that these who were helping their neighbours did not know when their own houses were burning, in so much that, before nine o'clock at night, not only all the houses but the most part of all the goods therein and several merchant shops of considerable value and above 4,000 bolls of victual in 'girnells' and all the corn stacks in the town were utterly laid in ashes, during which time the fury of the flames and the rage of the smoke were so great in all places of the town that with great difficulty, sick and infirm persons and infant children could be carried away from the danger to the open fields, by which sad visitation 306 families, conform to a list of the householders' names given in herewith, have had their dwelling houses within the said town utterly burnt down.
>
> And of them not 20 will ever be able to rebuild again upon their own means and expenses. And the loss of merchandise is so great that it cannot well be known, the particular loss of some of them being valued above £20,000 Scots and of the others above £1,000 sterling; and the more indigent people have lost the whole substenance of their livelihood through the burning botts of their houses and corn, so that with much difficulty they have been hitherto supplied with the charity of their neighbours, which will not serve long to sustain them without the Lords of the Privy Council, in commiseration of their necessitous condition, shall graciously be pleased to provide for them a more universal and seasonal supply and humbly supplicating the council would recommend them and their desolate and indigent families to the charity of the whole kingdom, and grant order and warrant for that effect in the manner underwritten.

The Lords of the Privy Council granted aid to Kelso. An Edinburgh advocate, Robert Burnett, was hired to collect contributions from every parish in Scotland, Cash was provided almost instantly by the government when they diverted a fund got up to pay for prisoners taken by the Turks (not needed at that moment) to Kelso. The cash collected by Burnett was distributed by Sir William Ker of Greenheid, Francis Pringle of Rowiston (apparently a political survivor of some skill and if he could maintain his position in the town after the events of 1679), William Ker of Chatto, and James Lorimer the minister.

The great fire of 1684 represents a turning point in the history of Kelso. After it almost all of the town had to be rebuilt —probably in the form that we know it now. Wester Kelso seems to have largely perished in the flames leaving only the stone market cross. Kelso Square may have begun to

Slezer's view of 1695

assume its present form after 1684, acting as the central market-place for the whole town.

The first pictorial record of Kelso comes in 1693 with Slezer's view of the town. It is a recognisable view. Little more was left of the Abbey then than there is now. The bridge over the Tweed was not yet built, the crossing being made by ferry. But nevertheless the shape of Kelso at the end of the seventeenth century was the identifiable seed from which the modern town grew.

Part Six

THE EIGHTEENTH CENTURY began badly for Kelso. Here is a petition sent by the inhabitants of Kelso in late 1699 to the Earl of Marchmont, the Lord High Chancellor of Scotland:

> Your petitioners for the foresaid Burgh of Barony of Kelso humbly represent that the great scarcity and coninuall quartering of souldiers upon the said Town of Kelso, which was so lately burnt to ashes by an universal conflagration, hath made such a decay of trade, that the few traders who lived therein, about the time of the said conflagration, hath since removed to follow their trade to other places of the Kingdom, whereby the remaining inhabitants are rendered altogether incapable to pay so much as the one half of what was demanded formerly from them, (during the time of Mr John Buchan's task).

The Chancellor took pity on the plight of Kelso and he agreed to reduce taxes by half. The petition shows how catastrophic the fire of 1684 had been. Even 15 years later the commerce of the town had not recovered. Traders had left to work elsewhere — in 1699 Kelso was literally only half the town it had been in 1684. This may be a formal recognition that Wester Kelso had ceased to be a place of much importance and that future development was to happen around the ruins of the abbey.

Kelso's straitened circumstances at the start of the eighteenth century could sometimes be expressed in smaller, more personal ways. One of the obligations of the town's trade guilds was to provide mort-cloths or shrouds for their members. In 1701 this clause was added to their rules about this provision:

And if it shall happen, as God forbid, that he who is keeper of the said clothes shall loss them by any extraordinary way, as by fire, water or WARRES, that then and in that caice, it shall (be) loss generally to us all, gif we are made sensible that they or any of them be so lost.

Despite this depressing set of circumstances at the beginning of the century, life in Kelso did improve gradually over the following hundred years. Modest growth, both economic and geographical, took place. The town began to assume its basic modern shape and several institutions were founded in the 1700s which still survive.

Kelso's main asset was its location — in the heart of rich farmland. During the eighteenth century agriculture developed and became more productive and the town was the obvious place for the markets where landowners could sell their produce. Rutherford's guide to Kelso makes the point eloquently:

It may give some idea of the central position of Kelso when we state that its radia of eight miles include two kingdoms, three counties and twenty parishes. All these parishes are in the highest state of cultivation; and, of eighteen of them, Kelso is the market town and natural outlet.

1 A Rudimentary Plan

The eighteenth century saw the erection of stone buildings in Kelso, in Easter Kelso, which still survive. Their location gives some sense of a rudimentary town plan. We already know that Roxburgh Street was an established thoroughfare extending from the market cross at Wester Kelso to the west door of the Abbey. Number 9 Roxburgh Street existed as a substantial stone-built house in 1666. In what is now Bridge Street, but what may have been an extention of Roxburgh Street, there exists a large cellar dating from the late seventeenth or early eighteenth century. The building above it is now a cafe and was built at a later date than the cellar. This house, numbers 5 and 7 Bridge Street, was owned in the eighteenth century by the Ormiston family. They were prosperous merchants who channelled their trading business through Berwick Upon Tweed, although they suffered an important disability in that they remained catholics after the Reformation. There is a tradition that catholic worship was carried on secretly in the house — possibly out of sight in the cellar. This is an unusually large room measuring 30 feet by 23 feet with a barrel-vaulted ceiling. There is evidence of two doorways in each of the side walls. To the east there were three windows, now built up, while to the north there is a fourth still open to the street. It shows that the gable-end is ten feet thick.

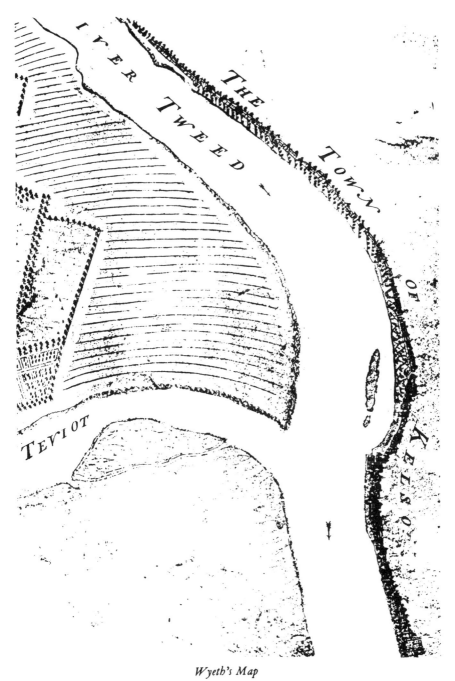

Wyeth's Map

Five iron rings used to be fixed to the ceiling so that the winter's store of salted carcases could be hung there.

What is now called Turret House dates from at least 1678, making it contemporary with the other two buildings. The alignment of the three old houses seems to support the notion that Roxburgh Street pre-existed the Square. Roxburgh Street probably ran past the west door of the Abbey and down to the Tweed to the place where ferries set off for the opposite bank of the river.

2 *Wyeth's Map*

The earliest map of Kelso that exists was drawn by a man called Wyeth. He did it in 1736 although it is likely that he worked from material prepared slightly earlier. Kelso only just makes it into the bottom right-hand corner of the map, since its purpose was not to show the town but to serve as a plan of the Duke of Roxburgh's estates. Friars Farm is at the centre and although Floors is marked it is not given the prominence one would expect for the house that became the ducal seat. Sir John Vanburgh designed Floors in 1718 and its position at the top of the map and not its centre suggests that Wyeth's survey was probably done before that date.

At all events, this piece of work represents one of the earliest glimpses of Kelso. Wyeth essentially, did a rough perspective drawing rather than a ground plan map. This method allows a certain amount of inaccuracy (some buildings are almost certainly hidden by others) and artistic licence, but even so, it is an immensely useful document.

Wyeth depicts the Abbey much as it is now, that is to say by the early eighteenth century its destruction had come to an end, probably as a result of the Parish Church and manse attached to it. The map shows no clear evidence of either of these additions. The abbey glebe is now an open field where animals graze but in the time of Wyeth's survey it was heavily wooded, perhaps with the fruit trees implied by the name 'Orchyairds' that appear in seventeenth century documents.

The other identifiable building is the Abbey Mill which seems to be in a working condition. The map shows another mill on the site of what is now called Teviot Mill, or Maxwellheugh Mill although at that time it was probably known as Bridge-end Mill. It served the village of Maxwell.

Housing in Easter Kelso is shown as being more dense than in Wester where, (as geographers would say), there is only ribbon development along Roxburgh Street. The houses in Wester Kelso have gardens running down the bank to the Tweed, as they do now, but the Easter Kelso houses have no gardens. The reason for this is that the Chalkheugh, where Kelso gets its name, was much more of a chalk cliff in the early eighteenth century. During that period it actually overhung the river and streaks of white gypsum were visible in it. By 1810 the occasional floods of the Tweed had undercut the cliff so much that it had become dangerous. It was cut down into terraces (which are very obvious on that part of the Chalkheugh opposite St John's Church, below the place where benches have been sited for people wishing to enjoy the view in comfort) and sloping gardens and defended from the river's force by a strong retaining wall.

Before coming to the main observation of Wyeth's map it is worth noting that there is no trace of St James' Church on the Fairgreen or indeed of the town of Roxburgh itself. Although it is known that the congregation of St James' numbered only six communicants by 1649, it is a surprise to see no trace of what was a working church only half a century before. Since there is not a trace of any building in Roxburgh itself — or even any sense of its having been there, the town must have completely vanished well before Wyeth came on the scene. However he does note one interesting detail. The old road from the Roxburgh ferry is still visible, probably serving Friars Farm.

The main point of Wyeth's map is a simple one. There is no indication that the shape of early eighteenth century Kelso was anything other than the length of Roxburgh Street. The creation of the Square was still in the future, just.

3 From Wester to Easter Kelso

In 1715 the Jacobite army entered Kelso and the Earl of Dunfermline proclaimed the Old Pretender as King at the Market Cross. Now the only Market Cross in Kelso at that time was the old cross at Wester Kelso. This choice of location for an important event is informative. The Market Cross at Wester Kelso was still, in 1715, seen as the focal point of the town, the place where markets took place. This suggests that the market place or The Square had yet to come into being.

An important clue to the dating of the shift away from the cross at Wester Kelso to the Square in Easter is offered in a series of documents held in Edinburgh at the High Court. Known as 'Services to Heirs' they list and ratify changes in the ownership of property. In 1725 there is an entry concerning Kelso. Alexander Slowan, a slater, agreed to pay his father, Andrew, an annual rent of £24 for a tenement of houses 'at the Council House of Kelso', and a tenement in Oven Wynd. The importance of this is not in the first appearance of the street name 'Oven Wynd' but in the fact that by 1725 Kelso had a 'Council House' or town hall. If this building is the same one which stood on the site of the present town hall, then 1725 looks a likely date for the opening out of Kelso Square — probably this took place between 1715 and 1725.

Here is some supporting evidence. Numbers 1, 3 and 5 Woodmarket were built in the early part of the seventeenth century — around 1725. The front of the building, leaving aside the remodelled shop fronts, is largely untouched and easily recognisable as an early Georgian town house. But what suggests that this building's creation is co-existent with that of the Square is its position. Although its address is Woodmarket it is set well back from the alignment of that street as if it were not intended to be part of it, but part of the new Square. The facade of the house is expensive and, for that period, quite exceptionally good looking — not the sort of facade to hide from view in a narrow street but one to be admired from a distance, possibly from as far away as the entrance to Roxburgh Street, across a new square.

At some point at the beginning of the nineteenth century, John Duke of Roxburgh decided that Floors needed an imposing entrance, and, more practically, with the disappearance of those at Friars Farm, the ducal seat needed a new garden. The obvious place for both of these requirements was the head of Roxburgh Street on the site of Wester Kelso. An undated, unprofessionally drawn plan has come down to us which solves all the riddles about the location and layout of Wester Kelso. It seems to be some kind of preliminary sketch of the ducal garden but the fascinating thing is that the plans have been superimposed over an old map of Wester Kelso. Garden number 3 has been placed 'Over Market of Kelso' and to the immediate south west of that the 'Old Road by the Water Side' is indicated. To the west of garden number 3 the outer garden has been laid out 'Over Ferry Road' while across number 1 lawn ran the 'Barras Loan or Old Road to Kelso'. The Fair Cross is not clearly marked but its location is already known from the Ordnance Survey.

So, Wester Kelso had three street names; Ferry Road, Barras Loan and the Old Road. Its plan was a T-shape with the Ferry Road and Barras Loan forming the cross-piece and the Market with Roxburgh Street the stalk.

It is clear that the Duke had to undertake significant demolition work to have his gates and garden but it seems unlikely that much eviction took place. In 1715, the date the Old Pretender was proclaimed from the Fair Cross and certainly before the plans to turn Wester Kelso into a garden were conceived, the Kirk Session records contain a complaint about vagrants living in empty houses at the 'Townhead'. These belonged to John Waldie and William Yett who were instructed to eject the squatters.

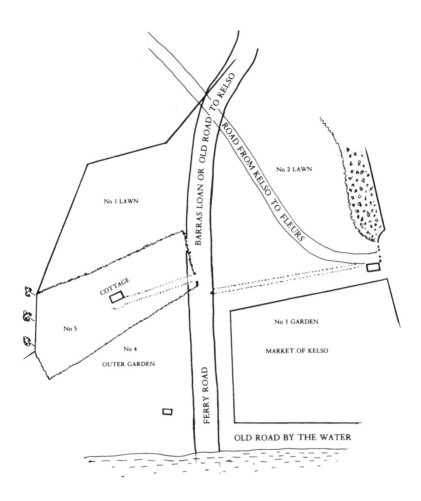

Wester Kelso

4 Country Seats

Around the embryonic town local grandees began to build their country seats. In 1718 Sir John Vanburgh (perhaps better known as a playwright) designed Floors Castle for the first Duke of Roxburgh. The house was an oblong measuring 412 feet in length. It had two wings enclosing a courtyard to the north west. On each corner of the main block it had a tower which was gabled and pedimented. The overall effect was dull and relieved only by the beautiful siting of the house on terracing above the Tweed. In 1838 the sixth Duke called in W H Playfair of Edinburgh to remodel the exterior of the house. Playfair was working at that time on Heriots School and the new Donaldson's Hospital and the three buildings have pronounced similarities — not least the use of the pepperpot towers. Nonetheless Playfair's work undoubtedly improved Floors Castle bringing Vanburgh's original building into proper scale with its dramatically beautiful surroundings.

A year later work was completed on Broomlands House. It was built for John Don of Attonburn (a relative of Patrick Don and a wealthy man) and was designed by William Adam, father of the more famous Robert. Although the house is much altered since 1719 it is still possible to see the basic design — a simple and attractive square house with a basement and two upper floors.

Not all the country houses around Kelso had a tranquil history. Near the graveyard of St Michael's Church on what is now the Border Union Showground stood Bridgend mansion house. It was the property of Sir William Ker of Greenhead (he sold the estate, as Springwood, to the Douglases in 1750). In 1714 Bridgend was burnt to the ground by a band of gipsies, revenging themselves on Ker for some misdeed. They were caught and eight of them (six women and two men) were transported to American Plantations. Their leader, Patrick Faa, had his ears cut off and was whipped and pilloried in the streets of the royal burgh of Jedburgh.

5 The Jacobites of 1715

The following year the Jacobite rebel army descended on Kelso. Two months before this the inhabitants of Kelso had met in the Parish Church and had agreed to stand by the Hanoverian succession, the Protestant religion and to oppose the popish Pretender. A local militia of 120 was raised and armed and put under the command of Sir William Bennet of Grubbet and Sir John Pringle of Stichil. As the rebels approached Sir William and his militia barricaded the town but discretion overtook their valour and the night before the Jacobites' arrival they left Kelso. The Old Pretender's army entered Kelso unopposed. This was a mainly lowland force and part of the reason for their occupation of Kelso was so that they could link up with a Highland army which has crossed the Forth under the command of Brigadier Mackintosh. The lowlanders marched out of Kelso to meet Mackintosh's men at Ednam Bridge and escorted them into the town with bagpipes playing. Apparently it was raining and the Highlanders had a day's difficult march behind them. The effect on the townspeople was negligible. Just as their bold militia had opted to leave, so the remaining Kelsonians did nothing to aid or resist the damp Jacobites.

The following day was a Sunday, 23 October 1715, and the troops mustered for divine service. They held it in a place they called 'the Great Kirk' which must mean the Abbey. Their chaplain, Mr Patten, preached a sermon based on Deuteronomy xxi 17, 'The right of the first-born is his'. Next morning, the troops, having paraded in the church yard, were marched with drums beating, colours flying and bagpipes playing up Roxburgh Street until they reached the Market Cross at Wester Kelso. They drew up in circles around the cross with the leaders forming the centre. The soldiers fell silent, a trumpet sounded and the Earl of Dunfermline, Seaton of Barns, proclaimed the absentee Chevalier as the rightful King of Scotland, England, France and Ireland. After this a document was read out. It contained a condemnation of many oppressions and grievances including high taxes. Now, it was not raining on that day and some of the townspeople of Kelso had turned out to watch the spectacle at the old Market Cross. When lower taxes were mentioned they began to chant 'no union, no salt tax, no malt tax'. Only days before they had sworn allegiance to the union, the crown and had been drilling a militia armed with muskets. Considering Kelso's recent history as a town struck in the middle of two warring nations, a number of warring factions and being the sufferer from a good deal of natural calamity, such a talent for bending with the prevailing wind must have been inborn. After the rebellion fizzled out, a commission of Oyer and Terminer went around Scotland to root out Jacobite collaborators. The commission sat in Kelso, but no charges were brought against anyone even though the town had been occupied by a Jacobite army. Remarkable.

6 Freemasons and Whipmen

Turning away from war and violent revolution back to the domestic life of Kelso, a number of institutions that still survive in the town had their beginnings in the early eighteenth century. The minutes for a meeting of the Freemason's Lodge Kelso (no 58) held on 27 December 1701 are extant. They refer to earlier meetings and the lodge may date from 1658. There exists a register dated for that year which lists the 'Fyf treads of Kelso —Hammermen, Wiwers, Showmakers and Glovers'. The Hammermen covered all those trades using the hammer; metal-workers, woodworkers and masons. George Faa, who was master of the Kelso Lodge in 1702 was a deacon of the Hammermen's guild.

The lodge was under the protection of St John, perhaps not co-incidentally one of the saints to whom the abbey of Kelso was dedicated (St Mary being the other). Local landowners were honorary members of the Freemasons and one of these was the owner of Bridgend mansion, Sir Andrew Ker of Greenhead. The lodge master, George Faa, sounds like a relative of Patrick Faa, the man who set fire to Ker's house.

The lodge still acted as a craft guild for masons but their main function seems to have been as a friendly society for masons' widows and those masons too old to continue working. They held frequent meetings where they dined and drank and in 1726 the lodge met at Thomas Winter's house to sort out the lodge accounts — one of these was a large bill from James Purves, a vintner of Kelso. In 1732 another hefty drinks account came in and the lodge resolved that 'all drinking after closing of the sederunt shall be out of every man's privatt pockett'. Despite this stricture the masons continued to do very well for themselves at their meetings. In 1748 they held their annual general meeting in the Town Hall and their records state that they not only had a good dinner but paid relatively high sums for entertainment after the meal; 'a guinea each to the fiddlers, 15s to the hautbois [oboe] and 10s to the bass'.

At the other end of the social scale in seventeenth century Kelso was another society: the Whipmen. They are remembered today in the celebrations at Civic Week. Here is a colourful description of the Whipmen from a contemporary writer who clearly sneered at them, the proles at play:

> There is a society, or brotherhood, in the town of Kelso, which consists of farmers' servants, ploughmen, husbandmen, or whipmen, who hold a meeting once-a-year for the purpose of merriment and diverting themselves; being all finely dressed out in their best clothes, and adorned with great bunches of beautiful ribbands, which hang down over their shoulders like so many streamers. By the beating of a drum they repair to the market place, well mounted upon fine horses, armed with large clubs and great wooden hammers, about eleven o'clock in the forenoon, when they proceed to a common field [the Berry Moss] about half a mile from the town, attended all the way with music and an undisciplined rabble of men, women and children, for the purpose of viewing a merriment of 'cat in a barrel', which is highly

esteemed by many for excellent sport. The generalissimo of this Regiment of Whipmen, who has the honourable style and title of 'My Lord', being arrived with the brotherhood at the place of rendezvous, the music playing, the drum beating, and their flag waving in the air, the poor timorous cat is put into a barrel partly stuffed with soot, and then hung up between two high poles, upon a cross-beam, below which they ride in succession, one after another, beseiging poor puss with their large clubs and hammers. The barrel, after many a frantic blow, being broken, the wretched animal makes her reluctant appearance amidst a great concourse of spectators, who seem to enjoy much pleasure at the poor animal's shocking figure, and terminate her life and misery by barbarous cruelty.

The cruel brotherhood having sacrificed this useful and domestic animal to the idol of cruelty, they next gallantly, and with great heroism, proceed with their sport to the destruction of a poor simple goose, which is next hung up by the heels, like the worst of malefactors, with a convulsed breast, in the most pungent distress, and struggling for liberty; when this merciless and profligate society, marching in succession, one after another, each in his turn takes a barbarous pluck at the head, quite regardless of its misery. After the miserable creature has received many a rude twitch, the head is carried away.

The day's sport ended in clumsy races: the usual prizes were a riding and cart saddle; and frequently the company were amused by donkeys running for a small sum. The whole concluded with a dinner and ball, to which all the friends of the society were invited, and the evening generally ended in peace and harmony. The custom of 'cat and barrel' has long been given up, and it is very unlikely it will ever be revived.

Even allowing for the evident distaste of the writer, a Mr Brand, who wrote several volumes entitled *Popular Antiquities*, this does dound like a grim series of rituals. Without stretching the point too far, there may be some relationship between the cat and the goose and animal sacrifice on a solstice.

7 Fornication

Whatever the origin of the Whipmens' festival, Brand's description does offer an early insight into the ways in which ordinary people enjoyed themselves. In a more oblique way the records of Kelso Parish Kirk Session relate other pastimes enjoyed by Kelsonians. Oblique because of course the Kirk Session was the court which heard the pleas of sinners; not large sins but the more everyday sort. Fornication was popular in Kelso, or perhaps it only seemed popular since, in the days before contraception, the net result of fornication was always so obvious. First a funny story and then a sad one.

The Parish Kirk Session records for 15 June 1755:

William Dryden being cited to this diet upon a Frama of a scandalous

135

behaviour betwixt himself and Isobel Garline, compeared and being interogate, said that upon Saturday beggone three weeks between the hours of twelve and one in the morning he was overtaken with liquor, that after this he drank three bottles of ale in company with Walter Anderson in Adam Hume's brewhouse, that Walter Anderson went away, and that himself had a good time after in the brewhouse, where Isabel Garline and Elspath Selkirk were brewing. That he, intending to go home betwixt five and six in the morning, Isabel Garline went along with him, through the Long Entry, and that he, the said Wm, hearing a cough and being ashamed to be seen in the said Isabel's company at such an early hour, he run into James Nelson's kiln and desired her to go into the street or come into the kiln, and that she coming to the kiln-door, he pulled her towards him that she might not be observed and in pulling her she fell back — that a dog coming to the door, the Declarant endeavoured to conceal himself upon the ground and that immediately after John Sinclair came in the door and George Learmont in company, and being further interogated answered that he and Isabel Garline were not in the kiln above two minutes.

How you interpret that is largely a matter of taste but Sinclair, and Learmont's testimony was very different. The Kirk Session preferred to believe them and Garline and Dryden were rebuked for their behaviour.

And now the sad story. In 1723 two young men, James Hislop and William Young, were walking through the parish churchyard when they heard a young woman crying bitterly. Her name was Agnes Pringle and she was crying because she had just been raped. The culprit was later found to be a dragoon visiting the town by the name of Greenham. Agnes Pringle was summoned before the Kirk Session and told:

that since guilt could not be proved against her, the Session would wait until Providence should in time discover if she were so or not, in the meantime, she was exhorted to be circumspect.

When it was apparent that Agnes was pregnant, she was rebuked before the congregation. Another sad story from 1756:

Phyllis Brown, unmarried woman and native of Berwick [had got] herself with child, said that John Bennet the shoemaker was the father . . . said the guilt [sic] was committed in the harvest time about five weeks before the Winter Fair at Kelso, in the way from Ednam to Kelso as she was returning from the shearing.

She was also rebuked by the Kirk Session. Clearly the shame of being so publicly identified as a fornicator was very great. Both man and woman suffered it but of course the woman had the huge burden of bearing and caring for the bastard child. Although it is not recorded what happened to

Agnes Pringle and Phyllis Brown's babies, the session does record the murders of several babies, killed by their desperate unmarried mothers. The callousness and smugness of the men who sat on the Kirk Session seems appalling now, but their actions would seem entirely normal in the middle of the eighteenth century in Presbyterian Scotland.

8 Remarkable Schoolmasters

While the moral education, such as it was, was emphatically in the hands of the church, the secular education of children in Kelso was in the care of a remarkable series of schoolmasters. In 1690, James Kirkwood came to Kelso from Linlithgow to be Rector of the Grammar School. He was an intellectual of considerable power; he rewrote Despauter's Latin grammar because he thought it required improvement and when he left Linlithgow after a row with the town council he wrote and published a satirical pamphlet *The Twenty Seven Gods of Linlithgow* addressed to the 27 members of the council.

From the outset he was a controversial figure in Kelso. The Rector of the Grammar School was generally made Session Clerk (because his literacy and numeracy were to be relied upon) but Kirkwood was not. The fact that he was not appointed may have something to do with his work as Session Clerk for the Episcopal Meeting House in Kelso. He compounded his unpopularity with the Parish Kirk by refusing to take responsibility for his pupils' behaviour in church. The Session rebuked him twice for their unruliness but Kirkwood seems to have paid no attention. His refreshing obstinacy and aggression is best illustrated by an incident that took place on 30 December 1696. The Parish Kirk Session met to hear any objections that might be made to a group of men chosen to serve as kirk elders. The bold Kirkwood appeared with a party of his supporters, doubtless with a drink or two in them, and 'in a rude and noisy manner' they made many objections to each elder as he was proposed. The Moderator of the Presbytery is said to have ruled their remarks as 'irrelevant'. Kirkwood sounds like an extremely attractive man.

David Chystie followed as Rector in 1708, and was duly appointed as Session Clerk. During his tenure there was a controversy over the question of schools in Kelso other than the Grammar School or the 'Highe School' as it was sometimes known. Evidently several private schools existed and these were explicitly banned in this bit of the Bailie Diet Book (a record of town council meetings) for 30 January 1717:

It is found that no persons can teach schollars, or set up schools within the town of Kelso without allowance and consent of the Duke of Roxburghe of his Bailly, as the samyn more fully bears: yet for notwithstanding thereof, Ther are several persons, inhabitants within this burgh and town, who gott up publick schools, and teaches schollars thereat without allowance or consent of the faimly of Roxburghe or their baillys. Therefore and for protecting the lyke in time coming. The Bailly by force of this act discharges all persons within the burgh and town of Kelso from Candlemass next from keeping any publick school, or teach maille children thereat above seven years old other than at the High Schoole of Kelso.

Concealed in the above may be a major reason for the demand for private schools. Only 'maille' children were taught at Kelso High School in the early seventeenth century. It may be that the private schools catered for the educational needs of the little girls of the town.

When Chystie's successor, George Ogilvy, was appointed, the Bailie Diet book offers two interesting pieces of information. One of the witnesses to Ogilvy's appointment was a Mr John Gibsone, Doctor of Medicine. This in 1720. In 1731 the Register of Sasines (a set of documents concerned with land ownership, kept in Edinburgh) mentions a Mr John Ker, 'chirurgeon of Kelso'. Two doctors, one of medicine the other a surgeon, in the space of a decade: another indication of the development of Kelso as it pulled itself out of the wretched condition in which the town saw the opening of the century.

Ogilvy lasted a long time as Rector of the school — until 1752, and in his time the scope of education available expanded. Out of his salary he hired two assistant teachers; John Hall to teach Latin and John Dawson to teach English. No mention is made of the school building itself expanding to cope with the extra classes. That comes later.

9 A New Bridge

Further evidence of the development of Kelso occurs in 1752. Before that date and indeed for the period since the mediaeval bridge across the Tweed from Wester Kelso to Roxburgh had fallen, the passage across the River had been made by ferry (or the 'cowbill'). In his *Theatrum Scotiae*, Slezer includes a print of Kelso made just before 1690. It shows a ferry or coble plying between what is now Bridgend Park and the foot of the brae beside the glebe field. By 1752 this hazardous (in time of flood) and limited form of crossing had become obselete. Kelsonians wanted a more dependable link with the south bank of the Tweed. The records of the masonic lodge for that year record a vote of £50 towards the costs of building a bridge. Every working mason promised a day of his labour on the project and the following year the lodge voted more cash to the building fund, the rest of which was compiled by subscription. The result, completed in 1754, was a six arch bridge, slightly hump-backed. It was the only structure spanning the Tweed between Peebles and Berwick.

Kelso Masonic Lodge took part in the laying of the foundation stone on 17 June 1754. The masons processed from the Town Hall with music playing (2 French horns, 2 oboes and a bassoon) and wearing new aprons and gloves. Medals were struck to mark the occasion and they had carved a suitable Latin inscription on the foundation stone. Ralph Walker, the overseer in charge of building the bridge, was admitted to the lodge and enjoyed their well known hospitality. It had cost £3,000 but, crucially, no allowance had been made for the upkeep of the new bridge and no tolls were charged to provide any cash for maintainance.

On Friday 22 October 1756 disaster struck. The middle arch of the bridge fell and six people were killed. The Kirk Session records two days later:

> a collection from house to house is ordered . . . in favour of the sufferers by the dismal calamity of the falling of one of the arches of the bridge . . .

A short time later the Session began to organise the collection of money to repair the bridge. They did this systematically, dividing the town into several quarters. This is informative because it shows how Kelso was shaping in the middle of the eighteenth century. Collections were to be made in:

1. The Easter quarter.
2. The Mill quarter.
3. The Townhead.
4. The country part of the parish.
5. Maxwellheugh.
6. Brox-law barony.

The 'Easter' quarter is listed first because it comprises the area around the Town Hall and probably Horsemarket and Woodmarket. Working outwards the 'Mill' quarter is easy — the area between Roxburgh Street and the Tweed. 'Townhead' sounds like the new name for what remained of Wester Kelso at the top end of Roxburgh Street. 'Maxwellheugh' is new and shows that the village of Maxwell had crept up the hill away from the danger of flooding in its old location on the Border Union Showground. The creation of the bridge (however unreliable) must have helped the growth of Maxwellheugh greatly. The 'country part of the parish' is straightforward but what is less so is the re-appearance of 'Brox-law' an ancient name for the bit of land near the outflow of the Stodrig burn into Tweed. A name remembered only in one of the Duke of Roxburghe's more obscure titles and not in the common memory of people who live in Kelso.

10 More Jacobites

The middle of the eighteenth century saw only one occasion when national politics interrupted the town's peaceful life. In 1745 Bonnie Prince Charlie marched into Kelso at the head of his Highland army. He was met with the same apathy that greeted Brigadier Mackintosh in 1715. Prince Charlie is said to have remarked that although he had many drinking friends in Kelso, he had few fighting ones. No Kelsonian joined his army to fight and those who were pressed into service to convey the baggage returned home as soon and as safely they could.

Just as in 1715, Mr Ramsay, the Parish Kirk minister, made sure that none of his parishioners were tainted with sedition. Before the rebels arrived in 1715 he discreetly warned any potential Jacobite sympathisers that he would note their names and make them known to the government in the aftermath of the rising. Ramsay was confident that both the '15 and the '45 would fail and he probably managed to persuade any waiverers of the same. He became Kelso's minister in 1708 and lasted in the job until his death in 1749. His conduct before and during the rebellions shows his tremendous influence as a community leader.

11 Dissent

The Duke of Roxburghe chose the minister of Kelso at that time and when Ramsay died the Duke selected Cornelius Lundie to follow. But many of the congregation dissented from this and 112 signed a petition which was presented to the Duke. When his grace ignored their arguments and the 112 took themselves out of the Parish Kirk congregation and formed the Burgher Church. They bought a place called the 'Riding School' and fitted it out as a church. The group was joined by a like-minded congregation from Stichill whose preacher, Mr Potts, came to Kelso to work permanently.

This example of dissent from the all-pervading power of the Duke, the Burgh Superior, is not an isolated one. In 1757 the English House of Lords (not, theoretically, empowered to hear Scottish appeals either then or now) heard an appeal in the case between 'the Duke of Roxburghe (named John) versus Ninian Jeffrey and others, the Representatives of the Several Corporations of the Borough of Kelso'. The argument was about which party had jurisdiction over Kelso Mill and the anna in the Tweed. The House of Lords made a split judgement and agreed with Duke John that he had jurisdiction over the mill and that he could collect customs from it. But they also said that the anna should at all times be accessible to the inhabitants of the town for the purposes of comfort or utility. They probably used the anna for drying and bleaching clothes.

These incidents taken together show that Kelso, as a community, had begun to find an identity. Fifty years before, the representative of the town had been begging the Lord Chancellor to reduce their taxes by half since the town was in such an enfeebled state.

Population size is a good measure of stability and growth and in the second half of the eighteenth century, Kelso's began to expand. In 1755 2,781 people lived in Kelso compared with 4,324 in 1793.

12 The Parish Church, the Dispensary and a Library

Population expansion and relative prosperity resulted in the building of a bridge in 1754 and by the 1770s two more projects underlined this trend.

Since the Reformation Kelsonians had worshipped in a makeshift church built into what remained of the west end of the Abbey Church. By 1773 this had become unsatisfactory. There is a tradition that the congregation was spooked by a fall of plaster from the ceiling of the kirk because it was seen as the fulfillment of a prophesy that 'Kelsae's kirk would fall at its fullest'. What is more likely is that the old makeshift kirk became too small. Plans were drawn up by James Nisbet, the architect of Ednam House, John Laidlaw and John Purves. The building was completed in 1773. The design is odd and it has prompted scathing reactions. The historian John Mason:

> The parish church is a misshapen pile, bearing some resemblance to a mustard pot of immense size, and pollutes the lovely scene amid which it stands.

Another historian, Rutherford, writing in 1880:

> The present parish church of Kelso built on an octagonal plan has the peculiarity of being, without exception, the ugliest and least suitable in its architecture of all the parish churches in Scotland —and that is saying a good deal — but it is an excellent model for a circus.

Hard words, but in fact many Scottish parish churches are polygonal — St John's Edenside to name but one — because that shape suits the particular needs of the presbyterian religion. Nonetheless it is not a beautiful building, which is surprising when one considers the architect. James

Nisbet designed Ednam House in 1761 for James Dickson and made one of the most beautiful Georgian manions in the Borders. Dickson came from Ednam and Nisbet was a native of Kelso. Dickson had, as a youth, committed the crime of breaking the pant-well which stood in the Square. Rather than face justice he had run off to London where he made a fortune trading with the West Indies. His business is remembered in Kelso by the street-name of Havannah Court. Nisbet also worked out of London with a practice based in Berners Street. It is possible that the two exiles met in the capital where they conceived the idea of Ednam House.

At all events Dickson returned home as a wealthy grandee in need of a suitably grand house. And he got one. Ednam House has a unique site on the river just above Kelso Bridge. Nisbet took advantage of the location and created a terrace (where newly married couples are often photographed — the building is now a hotel) with, originally, a summer house and a garden house (which still survives). Ignoring the later additions, the 'town side' of the house or the front entrance is a stunningly harmonious composition. Inside there are plaster relief ceilings, beautiful marble mantlepieces, friezes and carved mahogany doors. Dickson got his money's worth.

Soon after the Parish Church was completed Kelso got another, equally important institution. Mrs Bailie of Jerviswood, a local landowner, provided a sum of money for the creation of a public dispensary. This was to become, in effect, the town's hospital and surgery. The building is in Roxburghe Street and is now a family house, occupied by Jock and Sheila Hume. After its completion the dispensary was maintained by voluntary subscription. Patients who received treatment were not charged for it and in times of epidemic it was used as a fever hospital where patients with contagious diseases could be easily isolated.

The Dispensary was run by Dr Christopher Douglas, a local doctor who later compiled the First Statistical Account for Kelso. He kept concise records. In its first year the new hospital treated 302 patients. They suffered from a wide variety of diseases, and chief amongst them being fever, ague, asthma, dropsy, rheumatism and two cases of smallpox. Scurvy, scarlet fever and cholera all visited Kelso. In one year 40 people died from cholera.

Some years before the establishment of the Dispensary, Kelso got another useful institution. In 1750 Kelso Library was founded making it one of the earliest municipal libraries in Scotland. It was paid for by subscribers and in the first forty years of its existence it accumulated more than 3,000 books.

One of these might have been Wight's 'Husbandry in Scotland' written about 1778. It records a remarkable trade that grew up around Kelso in that period and gave the town one of its street names. In 1778 the planting of tobacco was introduced by a Dr Jackson of Nicholatownfield (a name that used to be used for Rosebank) a farm near Kelso. Jackson had been a doctor in the former colony of Virginia and when he returned to Scotland he brought tobacco seeds with him. His experiment caught on and Alexander Blackie, a local gardener and seedsman, also began to plant the weed. The London market liked Border tobacco and compared it to third quality Virginian. In a very short period more than 1000 acres were planted between Eyemouth and Hawick. The street-name it gave Kelso is, of course, Drying House Lane — nothing to do with clothes but everything to do with tobacco leaves.

13 James Palmer and the Kelso Chronicle

On page four of the *Kelso Chronicle* for Friday, August 29 1783 tobacco was the subject of a story, the burden of which concerned the amount of duty to be paid on it. This was not the first issue of the *Chronicle* but the twenty-sixth, having made its first appearance on March 7 1783. It is a remarkably early date for the foundation of any newspaper, never mind that of a country town. The *Kelso Chronicle* is as old as the *Glasgow Herald* and older than *The Scotsman* — and older than almost every English newspaper (save *The Times* and one or two others). Perhaps the directors of the *Tweeddale Press* were aware that the *Chronicle* was almost 200 years old when they closed it and waited for its bicentenary before they ceased production. Then again perhaps they were not.

The edition of 29 August 1783 is very odd. Odd because for a local paper it carried very little local news. The tobacco story is actually a notice from the Customs House of Edinburgh which gives planters information on how much excise duty they will have to pay on their crops. It also, by the way, shows what a lucrative business it must have been, in the aftermath of the loss of the American colonies and the temporary drying-up of the tobacco supply. The only other bits of local news concern the grain prices being made at Kelso and at Haddington. This is disappointing but not altogether surprising. The *Kelso Chronicle* was not considered by its readers to be a local paper — it was the *only* paper they saw. Therefore it had to contain all the news available. That is why page one carries a story about conditions on board naval ships, page two reports on the appointment of ambassadors to the Tsar's court at St Petersburg, naval stories from Naples and Cadiz and, most interestingly, the latest news on what was happening in America. Most if not all of this seems to have been cribbed from the *London Gazette* and government notices. There is the occasional bit of flowery poetry of the sort that was fashionable in 1783. It seems to have been used as a column-filler when the main page-lead story ran out, but a complete poem does appear in the first column of the front page. Readers of that edition of the *Kelso Chronicle* were greeted with:

> Awake my Muse, and view the pleasant fields,
> Cloth'd with the gorgeous robe which Autumn yields.
> See, who the whit'ning fields of waving Corn
> The verdant hills and dales around adorn;
> To where the landskip meets the bending skies,
> O'erspread with waving Corn the mountains rise;

Waving corn — either the editor of the *Kelso Chronicle* was very daring or very pretentious, or stuck for a page-lead. Right at the end of the paper his name appears. He was James Palmer and without doubt, a remarkable man.

Palmer edited and printed his newspaper in a building which still stands and is now occupied by Swan's toyshop. His nickname was 'Black Neb' a name given to those who sympathised with the aims of the French Revolution. In line with his political beliefs, Palmer's *Chronicle* took up a thoroughly independent position. He questioned the 'divine right' of government to abuse its powers by repressing liberty of speech and denying political rights to the people; and of the country gentry to take advantage of their social and political power to lord it over their less wealthy fellow citizens. In the period after the American Revolution (whose upshot was a bill of rights which declared that all men are equal under God) and in the run up to 1789 and the French Revolution, these views were not unknown but they did make Palmer highly unpopular with the great and powerful in and around Kelso. From time to time he was imprisoned in Jedburgh Castle jail for his views.

His paper was nicknamed the 'Palmer-worm' by local gentry who occasionally suffered attacks in the Chronicle. He ran a campaign against cock-fighting which offended many of the local grandees. What offended them more was this kind of political statement, which appeared in the first number of the *Kelso Chronicle*: Palmer is writing just after the end of hostilities in the American War of Independence:

> The publisher, after such a long, expensive and unsuccessful war, is happy, in his first paper, to congratulate his readers on the approach of peace; although the preliminaries have not answered the expectation of the public, nor been cordially approven of by the House of Commons. In time of war people in general are naturally most anxious for news; yet the most brilliant victories are

144

only tales of woe, and everlasting monuments of the depravity of mankind,
which, to very ingenuous mind, must give less pleasure than to hear of the
flourishing of agriculture, manufactures, and commerce, — the true support
of the nation, and which the blessing of peace cannot fail to promote.

Anti-war stuff like this must have alienated Palmer greatly —especially in a
small community like Kelso. Ten years after this he again adopted an
unpopular stance. In the *Chronicle* he constantly advocated a policy of non-
intervention in the French Revolutionary Wars and although he was
supported in this by merchants and manufacturers (who took
advertisements in the paper) Palmer's pacifism ultimately led to the
establishment of a rival publication.

14 The Mail and the Chronicle

In 1797 the Ballantyne Brothers began printing the *Kelso Mail* in offices
almost exactly opposite Palmer in Bridge Street. The *Mail* was a
conservative newspaper which was immediately adopted by the gentry,
the freeholders and heritors of Roxburgh, as the 'county' paper. It
professed an impartiality in politics and turned its attention to other areas
such as law reporting and agricultural affairs, much like the *Chronicle* as it
used to be until its recent demise. The Ballantyne brothers, although they
found themselves in the same street and the same town tended to behave
as though the *Chronicle* did not exist and there seems to have been little
sense of rivalry between the papers. After Palmer died his sons attempted
to carry on the business but finally gave up in 1803 when the *Kelso Chronicle*
ceased, temporarily, to be published.

The Ballantynes were friendly with the young Walter Scott who had
come to stay with his aunt in the house now known as Waverley Lodge.
Evidently Scott's health, as a boy, was poor and it was thought that the
fresh air of Kelso would do him good —compared with that which he
inhaled as a pupil of the Royal High School in Edinburgh. Scott attended
Kelso High School where he was taught by the Rector, Lancelot Whale,
and where he met James Ballantyne. This was in 1783. The two young men
met again at Edinburgh University as members of the 'Young Teviotdale
Club'. After graduating, James Ballantyne returned to Kelso where he
began to practice as a solicitor in 1795. Apparently his business did not
succeed very well because he:

willingly listened, in the summer of 1796, to a proposal of some of the
neighbouring nobility and gentry respecting the establishment of a weekly
newspaper, in opposition to one of a democratic tendency then widely

circulated in Roxburghshire and the other Border counties. Ballantyne undertook the printing and editing of this new journal, and proceeded to London in order to engage some correspondents and to make the other necessary preparations.

He also went to Glasgow to buy type and on the carriage back to Kelso, Ballantyne met Walter Scott. While Scott was staying at Rosebank in the autumn of 1799 he called on Ballantyne with a few paragraphs on some of the legal questions of the day, which he had written out for publication in the *Mail*. During the course of this transaction, Lockhart, Scott's biographer, believes that the two men discussed the proposition that the *Kelso Mail's* press and types should not lie idle four days a week but that Ballantyne should try some book printing. Accordingly, he published twelve copies of *Apology for Tales of Terror* in 1799. Scott was apparently impressed with the quality of the printing (he made no recorded comment abut the literary merits of the book) and he suggested Ballantyne should publish a collection of Border ballads which he had been compiling for some years. Called *The Minstrelsy of the Scottish Border*, two volumes of this work were brought off the Kelso presses in 1802. Scott was launched on his literary career and Ballantyne, so he thought, on that of a successful publisher. While the third volume of the *Minstrelsy* was in preparation, the young printer and publisher left to set up his business in Edinburgh. He found premises near Holyroodhouse and began a career that was to end in financial catastrophe for both Ballantyne and Scott. The business went spectacularly bust and Scott spent the last years of his life working long hours writing so that he could repay what he and Ballantyne owed. The work broke his health and led to a premature death.

The *Kelso Mail* continued, now run by the Jerdan family, and in 1832 the *Chronicle* resumed publication. The two newspapers co-existed reasonably in the early nineteenth century although at elections they were at each other's throat.

The circulation of the rival papers did fluctuate very considerably and sometimes according to the prevailing political climate. The *Chronicle* tended to support the Liberals while the *Mail* was conservative and defended the interests of the Roxburghshire landowners. Here is a table showing the relative circulation of the two papers:

	1837	1839	1840	1841	1842	1843
Kelso Mail	550	1000	500	450	385	469
Kelso Chronicle	300	615	307	700	769	384

Occasionally the *Mail* and *Chronicle* would unite to campaign in favour of a single issue. For example, they combined behind moves to improve the quality of the postal service between Kelso and Edinburgh in 1843.

As Scotland began to acquire national papers and as the distribution of these became more widespread Kelso's newspapers became more local in their news content and by the middle of the nineteenth century they are a fertile source of information.

15 Kelso at the Theatre

This development was too late, however, to cover what was a remarkable phenomenon in the cultural life of the town. Between 1791 and 1809 Kelso had a permanent theatre which was visited by numerous touring companies, and on one occasion by the most famous actor of the day, John Kemble. The theatre was located in Horsemarket in a close remembered until recently as Theatre Close. At the head of Theatre Close there existed an outside stair which led to a large room. This was Kelso's theatre.

Much of the evidence for this unusual development comes from a series of playbills which have come down to us. The first of them is dated 9 December 1791 and it was published by Mr Stordy's company. He presented a 'favourite new comic opera (never acted here) *The Highland Reel* with a prologue by Mr Peafeld previous to the play'. This was a comedy about highlanders of the sort common after the '15 and the '45. After the *Highland Reel* there were two monologues (or perhaps recitals) *The Golden Days of Good Queen Bess* by Mr Stordy and *A Sailor' Life's a Life of Woe* and then after those, a farce, called *All The World's a Stage*. This extraordinary full evening's entertainment was on offer at two prices 2s and 1s with the curtain rising at 6pm.

Judging by the name on the cast list and the plays on offer —*Good Queen Bess* — it seems likely that this was an English company. Their actor-manager, Mr Stordy, sold the tickets himself at Mr Middlemass' shop at the head of Woodmarket or at the inns of the town. The price differential on the tickets offers some clue as to the interior of Kelso's theatre. It was 2s for the pit and 1s for the gallery. The pit was probably a floor-level area near the stage and the gallery a raised area at the back of the room.

Mr Stordy's company did come back to Kelso in the 1790s but no playbills survive from that period — nor do they survive from a visit supposedly made by an earlier company during Kelso race week in the 1770s. The next bit of evidence is a bill for 1801. This advertises performances of Sheridan's *The Beaux Stratagem* with a new song between every act, a pantomime called *Harlequin Skeleton or the Chapter of Accidents* imported from *The Circus, Edinburgh*. All of this was to be followed by a dance. This company was run by a Mr Rutherford. The playbill carries the usual information but with one change from the 1791 publicity. Performances are to be at the *new* theatre and the prices are lower, suggesting a new room or a new building.

Alexander Ballantyne printed the playbill of 1802 for Mr Stanfield and made a good job of it. On 4 June of that year Stanfield mounted a production of *Bluebeard* or *Female Curiosity* with new machinery and scenery. It had a cast of fourteen and an elephant. Nothing, but nothing like that happens in Kelso now. The elephant and the large cast imply a large building, which they would doubtless need with a title like that. Interestingly the playbill stipulates that there be 'no admittance behind the scenes' during the performance of 'Bluebeard' or 'Female Curiosity'.

1803 saw a long season, judging by the number of playbills which survive. Performances, again by Stanfield's company, went on every three days. Either they toured to nearby towns on the other two days or they were so exhausted by their marathon bills that the company needed two days to recover. Tickets were sold at the *Kelso Mail* Printing Office (where they were probably printed), at Mr Bruce's the Innkeeper in Horsemarket (possibly the Black Swan) and by Mr Robertson, the Shoemaker of Woodmarket —an interesting continuity this. Robertson's was probably a handy place near the theatre entrance for a daytime box office.

On 18 November 1803 a star came to perform at Kelso. Mr John Kemble took the lead in *Wheel of Fortune* and on 22 November he played John Locke in *The Miller of Mansfield*. A London star in a London production. The playbills stop in 1809 but there is reliable evidence that the theatre carried on. It was maintained and used by French prisoners of war who put on their own entertainments, which were much enjoyed by the townspeople.

Throughout this colourful period of Kelso's history there is, curiously, no murmur of disapproval from the Kirk. The theatre was and sometimes still is a bugbear with the Church of Scotland. The minister at that time was Cornelius Lundie. He followed James Ramsay, who held the living between 1707 and 1749. Lundie in turn held the post of parish minister between 1749 and 1801, a remarkable record with two men spanning and entire century in one place. Lundie must have been an old and wise man when the theatre came to Kelso and it seems he knew when to leave well alone.

16 The First Statistical Account

1793 saw the publication of the *First Statistical Account*. This document, 700 years later than England, was Scotland's *Domesday Book*. Each parish was described, measured, had its history noted down and its population counted. Kelso was written up by Dr Christopher Douglas, a physician who worked in the town and at the Dispensary. It is elegantly, crisply written and it provides a historical snapshot of Kelso taken in the period prior to 1793. There is little point in paraphrasing Douglas' prose or taking short extracts from it. Here is an edited version of the account:

> This district, formerly consisting of three separate parishes, viz. Kelso, Maxwell and St James, is situated in the lower division of Roxburghshire or Tiviotdale. It is of an irregular triangular figure extending in length, from North to South, 4½ miles and in breadth from East to West 4½ miles. On the East the parish of Sprouston separates it from Northumberland. The rivers Tweed and Tiviot unite at Kelso. The former divides the parish nearly into two equal parts. St James lies between the two rivers; Maxwell on the south east and Kelso in the north and west of both.
>
> The valued rent is 15,300 pounds Scotch. The real rent, including the land in the possession of the proprietors, which is by far the greatest part of the parish, is from 7,000 pounds to 8,000 pounds Sterling. The land in this part of the country is all measured by the English acre. The Duke of Roxburgh, superior of the town and the greatest part of the parish, resides above half the year at Fleurs. Besides his Grace the following heritors also reside in the parish; Sir George Douglas, Bart. Rear-Admiral William Dickson, Robert Davidson of Pinnacle-hill, Robert Walker of Wooden, John Proctor of Softlaw Tower, Esqs. Capt Scott of Rosebank, Rev. Dr Panton, Dr Blaw, and many others of smaller property.

Having set down the extent of Kelso parish, its monetary value and a list of the powerful people who control it, Dr Douglas goes on to give a geological description of the land. He follows this with a breakdown of the different crops grown around Kelso; turnips, potatoes, barley, spring wheat and hay, and then mentions that sheep and black cattle are pastured on 'a considerable part' of the parish. Douglas turns his attention to the town itself:

> At present Kelso is a handsome town, containing many good houses, with a spacious market-place 300 feet in length, and 200 in breadth; from hence, as a centrical point, proceed four long streets, and two considerable lanes. In the square stands the town house, the principal houses, and shops, many of which would do no discredit to the capital of any country.

Three of the long streets must be Roxburgh, Horsemarket and Woodmarket but what about the fourth? Bowmont Street had no proper entry into the Square at that time and was in any case a long back lane. The fourth 'long' street could be Bridge Street —perhaps Douglas' definition of 'long' was elastic enough to include it. At all events this description is the first complete record of the shape of modern Kelso. Here is Douglas with a good description of the government of the town:

> Kelso is governed by a Baron Baillie, appointed by the Duke, and fifteen stent-masters, of whom the Duke nominates seven. The other eight consists of the Preses of the Merchant Company, a Deacon Convenor, the Deacons of the five following corporations, Hammermen, Skinners, Shoemakers, Taylors, Weavers, and the Deacon of the Butchers, although they are not incorporated. The stent-masters, under the authority of the Baron Baillie, are entrusted with the power of imposing a stent or tax upon the inhabitants, as they judge their circumstances may afford. This is levied with the purpose of supplying the inhabitants with water, conveyed by leaden pipes, to different parts of the town, for repairing the streets, keeping the town clock in order, paying part of the school-masters' salaries, and for several other incidents.

By the late eighteenth century a certain degree of religious tolerance grew up. Kelso had its share of different sects:

> Besides the established church (the parish church), and an Episcopal chapel, there are a number of sects, each of which has a house for public worship, and some of them are even elegant. These are the kirk of Relief, Burghers, Antiburghers, Cameronians, Methodists, and Quakers. There are three Roman Catholics and one Jew in the parish. The major part of the inhabitants, particularly of the genteel class, attend the parish church and the Episcopal chapel. The meeting-houses are chiefly supported by the inhabitants of different parishes in the vicinity. This place, being centrical and convenient, induces them to build here. The Parochial church and Episcopal chapel are both new; the former a spacious octagon, with a handsome dome, and constructed to accommodate three thousand hearers; the latter, a small neat gothic building, and has lately been ornamented with an organ.

Next, Douglas deals with population — in fascinating detail:

> In the year 1749, the number of inhabitants was 2900. The return from Dr Webster, in 1755, was 2781, and the number at present amounts to 4324. The annexed table contains an exact statement of the number of houses, families, males and females, in the town and country divisions of the parish, as drawn up from an actual survey made last year, 1792.

Census

Houses in the Town	376	Houses in the Country	126
Families in ditto	826	Families in ditto	127
Males in ditto	1644	Males in ditto	365
Females in ditto	1913	Females in ditto	402
Number of souls	3557	Number of souls	767
Under 10	933	Under 10	193
From 10 to 20	713	From 10 to 20	141
From 20 to 50	1416	From 20 to 50	334
From 50 to 70	393	From 50 to 70	78
From 70 to 100	102	From 70 to 100	21

Occupations

Skinners	20	Medical Practitioners	6
Weavers	60	Writers or Attorneys	11
Optician	1	Schoolmasters	7
Dyers and Clothiers	3	Booksellers and Printers	2
Tailors	47	Shopkeepers	30
Upholsterers	2	Bakers	32
Brewers	2	Butchers	24
Plaisterers	6	Inn & ale-house keepers	40
Carpenters	60	Saddlers	12
Midwives	6	Shoemakers	147
Masons	40	Stocking weavers	7
Smiths	15	Gardeners	10
Copper & white ironsmiths	6	Nailers	7
Staymakers	3	Cutlers	3
House Painters	2	Watchmakers	4
Glovers	4	Glaziers	2
Carriers	3	Barbers	6
Carters	40	Milliners	4
Labourers	162	Mantua-makers	8
Clergymen	7	Pastry cooks	2

The disproportion between the average number of each family of the town and country, is owing to the number of widows and single women, who live more conveniently in the town, and get employment more readily than in the country. In 38 years, the increase of inhabitants has been 1543. This great increase may, in part, be accounted for, from the destruction of many villages in the neighbourhood, occupied by small farmers and mechanics (workers). From the enlargement of the farms, many were obliged to follow other trades, and Kelso being the metropolis of the district, they flocked there for habitations and employment; and, in proportion as labourers and mechanics have become fewer in the country, Kelso has increased in population.

Douglas' broad analysis of the population movement falls in with what was happening throughout Scotland at the end of the eighteenth century. As farmers began to enclose their land and modernise their methods of production, agriculture became less labour-intensive. People left the land and came to Kelso for jobs.

Looking more closely at these figures a number of things are surprising. Life expectancy, on average, looks higher than in other parts of Scotland at 47. There are many who survive beyond 50 and 102 beyond 70. With more than twice the number of families than there are houses in Kelso, this suggests tenement living on a wide scale.

The occupations list shows a thriving economy, and a relatively sophisticated one. Six doctors, eleven lawyers, four watchmakers, and two printers — more in each category than exist in Kelso now. The spread of occupations shows that there must have been a demand from the surrounding countryside, as well as the town, for all of the goods produced. The large number of skinners, weavers, tailors and shoemakers suggests that there was some export of locally finished goods outside the area.

Having listed the occupations of Kelsonians, Douglas goes on to describe how they sold what they made:

> The weekly market day is Friday. There are twelve high markets in the year, two before and one after the term days of Whitsunday and Martinmas; the two first are for hiring male and female servants, the last is generally employed by the servants in mirth, and in laying out their wages before they enter again into service. On these days, the concourse of people being great, and beyond what is known on the like occasions in any part of Scotland, it is productive of immense profits to the shopkeepers, milliners etc among whom they lay out incredible sums of money, principally for wearing apparel, and female ornaments. The other six high market days are in March and the end of Autumn; the former for purchasing horses for summer work, such as, driving lime, coal etc; which being over, they sell the horses again before the winter sets in, owing to the high price of fodder at this season.
>
> There are three fairs in the parish, including St James's, which is held on the 5th of August; two in the town, one of these on the 10th July, the other on the 2nd of November. When these fairs were established they were wisely designed; the first was for buying lean cattle, to be fed during the summer and autumn months, upon meadow and pasture ground; and, when fat, they were brought to market, and sold for winter and spring food, called Marts, being immediately killed and salted. In these days fresh meat was not to be got during the winter; but, since the introduction of turnip husbandry, the market is plentifully supplied with the very best fed cattle during the whole year. The summer fair being no longer of its original use, it would be a great

advantage to the stockholders, to have it altered to the end of August; this would suit dealers in cattle to purchase, at a convenient time, to drive them south to Woolpitt market, held in September. Fairs ought to succeed one another from north to south, until flocks arrive in London, the *ne plus ultra*.

At the markets and fairs people, of all classes, spent money. It was the reason to come into town, to get supplies. Douglas mentions that you could buy:

> all kinds of woollen drapery, haberdashery, hosiery goods, groceries and hard wares, grass seeds, gin, brandy, wine, green tea, black tea and coffee, beer, bread . . .
>
> The butchers have lately been acommodated by the Duke of Roxburgh, with a large and excellent market place. Upon an average, they kill annually;
> Black cattle 700
> Calves 620
> Sheep and lambs. 8000
> Swine. 600
> The dressers dress from 70,000 to 80,000 sheep and lamb skins. They also send to Manchester and other places, the wool of 40,000 or 50,000 mort skins. These are the skins of lambs, either brought forth dead, or which die early. They likewise collect and send away above 5000 hare skins and of rabbit, fox, polecat and otter skins, from 500 to 600. The shoemakers, by far the most numerous class, make annually 30,000 pair of shoes, and from 300 to 400 pairs of boots. These are all sold at different fairs in Northumberland, and in Kelso market. The high wages the journeymen receive, and the price of leather, precludes masters from the benefit of exportation.
>
> The weavers yearly make about 20,000 yards of flannel, or what are locally called, plains; and from 9000 to 10,000 of different kinds of linen, which they call custom work. Stocking weavers work annually from 300 to 400 dozen of pairs. Dyers and clothiers are principally employed in dying and dressing, what they call country work, made by individuals for private use, in pieces from 50 to 60 yards in length. They also dye home-made cotton pieces for private wearing. The copper and white iron smiths, sell every article of kitchen utensils, tea kettles etc and have a great demand for them at all the markets.

Douglas writes after this passage about the price of food in Kelso, the export of fresh salmon to London and the trade in coal from the coast. Next the church, and then education:

> The stipend is in money and victual, 100 guineas, per annum, exclusive of a house and garden, and a valuable glebe, measuring between six and seven acres. It is worthy of remark, that, during this century, there have been but two incumbents (of the office of parish minister) Mr Ramsay, and the present much esteemed and worthy pastor, Mr Cornelius Lundie.

> There are two established schools, one for Latin, and the other for English. The tutor has a salary of £22 per annum, a house and garden, and 5 shillings per quarter for each of his pupils. He has about 50 scholars. The office of session-clerk is generally annexed to his employment, which is worht about £12 a year. The English master's salary is £5. 13 shillings, 2/6 and 3/6 per quarter from his pupils; the first for being taught reading, the second reading and writing; and the third arithmetic, in addition to the other two. His scholars are from 100 to 130. There are also four other English schools, one of them taught by the clerk of the chapel, and in good reputation. Besides these, there are female teachers, for instructing girls in sewing. A recent institution, which does credit to the founders, and which it is hoped, will turn out to their advantage, and to that of the public in general, is a School of Industry, in which employment is given to poor girls, who have stated hours for sewing, knitting and tambouring, for learning to read and write, and for inculcating moral duties.

Judging by the numbers of children attending the two main schools — about 180 — and the existence of four other schools, and the fact that these institutions only taught male children, it looks from Douglas' statistics that education in Kelso was enjoyed by all and not limited to those who could afford it. He goes on:

> A public library, which has existed upwards of forty years, and can now boast a collection of the best modern authors, being regularly supplied with every publication of merit; together with a coffee house supplied with the London, Edinburgh and Kelso newspapers. The proprietors of the library have lately resolved to erect a neat elegant house for the books, and for the accommodation of the librarian.
>
> It is much to be regretted, that the elegant square in which the market is held, is not ornamented with a better townhouse. The present is old and ruinous, and, from its construction, the receptacle of filth, and the harbour of vagabonds, who here lay their plans of depredation, which are too frequent among the idle and low class of whisky companions.
>
> It is a matter of serious regret to every person of feeling and reflection, it strikes strangers with surprise, and impresses no favourable opinion of the inhabitants, that the churchyard, from being uninclosed, should have a number of roads running through it; and that it should be covered with the skins of animals, which the skinners take the liberty of drying on it; and, owing to the same cause, there is nothing to prevent even swine from turning up the graves. The respect which mankind, in all ages and countries . . . have paid to the ashes of their ancestors . . . should induce the heritors and inhabitants to inclose it.

It is significant that Douglas should end his elegant and painstakingly researched account with two complaints. It shows a hurt civic pride — a wish to make Kelso even better looking than it is. Throughout his essay Douglas' affection for Kelso is evident and from his statistics it is equally obvious that Kelso's was a local economy on the move. The contrast between the portrait of a prosperous and sophisticated society compares with the picture of abject distress at the beginning of the century.

Part Seven

---

1 *A Cataclysm*

JUST AS THE eighteenth had, the nineteenth century began in Kelso with a cataclysm. Here is a full extract from the *Edinburgh Magazine* of 1797:

> On the evening of Friday last, October the 25th, we experienced one of the most tremendous storms of rain and wind which we recollect to have ever witnessed in this part of the country. The storm began at six o'clock, and continued to rage during the night with constantly-increasing violence. On Saturday morning the atmosphere continued gloomy, and the rivers were every moment swelling. The Teviot overflowed the island formed below Maxwellheugh-mill by itself and the mill-dam, together with the public road from the new bridge (across Teviot) to Kelso Bridge as well as a considerable portion of the adjoining fields. The island in Tweed, at its confluence with the Teviot, was so deeply laid under water, that the trunks of the trees growing in it were half immersed; whilst an immense body of water, from both rivers, descended with great velocity towards Kelso Bridge, rose very high behind the piers of the arches, and overflowed the banks below on both sides, inundating the road and fields from the bridge to the bottom of Maxwellheugh-mill — forming altogether a spectacle truly sublime!
>
> It was observed early in the morning that the third and fourth arches had sunk a little below their usual level; from which it was concluded that the foundation had been completely undermined, and that, of consequence, these arches might every hour be expected to fall. Business and curiosity, however, induced a great number of people, most of whom had been warned of their danger, to pass the bridge on horseback and on foot. About twelve o'clock, a great number of persons belonging to the town, as well as many of the ladies and gentlemen connected with the Caledonian Hunt, assembled at the east end of the bridge, and on the adjoining ground, for the purpose of witnessing the event, which, from the evident sinking of the two arches, was every instant expected to take place. At the time two men were rash enough to pass the bridge on horseback. Many persons made signals, and called loudly for the

return of some foot passengers, whom curiosity had led to the opposite end of the bridge. They remained, however, apparently ignorant of their danger, till a young man, whose brother was among the number, rushed forward, almost to the middle of the bridge, exclaiming, 'the bridge is falling!'. His brother and another relative were the only two who ventured to return, while they felt the bridge shaking under their feet. The rest continued on the other side.

In less than five minutes the two arches sunk very fast; a rent which was formed at the bottom of the lower side of the pier which supported them, widened rapidly; and some large stones separated and tumbled from the top of the parapet into the river. In an instant the pier fell to pieces; the two arches sprang together, and their disjointed materials sunk almost wholly beneath the water in the twinkling of an eye. The foam ascended to a great height all around, and the water was dashed on either shore beyond its former limits for a considerable way downwards; whilst the agitated countenances of the anxious spectators greatly increased the awful solemnity of the scene. Fourteen persons now remained at the west end of the bridge; but were at length rescued from their disagreeable situation by the exertions of the people of Maxwellheugh. The active interest taken by several gentlemen of the Caledonian Hunt, previously to the accident, on behalf of the people whose curiosity overcame their sense of danger, was highly honourable to themselves, and has probably been the means of saving lives. Mr Monro Binning of Softlaw, in particular, exerted himself by rushing to the bridge and loudly warning people of the impending event, not many minutes before it happened. Providentially not a life was lost.

2 Rennie's Bridge

What Kelsonians did lose was a very valuable asset. The destruction of Kelso Bridge caused severe disruption; in order to travel to Maxwellheugh it was necessary to make an eighteen mile detour via Coldstream Bridge. There was no question that another bridge would have to be built as soon as possible and funds were mobilised almost immediately. Shares were sold to local people who could afford them and John Rennie of Haddington was engaged to design a new bridge. He fixed on a site about fifty yards downstream from the original structure. Contracts were signed with two builders: Murray of Edinburgh and Lees from Rennie's home town of Haddington. Work began in late 1793 and was completed in 1803.

Rennie's design was revolutionary in that he used for the first time the concept of the semi-elliptical arch. He repeated this idea when he went on to build three of London's bridges, including the famous Waterloo Bridge. Its lamp standards were placed on the original at Kelso when Waterloo Bridge was replaced.

The new bridge caused several outbursts of civic pride. In the *Second Statistical Account* of 1839 the Rev J McCulloch first gives its dimensions:

The total length of the building is 494 feet, the breadth of the roadway is 25 feet, and its greatest height from its foundations, which extend 15 feet below the bed of the river, is 57 feet. The span of each arch is 72 feet and that of the piers 14 feet.

He then goes on to enthuse:

it is by far the most perfect specimen of modern architecture in the parish ... uniting in a remarkable manner simplicity with strength.

The singular elegance of the bridge is the more fortunate as its situation renders it the most prominent object of some of the finest landscapes on the Tweed. Connecting two banks, each remarkable for its beauty, it forms the eye of a vast variety of pictures, while by its breadth of mellow light, it affords a striking contrast and relief to the dark colour of the wooded scenery on either side. This bridge forms the entrance to the town from the south; and few scenes are more imposing than that which opens upon the tourist as he descends from the opposite village of Maxwellheugh with the prospect beneath him of this fine architectural object, the majestic Tweed, the picturesque town and abbey, and the noble background of the castle, woods and surrounding heights of Floors.

3 Mobbing and Rioting

The intitial cost of the building was £17,800 and the town managed to borrow £15,000 from the Exchequer. They planned to both repay and service the loan by imposing tolls on wheeled and pedestrian traffic. The town had no proper structure for collecting these tolls itself and so it held an annual auction of the right to impose and gather the money. At the beginning of the bridge's life this privilege was worth £900 and by the middle of the nineteenth century it had risen to £1400. After 50 years of this, many townspeople correctly concluded that the government loan of £15,000 must have been repaid at least once if not many times over. Someone or some group must have been making a tidy income from the bridge traffic. Matters came to a head in 1854. The *Kelso Chronicle* remembered its campaigning days under James Palmer and published a spirited article which articulated the discontent in the town over the tolls. The article ended with the demand 'Publish your accounts!' When the trust which managed the bridge did not oblige the people of Kelso took the law into their own hands. The local historian Rutherford was writing only 37 years after the event and he had a vivid memory of what happened:

The mob removed for several nights in succession and sent down the Tweed the barricaded gates, despite the presence of the metropolitan and county

police, infantry from Edinburgh, cavalry from Jock's Lodge, and the reading of
the Riot Act. The leaders of the mob and men who handled the saw on the
gate posts, although perfectly well known by the general population, could
never be discovered by the authorities. So much sympathy had all classes with
the rioters that the very toll-keeper passed out from his window a candle-end
wherewith to grease the saw.

After this incident and several others, less dramatic, the trust finally
withdrew the toll. The only tangible memory of the violence of 1854 is the
local tradition that the groove which runs the length of the bridge's
parapet was worn by thousands of 'reluctant pennies' paid by pedestrians
crossing the Tweed at Kelso.

4 Maps of Kelso

During the course of the nineteenth century it becomes increasingly
possible to *see* what Kelso looked like. Map-makers, photographers and
engravers began to record the town's appearance with accuracy and
regularity. Aside from written description, only Slezer's view of 1695 and
Wyeth's map/drawing of 1736 existed before this period. The nineteenth
century saw five detailed and highly informative maps as well as many
engravings, mainly of the Abbey and its immediate surroundings.

The first of the maps appears in 1805. It is a fragment covering only the
area around Chalkheugh, the geological feature which gave Kelso its name.
The streets and lines it sets out are not named but they are instantly
recognisable. It calls Roxburgh Street 'High Street', underlining its status
as the main thoroughfare in the burgh. Chalkheugh Terrace is merely a
'Road to Chalkheugh' and a 'Road along the top of the Chalkheugh Bank'
and Distillery Lane is a 'Road to Chalkheugh and River Tweed'. The only
building on the map which is still extant is marked as 'Kelso Library', the
institution which Dr Douglas is so proud of in the *First Statistical Account*. It
now forms part of the British Legion Club. Interestingly the Chalkheugh
itself is shown as just that, a chalky bank leading directly down to the
Tweed, without the wall which was built as a defence against the flood
waters of the river. The extreme left hand side of the map just clips the
corner of the Butcher market.

The names of those owning property in that part of Kelso are written
over their houses, with the Duke of Roxburghe appearing twice. Some of
the names hint at businesses, the most obvious being an area called 'Boyd's
Tan-yard', conveniently situated at the back of the area of the Butcher
market where the animals were slaughtered, and on a south-west facing
slope that must have been a handy place to dry skins.

The second of Kelso's nineteenth century maps was drawn in 1816 and it offers the first comprehensive picture of the town and its immediate surroundings.

It seems that the purpose of the map was a familiar one; it concentrates on the landward area of the parish as it carefully details the ownership of land. The cartographer was not interested in giving much information about the town but he spends effort on recording who owned even the tiniest bit of land outside Kelso. Nonetheless there is a great deal to be gleaned from this.

The date of the map is 1816 but it may be slightly earlier. It cannot be earlier than 1799 since the map-maker notes that Lady D Scott has bought some land in what is now Woodside in that year. The area covered is only that part of Kelso Parish north of the Tweed, and no mention is made of Maxwellheugh. The Old Roxburgh segment is called Dovecot Farm but no more detail than that is given.

But within these limitations it is possible to recognise, without difficulty, the familiar shape of the burgh. The street pattern radiates from the Square; Roxburgh Street is not marked down as such, only the name 'Cunzie Nook' is there as the street enters the Square, 'Horse Market Street' and 'Wood Market Street' are clear while Bridge Street is known as 'Abbey Close'. Three wynds, Oven, Mill and Duns are named. Locations are sometimes identified; 'Abbacy', 'Cloister' for some of the ruins detached from the west crossing, the Parish Kirk and its manse and glebe, the Episcopalian chapel, and near it Ednam House is recognisable but not named, the Butcher market or Fleshmarket and the abbey mill.

The road pattern around the town is traced in a precise way (this affected land-holding and was therefore important) and is also familiar. Leading out of Coalmarket is 'Bullet Loan', the street now called Shedden Park Road. The origin of the name is not obvious but might have something to do with the game of bowls. *Boule* is a French word for a similar game which is played with *boulets* or little balls. It may be that the French prisoners of war who lived at Kelso at the beginning of the nineteenth century played this game in the Bullet Loan. Also 'Land Bullet' is a Scots version of Bowls. This street name now applies to a lane that leads down to the Tweed at the end of Shedden Park Road. On the 1816 map this is called 'Lodge Loan', possibly a reference to the farm of Nicholatown-field and its lodge. The site of this farm is now occupied by Rosebank. Tobacco was grown at Nicholatown-field and across the Coldstream Road in the area now used as a cemetery. The 'Dry House' for the curing of the leaves is clearly marked on the map. It stood in what is now Drying House Lane on the site of the modern bungalows.

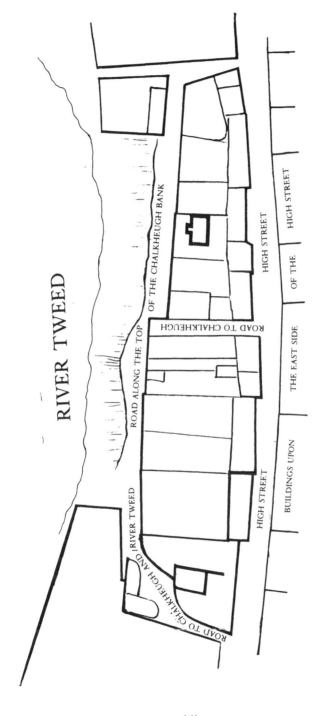

1805 map of Roxburgh Street and Chalkheugh

Further north runs 'Love Lane' along the line now followed by Inch Road. Lovers who spent summer evenings walking along it would have come to an area known as the Bleachfield in the early nineteenth century, and now known as Inchmyre. There was and still is a spring on that site, and it gave its name to Pipewell Brae. Bleachfield was where cloth was washed, dried and finished and doubtless the Pipewell spring came in very useful in that business. Across the brae is an area marked as standing water. It is called Spitle Loch, a direct reference to St Leonard's Hospital which stood nearby on the Ednam Road, and it was probably fed by the same source as the Pipewell. Before the present fire station was built, that corner of Eschiehaugh was always marshy, even in fine weather. In wet weather the marsh sometimes spread onto the football pitch.

The most remarkable aspect of the 1816 map, in the way of actually tracing Kelso's development, is how it shows the top of Roxburgh Street. In the perspective drawing of Wyeth's map of 1736 it is clear that there is housing in that bit of the town, but what the 1816 map shows is a plan of the remnants of Wester Kelso. Its general shape confirms what the plans of the Duke's garden had shown, namely that Roxburgh Street ran east to west at its head and that a road led down to a ferry at Tweed side. This map shows Roxburgh Street turning through 45 degrees almost exactly where the Catholic church hall now stands. It went on to meet the ferry road well inside Floors walls. Broad Loan is marked on the route it used to take before it was shifted westwards to allow the creation of the ducal garden, and the new entrance to Floors. The ground marked down to Mr MacIntyre and to John Lillie was absorbed by the Duke during this period. The fact that the 1816 cartographer indicates that there is still a ferry crossing available at Wester Kelso is an inkling that the village was still a going concern, if only just.

A comparison between this map and one drawn (and dated) only five years later in 1821 shows that the Duke had demolished what remained of Wester Kelso by that time and built his garden wall and fancy entrance. Broad Loan had been re-routed in what had been an extension of the lane running along the line of Bowmont Street. The area called the Townhead had assumed by this date the shape it still has.

The 1821 map is on a slightly larger scale than 1816 and it shows a little more information and a little more development. Bowmont Street is not marked as such but it is beginning to emerge with some housing built along its line at the south-western end. Winchester Row connects Bowmont Street with Roxburgh and forms a crossroads with Love Lane. Jamieson's Entry is unnamed but clearly there as it leads onto East Bowmont Street. Although Bridge Street is not called that, it too has been shaped as it now

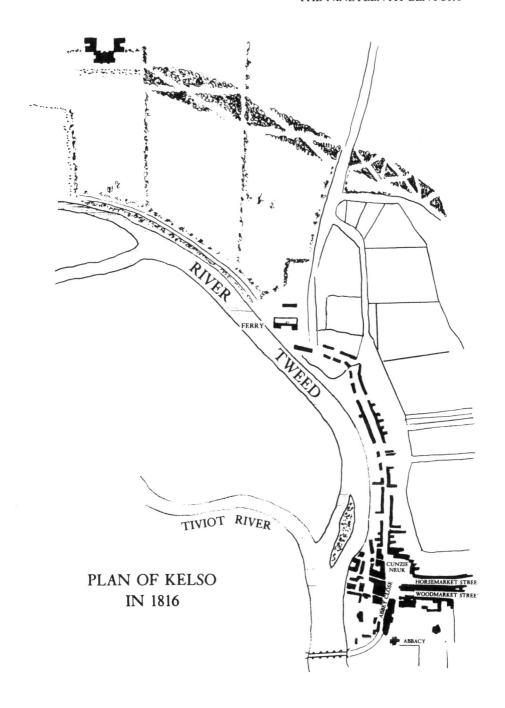

RIVER

TWEED

FERRY

TIVIOT RIVER

CUNZIE
NEUK

HORSEMARKET STREE

WOODMARKET STREE

ABBEY CLOSE

ABBACY

PLAN OF KELSO
IN 1816

is, with the spur road running off down Mayfield. The gardens of Ednam House are more clearly set out but the map does not show either of the two buildings in the grounds.

Both maps show the wooded ridge that encloses Kelso to the north. East and West Broomlands are shown simply as wooded country right up to where the woods stop at the Broom Loan (where Queen's House Hospital stood) but the trees at Angraflat are drawn as if they are a plantation, with rides running through them at right angles and diagonally. This is the explanation for the 'Meedies' being used for the natural woodland and the 'Plantin' for the man-made wood.

Antother innovation between 1816 and 1821 is the appearance of Teviot Bridge. Still spelled as 'Tiviot' it was the last major obstacle for travellers going west out of Kelso. Beside it is the farm of Fryers and what looks like a small perspective drawing of the remains of St Peter's Friary (only Kelso Abbey and the bridge get the same treatment). 'Dovecote Farm' or 'Dovecot Haugh' make up the site of Old Roxburgh along with 'Cooper's Croft'. All of these names seem to have passed out of use. The map does mark the route of an old road leading across the Fairgreen from the landing stage on the Roxburgh side for the Wester Kelso ferry, although the ferry itself is not marked. The line of the old road can still be seen now as it runs close to the edge of the ridge cut out by the flooding of the Tweed. The jumps for the point-to-point racing are set out along it as it parallels the river bank.

5 *A New Town Hall*

While this short spate of map-making was going on, the look of Kelso Square was changing. The Town Hall or Tolbooth was in the eighteenth century a building in the Scottish vernacular style. A contemporary print shows an arcaded ground floor topped by two storeys with a steeple. There was a clock and a weather vane on the steeple and there is a tradition that during a violent thunder-storm the weather vane was blasted off with such force that it landed in the parish churchyard. By 1816 Kelso had decided that the old Town House would no longer do. One writer described it (presumably meaning the ground-floor arcading) as a haunt of drinkers and ruffians. A new building was proposed. The Duke of Roxburghe donated the land to the town and cash was raised for the new Town House by subscription. Here is the local historian, John Mason, writing in 1839:

> It is an extremely chaste piece of architecture; built of beautiful freestone, surrounded by a handsome balustrade; and would be worthy of unmixed

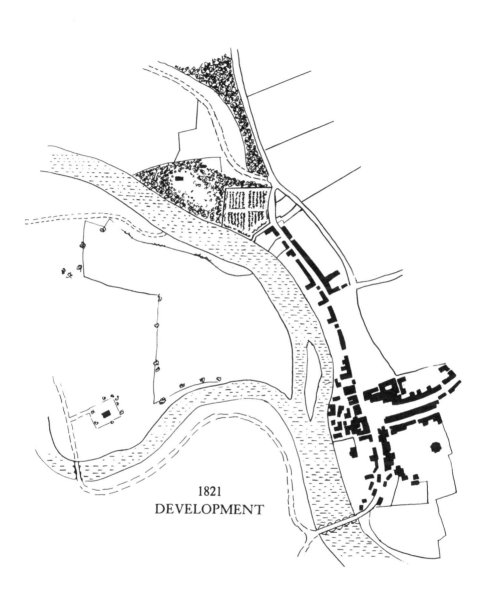

1821
DEVELOPMENT

admiration were its dome replaced by an elegant spire. The lower part of the town-house is railed in, and opened on market days for the convenience of those who expose butter and poultry for sale. Above is an excellent hall, extending the whole length of the building, in which the Justice and Bailie Courts are held, and in which the various incorporations of the place hold their meetings.

Between 1902 and 1908 renovations were carried out at the Town Hall and the arcading intended for market stallholders was built up to create more space for the town officials to work in. The cost of this was £3,000. Work was also done on the dome so disliked by Mason. Its shape was changed and the old weather cock replaced by a Wild Goose. Sadly the Goose proved useless since it was impossible to tell from it which way the wind was blowing, and so the old weather cock was put back.

Mason makes no mention of a clock on the dome but it is clear that a curfew bell was rung at 8pm each evening. There was certainly a clock in place by 1886, the date of the earliest photograph of Kelso Square.

6 Gaslight

Two years after the new Town Hall was built Kelso was the scene of a remarkable modern innovation. In James Palmer's old office in Bridge Street a local coppersmith, William Muir, lit his premises by gaslight. This was the first house in Scotland to be illuminated in this way. Muir probably got his supply from coal and his initiative paved the way for the creation of a private company formed to provide gas for the whole town. Here is a very formal minute from the Town Council:

> At Kelso, the twenty-seventh day of January, one thousand eight hundred and thirty one — A meeting of Shareholders of the Proposed Kelso Gas Company, called by advertisement in the *Kelso Mail*, was held in the Town Hall, this day at two o'clock afternoon.

The proposers of the company had done their market research and had been busy selling shares in the weeks prior to the meeting. By the end of January 317 shares had been bought and £1,585 worth of capital had been subscribed. The company's prospectus:

> to provide the manufacturing of Gas from Coal; to be disposed of at such prices as may be determined on, for the purpose of lighting the Streets, Shops, Houses and other Buildings within the Town of Kelso and in the immediate neighbourhood of the same.

The company bought a piece of land adjacent to the Knowes on the eastern side, near Waverley Cottage, from Mr Waldie of Hendersyde. They paid £350 for the land and estimated that a stone gasholder would cost £1,600 and a cast-iron one £1,700. The raw material for the production of Kelso's gas was to be coal and the company experimented with at least two sorts; from Dalkeith and from Newcastle. The price of gas was reckoned at 15s for 100 cubic feet. The company contracted to light the streets with the same number of lamps that had previously been lit by oil — the major difference would be that the pavements or streets would need to be dug up so that pipes could be run to each lamp.

Over the next two decades the consumption of gas leapt up; in one quarter of 1848 385,050 cubic feet was burned and for the same period in 1857 consumption was 636,000 cubic feet. The first Ordnance Survey was done at Kelso two years after this and it gives an accurate picture of what Kelso gasworks was like. There were three storage tanks, a large coal shed, a retort house, a purifying house, a lime house (a necessary chemical for the conversion process), a tar well, a meter room, a wash room, an office and a residence that fronted onto the Knowes. Clearly a big operation.

In 1866 the Gas Company arrived at a working arrangement with the Commissioners of Police (the forerunner of the Town Council) over the lighting of the burgh. The company agreed to provide gas lighting on Kelso Bridge and for Maxwellheugh Path, and to maintain the lamps by cleaning them once a week, coal gas being notoriously dirty. A leerie was appointed to light the gas each night and a contemporary account gives an idea of the scale of his job:

> At this time [1866] there were 133 lamps in the burgh. They are lighted every night for nine months, except when there is moonlight, the average lighting for each moon is 21 nights. 14 of the lamps will burn all night when there is no moon for 6 months in the season, and for the 3 winter months 30 will burn all night. The lighting to be commenced each night half an hour before dark and all the lamps to be lighted within the hour. The extinguishing to commence at half past eleven o'clock pm, and all to be out by half past twelve, those left burning all night to be out by daylight.

If the leerie had to get around either 103 or 119 lamps (depending on the time of year) in an hour and then find his way home in the dark, then he must really have had to hop.

The Kelso Gas Company ceased to exist in 1949 when the Labour government of the day nationalised the industry, and by 1958 gas production ceased at the Knowes. About the same time Kelso's street lights went over to electricity and the leeries had to find other employment.

7 Racing at Berrymoss

In 1822, four years after William Muir used gas to light his shop in Bridge Street, the foundation stone was laid for a very important new building for Kelso. That year the Duke of Roxburghe, after much encouragement from the townspeople, decided to move the site of his racecourse from Blakelaw to Berrymoss — much more convenient at only a mile from the town. Prior to this, the races had been held at Caverton Edge where there was a level site that afforded a track about three miles in circumference. The provision of stabling for the racehorses had never been good (they had generally been put up at Softlaw Farm) and the Duke built a new stand at Caverton to remedy this. However the stand brought problems of its own when gypsies took it over and used it as a base. Local farmers protested to the Duke about this (they claimed they were losing the odd animal here and there) and he finally agreed to take the structure down. What finally brought about the end of racing at Caverton Edge was the Duke's decision to plant the ground with trees.

Kelso races were an important source of income for the innkeepers and shopkeepers of Kelso, so there was great rejoicing when the masons set out in procession to lay the foundation stone of the new stand at Berrymoss. The Incorporated Trades of the town agreed to help in forming the racecourse out of the rough ground of the moss. The new stand was well appointed with a weighing in room, a main hall, a ladies room and much else. In 1822 an autumn meeting was held and it was agreed that Kelso Races were back to their former popularity after the problems of Caverton Edge and the decline of interest when they spent a short time at Blakelaw.

8 A Triumphal Arch

At the same time as the stand was going up at Berrymoss another, more exotic structure was being built on the other side of town. Springwood Park was built in 1756 by Rear-Admiral Sir James Douglas, first baronet of Springwood. It stood just outside the town in wooded policies bordered by the Teviot. In 1822 a magnificent entrance gate was designed by Gillespie Graham in the style of a triumphal arch. It acted as a terminal to the new bridge, whose architectural style it echoed. A beautiful object this, it has sadly fallen into a grubby and unattractive state.

9 John Wood's Map

The arch does not appear on the next and (by this stage) best of Kelso's

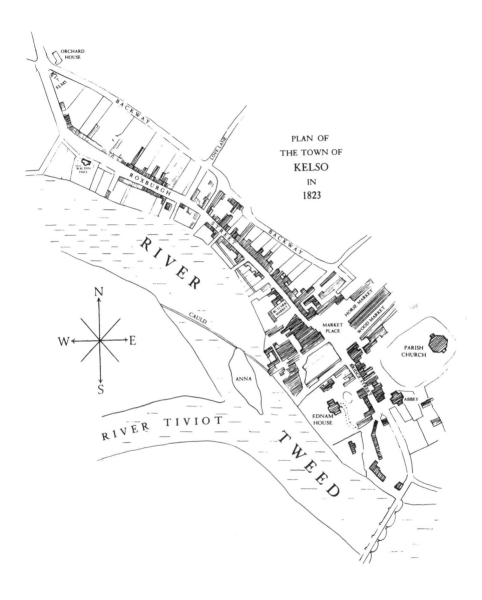

PLAN OF
THE TOWN OF
KELSO
IN
1823

town maps. Drawn in 1823 by John Wood as part of an atlas of Scottish burgh plans, this map is easily the most detailed, accurate picture of Kelso in the early nineteenth century to have survived.

For the first time, many of Kelso's street names come on record. In addition to Roxburgh Street, Woodmarket and Horsemarket and the three wynds (Oven, Duns and Mill), there is Bridge Street and its predecessor, Abbey Close, and at its foot Skinner's Brae. At the end of Woodmarket there is a square named as Cattle and Coal market. Leading off Bullet Loan is Hogg's lane which later became Suzy's Lane before finally settling on the more dignified Abbotsford Grove. Drying House Lane is used although by this time it is unlikely that tobacco was dried there since normal trade had resumed with America. The Knowes is given as such but without the 'e'. Crofts describes the area north of Love Lane and south of Broom Loan while to the south Tofts covers an area also marked as nursery ground. Two old names for open areas around Kelso survive; Short Whings lies between Rose Lane and Drying House Lane and beyond that to the east is Long Whings, although this has acquired the additional name of Woodside. Back Way is used to mark out the lines of both East Bowmont Street and Bowmont Street.

Wood's map picks out 15 buildings which have numbers attached and these are described in a key. Some of these are previously recorded in written material but others make their historical debut here. The key at the side of the map repays closer examination.

Number 1 is the Relief Church. It is located in Horsemarket and ultimately became the Roxy Cinema. The church was built in 1792 and had room for 778 worshippers. Its congregation was made up of people who did not wish to be part of the Established or Parish Church, as was the congregation of the United Secession Church which the map places on the site of Trinity North Church. In the *Second Statistical Account*, its author, Rev J M MacCullough shows a surprising degree of religious tolerance. He is writing in 1839:

> The United Secession and Relief congregations number among their members many persons of great respectability in point of wealth as well as character, and the Sabbath attendance is not only respectable but numerous, considering the distances which many of the members have to travel. One of them — the United Secession, is composed of persons collected from so many as thirteen parishes.

Marked as number 2 on the map is the 'English School'. This was located in a building which still exists as a garage and store for James Stewart & Son in the southern corner of Coal Market. Before it was a school this building was

'Beardie's' house — Beardie was Sir Walter Scott's great-grandfather. He died there in 1792 making that garage one of Kelso's oldest surviving buildings. Here is a good description of it written in 1880:

> Beardie's house in Coal Market, which still exists, certainly the worse for wear, but otherwise unchanged, except that its thatch has been replaced by slates, that one of its outshot attics has disappeared, having been blown away in a gale, and that its gable facing the churchyard is no longer crow-stepped. A peculiarity in the gable is an oddly-placed large window, within which, tradition asserts, Beardie used to sit and look down on the lads at their matches in the Butts, and the play and the traffic in the churchyard.

Almost next door, in the Butts, is a 'Charity School instituted by His Grace the Duke of Roxburghe'. This is almost certainly what the *Statistical Account* calls the 'Roxburghe School' which was endowned by the Duke for the teaching of girls. A female mistress was employed to run this school. Next door again was the town jail. It was described by MacCullough:

> The only place for confinement of delinquents is a lock-up house, the property of the burgh, which is employed chiefly for the temporary incarceration of vagrants.

It was a busy place. In 1829/30 437 people were lodged in it for one or more nights and this cost the town £31 and 14 shillings.

Number 5 is listed as the Bank of Scotland and it lay in Woodmarket on the site occupied until very recently by the same company. Behind the bank, with a frontage on Abbey Row was Kelso's Post Office.

Moving into the Square itself Wood picks out the Cross Keys Inn, one of the town's most imposing buildings. James Dickson of Ednam House built the Cross Keys in 1760. It had a large ballroom and a banqueting hall which was decorated with murals painted by a local artist, Mr Hume. The inn was a stopping-off place for coaches plying between Newcastle and Edinburgh and it still has the distinctive coach-entrance as its centre, now used as a shopping arcade. During Kelso Races the Cross Keys was traditionally the centre of social activity and its ballroom was occasionally used in the eighteenth century by visiting theatre companies to entertain racegoers.

Number 8 is the Town Hall while 9 is described as the Swan Inn, owned by Mr Curry. This is clearly the ancestor of the White Swan although in 1823 the inn occupied a larger building than it presently does. At that time it incorporated the corner site now used as a saddler's shop.

A few yards into the Square lies a small open space which led to Wester Kirkstile. Along with Easter Kirkstile in the southern corner of Coalmarket, it was the entrance from the town to the churchyard. There is an appreciable difference in the ground levels between this part of the Square and Abbey Row and this was probably due to hundreds of years of burial in the graveyard.

Very near to Wester Kirkstile and with a frontage onto the Square is a building marked by Wood as the Commerical Bank —what later became the National and Commercial Bank. It was run by Mr George Waldie Esq of Hendersyde the same man who sold his land to Kelso Gas Company in the Knowes. As a banker, Waldie doubtless saw an excellent opportunity there and secured a good deal for himself as well as a stake in the new company. In 1838 John Waldie succeeded George as agent for the Commercial Bank and he also took over responsibility for Kelso's Savings Bank. Founded in 1815, it was intended for the use of servants, labourers and young people. They could deposit small sums and when their deposit reached £10 it was transferred to the Commercial Bank itself. By 1838 223 people had accounts totalling £908 and 9 shillings. Working class people in Kelso clearly had some capacity to save, which in turn suggests a standard of living (for a few) that was above the breadline.

Wood notes an inn in Kelso which has disappeared. The King's Head stood in Roxburgh Street at about number 7 and was owned by Mr Russell. The Queen's Head, by comparison, has survived in the location given on the map in Bridge Street. Run by Mr Lauder this was a popular inn; the masons met there and social occasions were held in the large room at the rear. It was sometimes called Lauder Inn.

The office of the *Kelso Mail* was also in Bridge Street and is clearly marked as is the library in Chalkheugh Terrace. Another building at the foot of Oven Wynd on the right was described as the New Library. MacCullough calls it a reading room for newspapers, open to all who can pay the annual subscription, and to his personal satisfaction it closed on Sundays.

By 1823 many large private houses had been built in and around Kelso and Wood's map shows this development very clearly. Some of the houses are named; Orchard House at the head of Bowmont Street, near it Seven Elms (now simply the Elms), Croft House, Edenside, Tweed Bank, Hermitage, Rosebank (on the site of Nicholatown-field) and Pringle Bank. Marked but not named are Waverley Cottage and Abbey Bank in the Knowes. None of these houses appear on the map of 1816 or the map of 1821 but these lack detail and precision and may simply have neglected to note new building in the town. And both are more concerned with the land around the burgh than the burgh itself. Nonetheless it seems likely that a spate of house building did occur at the beginning of the nineteenth century. A good example is Walton Hall, built in 1820 by John Ballantyne, the bookseller and printer who made a great deal of money out of his association with Sir Walter Scott. It is an attractive Regency bungalow meant to be used in the summer. It has a projecting bay at the back with large windows overlooking its terraced garden and a stunning aspect over Tweed to Old Roxburgh and its castle. It is one of Kelso's best proportioned and best looking houses.

10 St James' Fair

Every summer on August 5 the occupants of Walton Hall could look out of their windows across the river to a scene quite different from the normal tranquil view of grazing animals. This was the day of St James' Fair, originally one of Roxburgh's fairs and probably the only tangible vestige of the now extinct burgh. Here is James Haig writing in 1825:

> St James's Fair, the greatest in the South of Scotland (St Boswell's excepted) is held on a green about a mile from Kelso, the site of the old town of Roxburgh.
>
> At this fair the show of cattle and horses to be fed on aftergrass and turnip, is generally large, and a great quantity of woollen and linen manufacturers are sold in wholesale; but the principal business of the farmer is the hiring of reapers for the ensuing harvest.
>
> This fair is looked forward to by the inhabitants of Kelso with peculiar pleasure and anxiety, as a great proportion of certain classes depend upon it for remuneration for the past year. It is a day of general festivity, and most of the young people repair to the fair in the evening, to regale themselves with their 'friends and favourites'.
>
> From a right which the town of Jedburgh acquired (at what time or how, we cannot ascertain, but suppose it must have happened at the period when Roxburgh lost its rank among the [royal] burghs of Scotland) to share in the emoluments derived from the privilige of holding this fair, a great jealousy for a long time subsisted between the two towns, which was always manifested on this day. It was formerly the custom for the Jedburgh people, coming on horseback, to enter Kelso by the bridge, and ride through to the top of the town, where they again crossed the Tweed by the ford, to go to the fair; which as it was going at least a mile out of their way, the people of Kelso regarded as an insult, and seldom failed to resent it; for, on these occasions, they were often pelted with stones, and frequent bickerings in consequence took place between them and the inhabitants. Happily these animosities have been put at an end to by the people of Jedburgh relinquishing this custom.
>
> The customs of the fair being divided between the town of Jedburgh and the Duke of Roxburghe, the magistrates of that burgh, attended by their officers, come regularly to open it, by parading over the ground at twelve

o'clock. Jedburgh receives one half of the revenue gathered, and the duke the other half.

This seems a very unfair state of affairs and the resentment of Kelsonians seems well founded. St James' Fair took place on their doorstep but they derived no income from its revenues. The reason for this is historical. In Scotland only royal burghs had the privilege of holding fairs on this scale. Roxburgh was of course a royal burgh but when it died the fair did not. The nearest available royal burgh was not Kelso but Jedburgh.

For this reason the Jedburgh officials 'cried the fair' by parading on the Fairgreen at noon and ringing a bell. Regulations peculiar to fairs went into force on August 5 and the purpose of 'crying the fair' was to remind everyone of these. St James' Fair finally ceased in the 1930s but its lineal descendant happens only a few hundred yards away at about the same time of year — the Border Union Show. Kelsonians sometimes mix up the 'Fairgreen' with the 'Showground', a good example of historical continuity.

11 The Second Statistical Account

The writer of the *Second Statistical Account*, the Rev J M MacCullough offers a great deal of information, mainly in the way of an update to Christopher Douglas' Account of 1792. He was something of a botanist and undertakes a short classification of plants. Throughout the *Account* he also classifies people into their social strata and is often patronising about the lower sort. But it would be inappropriate to dismiss MacCullough as a snob. His values may be unwelcome now but they were the norm in the nineteenth century. Not only did the upper classes feel superior, the lower classes usually agreed with their estimate.

MacCullough deplores the lower sort for not respecting the Sabbath and for drinking too much, but he does this with a resigned air as though he regarded this sort of behaviour as normal. His social attitudes are useful in that he gives us a precious passage on the elusive subject of what Kelsonians actually sounded like in the early part of the nineteenth century:

> One peculiarity of the pronounciation of this disrict has been already noted, — the tendency to give the dental sound of 'ch' the sound of 'sh'; as sheap for cheap. A second, is the habit of sounding the vowel 'a' in a mode precisely the reverse of the English usage: Thus 'water' (broad 'a') is uniformly pronounced 'water' (long slender 'a') and vice versa. The mode of enunciating the pronoun of the first person is also peculiar. It is sounded as if it were written 'aw': a native Kelsonian does not say, "I saw it", but 'Aw saw it".

In truth, in all that respects language, the natives of this district may be said to be *Scotorum Scotissimi*. Though at the distance of only five miles from England, they speak the Scottish tongue in the most Doric of its forms; nor does there appear any prospect of a speedy improvement in this particular. It would indeed seem, that, in proportion as the two countries approach their respective confines, the Scotch and Anglican tongues, instead of gradually losing each its distinctive character so as, at the point of junction, to interblend and coalesce in a common dialect, assume each its harshest and most intractable form; as if for the purpose of keeping their respective marches clear and distinct. At least the fact is unquestionable that, all along the south side of the east marches, we have the Northumbrian burr bristling, like a fence of thorns, to prevent the Scotch accent from penetrating into England; whilst on the north side, the latter dialect assumes a breadth of guttural energy, which effectually protects 'the ancient kingdom' against the inroads of the speech of the smoother-tongued Sassenachs.

MacCullough would find no 'improvement' today. Kelsonians still say 'witter' for water and 'Aw' for I. And at Carham the burr still bristles while a few hundred yards away at Redden the Doric drawls.

As a minister, MacCullough, complained about a lack of respect for the Sabbath but his words had a ritual ring to them. Kelso was, in the nineteenth century, a town intensely interested in religion. The *Second Statistical Account* gives a set of figures which show first the number the church could accomodate and then how many members it had:

Parish Church	1,314	2,631
Episcopalians	218	153
Reformed Presbyterians	320	66
Original Seceders	600	30
United Secession	955	1,034
Relief	778	598

Apart from the Reformed Presbyterians and the Original Seceders, most of the churches are doing well. At the time of the First Statistical Account there were even more sects; Burghers, Antiburghers, Quakers, Cameronians and Methodists. No indication of their numbers or where they worshipped is given but their diversity does show a particular popular interest in religion.

Judging by MacCullough's figures the church with the highest rating is the Parish Church or the Church of Scotland. The Kirk had almost exactly twice as many members as it could get into the building. To relieve this congestion it was decided to build another church, to be known as the North Parish Church. An open site was found at the corner of Love Lane and Back Way (or Inch Road and Bowmont Street) and a minister appointed, Horatio Bonar, the famous composer of hymns. The church was finished in 1842 and it cost £3,460.

12 The Disruption of the Church

Almost immediately after this the Church of Scotland suffered the Disruption. Many ministers and their congregations left the established church over the controversial issue of patronage —who appointed the minister, the congregation or the local laird(s) — and Horatio Bonar was one of these who left. The North Parish became the Free Church. The congregation decided to build a new, and bigger, church for Dr Bonar on a nearby site. Some houses were demolished in Roxburgh Street and work began on the new church in 1866. It was designed by Frederick Pilkington of Edinburgh in the Victorian Gothic style and is now called St John's Edenside. Its spire is an extraordinary thing, wholly out of proportion with the rest of the church, it broods over Kelso's skyline.

During the Disruption there was another free church in Kelso in Bullet Loan where M & J B Ballantyne have their yard. An architecturally attractive church is Trinity North. It was built in 1886 on the site formerly occupied by the United Secession Church marked on Wood's map, and is the third church in Kelso belonging to the Church of Scotland. Moving north up Bowmont Street, the next church one sees is the Baptist, built out of bright red sandstone in 1876 with money donated by Miss Scott MacDougal of Makerston. And then the Roman Catholic chapel of St Mary, erected in 1858 to accommodate 230 worshippers. In the *Statistical Account* MacCullough makes no mention of the Catholics in Kelso parish but he does list a small Episcopalian congregation. Their chapel in Abbey Court was replaced by the Church of St Andrew in 1868 — like Trinity North, a church built to suit its location and not to glower over it.

13 Water

By the middle of the nineteenth century Kelso was well supplied with churches and with gas, but it had always had difficulty in providing and maintaining a regular supply of pure water. Before Kelso began to grow, water had been taken from the Tweed and from a number of wells in the town. The Pant Well in the Square is the best known of these but there were others; the Pipewell, Lady Bennet's Well in the ground of Walton Hall, Tom Lillie's well in Wester Kelso (now in the Duke's garden). A spring exists on the property of A Middlemass & Son in Distillery Lane, and in Havannah Court there was a well which may have been used by the monks of Kelso Abbey. When building work went on in the street in the early part of this century, wooden (oak) water pipes were dug up. Pipes like these were used in the Middle Ages.

In 1843 a Tweed Water Company was proposed for the supply of water to Kelso. Nothing much was done until 1863 when the Police Commissioners gave notice that they wished to raise £1,500 to build a waterworks. Soon after this a steam engine and pump house were built at the Windy Gowl in Roxburgh Street to take water out of the Tweed for washing purposes. The water was pumped up to a tank located near the site of Queen's House, filtered there and fled into the town. Drinking water was taken from a spring in the grounds of Broomlands, the property of the Duke of Roxburghe. This was piped directly to a few houses but most of it went to a tank at the foot of Horsemarket. This tank fed the pant wells in the Square and elsewhere. This situation was not satisfactory; the Windy Gowl tank burst in 1867 injuring a little girl, and the Broomlands supply was too small. Also the purity of the Tweed's water was a problem.

By 1898 matters had come to a head. A scheme to dam the Heatherhope burn and pipe water from there was proposed. It was expensive but would have solved the town's water problems. An election was fought in November of that year on this issue. The supporters of the Heatherhope scheme, David Tait, T D Crichton Smith and J M Plummer, were all defeated. And this in turn brought the resignations of Provost James Smith, Peter Logan and Andrew Bulman. Although they had been elected they were advocates of the scheme which had been decisively rejected by the ratepayers.

James Melrose, George Henderson, James Strathearn and James Forsyth were elected in their places as opponents of the Heatherhope project. However if they and their colleagues hoped to find more water at Broomlands they were quickly disappointed. Less than six weeks after the election the Duke told the council that he would not allow further investigation for water on his property because he did not think it was in the best interest of the people of Kelso.

In 1902 Provost Forsyth, elected on the anti-Heatherhope ticket, resigned and one of the scheme's supporters, T D Crichton Smith took over. By 1911 the Royal Assent was given for the Kelso Water Order Confirmation Act. This allowed work to begin on the dam at Heatherhope. The water was piped downhill to a filter plant at Hownam and from there to two storage tanks at Softlaw, and then connected to the town's system. It cost £30,000 and could supply 420,000 gallons of water a day.

14 Kelso Becomes a Police Burgh

By the middle of the nineteenth century Kelso was a prosperous and stable community. With the arrival of the railway and the construction of the Royal Tweed Bridge at Berwick, communications with the outside world were good. The census of 1861 showed a populations of 5,192 for the parish with 4,309 in the town. Along with the rest of Victorian Britain, Kelso was expanding and outward looking. It must have seemed at best an anachronism that the town was still owned and governed by its feudal superior, the Duke of Roxburghe. And so on 14 November 1853 a petition, signed by more than the requisite 20 householders, was submitted to the Sheriff of Roxburghshire. It asked that the boundaries of the Burgh of Kelso be established and the effectual provision be made for regulating the Police, and for Paving, Draining, Cleansing and Lighting — and for improving these services. This was done unde the Police Burgh Act. On 22 December 1853 the petition was proposed to a large meeting in the Town Hall by James Smith of Maitland House, the Parish Church Minister, and seconded by John Bulman. It was opposed by Ebenezer Hardie, a grocer, and by Thomas Crosby of Kelso Mill but the meeting approved the motion by a large majority.

Kelso then became a Police Burgh instead of a Burgh of Barony under the titular control of the Duke of Roxburghe. For the purpose of electing 12 Police Commissioners, the town was divided into four wards. The first Kelso Town Council, in all but name, was James Stormonth Darling, James Tait, Charles Lauder, James Mitchell, John D Oliver, Adam Nichol, John Scott, Alex W Robson, William Robson, Alexander Nicholson, George Humble and George Craig. The Commissioners appointed James Stormonth Darling as their first Chairman and the Senior Magistrate. James Tait and John D Oliver were appointed Junior Magistrates. A lawyer, Robert Guthrie, became clerk to the Commissioners while Charles Robson was made Treasurer and John Guthrie, Collector of the burgh stent, or rates.

An administration was needed to run the services taken over by the Police Commissioners and they began by appointing a Superintendant of Police, a Procurator Fiscal and a Burgh Engineer. One of the first things they did was to rename two of Kelso's streets; the Back Way became Bowmont Street and the name of the roadway that ran from the foot of the Horsemarket round to the gates of the United Secession Church was changed from Caldrigs to Church Street — hardly an improvement since by 1859 it was known as East Bowmont Street.

At a meeting in 1855 the Commissioners discussed the appointment of an Inspector of Nuisances. Perhaps the kind of thing they had in mind was the practice of hanging out washing on the railings around the Abbey ruins. The Senior Magistrate, by this time known as the Senior Bailie, decided to discourage townspeople from doing this by sending round a drummer and an officer to read out a proclamation banning the use of the railings as a washing line. Doubtless both men managed to keep a straight face as they marched around the town.

More serious business was transacted by the Police Commissioners. In 1860 they authorised the building of a new sewer leading from the foot of Horsemarket down Bullet Loan (now called Shedden Park Road) to the top of Lodge Loan (now renamed Bullet Loan) and from there down to the Tweed. This sewer remained in used until recently. The cost in 1860 was £1,200.

Shedden Park was gifted to Kelso by the owner of Ednam House, Mrs Robertson. She named it Shedden Park to perpetuate the memory of her nephew, Lieutenant Shedden, who died in the polar regions while serving on the Nancy Dawson. His ship was searching for the Franklin expedition. Its mast and two of its guns were placed in the park at Mrs Robertson's request.

On 15 May 1893 Kelso got its first modern Provost. He was Mr James Smith of Maitland House in Forestfield. He got the title because the Commissioners decided to implement the Burgh Police Act of 1892; this officially changed the Police Commissioners into a Burgh Council and allowed them to elect one of their number as Provost.

15 *The Ordnance Survey Described*

The most important map of Kelso to appear in the nineteenth century is the Ordnance Survey of 1859 and 1860. Done on several scales it carries a wealth of detail not matched before or indeed since. Not only are the streets and houses precisely drawn so are the gardens, their paths, trees (both the size and location), rockeries, ponds — even large stones. It is a remarkable document. Too large to reproduce here, it demands close study.

Of these features of Kelso which have come down to us, many make their first appearance on the Ordnance Survey. Large houses such as Grovehill, Kerfield, Goshen Bank. The North Free Church is there and near it the Kelso Union Poorhouse, now Inch Hospital. There are new street names; Crawford Street, Union Street, Winchester Row, Edenside Road, Inch Road, the Pier Head, (recently absorbed into Kelso Mill). Simon Square is marked as the southern bit of the Coal Market, Forestfield was the given name for the two rows of houses fronting on to Inch Road, and not yet for the road which connected them to Edenside Road. Abbotsford Grove was known as Suzy's Lane.

The Tweed gets some of its local names for the different stretches; Coble Hole, the Put, the Back Bullers, the Cradles, Maxwheel, Hempseedford, Garden Foot and General's Bank for the water running past General Elliot's property at Rosebank. Jack's Plumb is marked on the Teviot at Vigourous Haugh.

Maxwellheugh is shown for the first time with its buildings grouped around the near-crossroads where roads from Sprouston, Yetholm and Hawick meet. This was the place where road tolls were taken. The railway is at Maxwellheugh by this time and both the station and goods yards have been built.

Unlike Kelso Station most of the streets and houses on the 1860 Ordnance Survey have survived and require little elaboration. More interesting are those things on that map which have disappeared. Beginning at the top of the town — or the Townhead, there was a nursery, called Sydenham Nursery, at the entrance to Orchard Park. Nearly opposite this was the old lodge and entrance to Floors and beside it stood a small gasometer which may have supplied the castle and home farm. At the top of Roxburgh Street many small houses are described as ruins, on both sides of the roadway. This looks like a legacy of the drift away from Wester Kelso after the creation of the Duke's Garden, which was still in place in 1860. Over in Bowmont Street, there was a long row of cottages recently built and certainly occupied. They lie near to Croft House and were called Croft Cottages. Had they survived they would have stood in the grounds of Kelso High School.

Both Roxburgh Street and Bowmont Street had small industrial premises in them. Behind the houses on the Tweed side of Roxburgh Street there was a tannery and skinnery, while on Bowmont Street, about 100 yards down from the Catholic chapel there was a skinnery. In Gray's Close there was a weaver's shop and near it a cooperage.

Connecting Roxburgh and Bowmont Street, running parallel with Winchester Row, was Lillie's Close. It was obliterated by the building of modern council houses on the site. Opposite was the Kelso Dispensary and such is the detail of the map that each room is described; the consulting room, waiting room, surgery and two fever wards. Equally clear is the plan of the Kelso Union Poorhouse erected in 1854 to provide accommodation and work for the Parish poor. Facilities for men, women, boys and girls show that, in Victorian fashion, the sexes were segregated. The building now used as a mortuary was a wash house and the walled in area on the Inch Road side was four exercise yards, one for each group of inmates.

Turning back to Roxburgh Street, the creation of St John's Edenside Church removed Davidson's Close which led to Bowmont Street on the same line at Beechtent Lane. Some names are noted for places which still exist although the nineteenth century names themselves seem to have passed out of use. Robson's Yard describes the stables that lead off Bowmont Street near the old fire station and Jack's Yard was the given name for R & W Charters' plumbers' yard. Opposite Jack's yard was the old Kelso Chronicle Office and printing shop, while behind it was one of Kelso's jails. It had four cells, a jailor's house, an office and a wash house.

In 1860 Cunyie Neuk was still being used for the foot of Roxburgh Street but the inn which Wood, in 1823, called the King's Head was now the Crown. The maze of wynds between Roxburgh Street and the river is virtually unchanged from earlier maps although it is worth noting that the Pier Head has now gone as has Kiln Wynd, which connected it to Mill Wynd.

Two locations in Bridge Street show a change of use. Part of the building that used to be known as Ormiston House (and is used for shops) was a branch of the National Bank. Further along, on the same side of the street, the Weigh House Inn makes its first appearance, complete with its weighing machine outside. On the corner of Abbey Court and Bridge Street there was a Smithy but its successor in the transport business Croall Bryson is not yet in evidence. The site of the coachworks is still marked as part of the Parish minister's glebe — the field was bisected by the road leading to Kelso Bridge. Opposite that site, still in Bridge Street were two buildings which stood very near the abbey ruins. One was Abbey House and the other was the office of the Procurator Fiscal, the man recently appointed by the Police Commissioners as Kelso's public prosecutor. Another inn making its debut in this area is the Spread Eagle, an extensive building according to the map.

At the corner of Bridge Street and the Square stood the British Linen Bank and next to it the Commercial Bank; the two companies were to remain in that location for more than a century. The White Swan Inn had contracted into its present premises with a frontage on both the Square and Abbey Row, while behind it, in a handy place for its patrons was a billiard room and reading room. Nearby was what must have been a new building at that time, the Corn Exchange. Further along Woodmarket at its corner with Simon Square was Kelso's Post Office, it abutted Beardie's house and now forms part of James Stewart & Son's premises. A few yards away, in the middle of the Coal Market was a weighing machine and next to it an office so small it can only have been a booth. Moving through the narrow opening that was Easter Kirkstile, the first building in the Butts is marked as

Roxburgh School, the institution described by Wood in 1823 as a charitable school for the education of girls. Next to it was the Police Lock-up with its office and three very small cells. Set back off the road was the Friends Meeting House, the place of worship for the small group of Quakers in the town.

In Shedden Park Road there stood a large church making its first appearance. This was Sprouston Free Church. It belonged to a group of Presbyterian dissenters, some of whom came from the village of Sprouston. They used the ferry at Hempseedford having crossed by the chain bridge onto Wooden Anna.

Rose Lane was the focus of a good deal of commercial activity. On its western side there were yards used by wheelrights, plasterers, carpenters and builders and opposite them a row of dwellings called Victoria Cottages, some of which still survive.

Cross Street is not given its name but the map places a printing works there — the same works which used to produce the Kelso Chronicle. Moving into East Bowmont Street another church makes an appearance. This was the R P Church and it stood on the site of the Territorial Hall. Along East Bowmont Street was another group of industrial premises: a coach and harness factory and near it a foundry and millwright's works — the forerunners of Hendersons agricultural engineering firm. Backing onto these locations were a series of closes which had their entrances in Horsemarket. Two of them are named as Townley's Court, which still exists, and Elliot's Court which is next to a new supermarket. Neither of these names seem any longer to be in use. Along Horsemarket, nearly opposite Cross Street was the town fire station. It stood conveniently on the site of the tank or reservoir which was fed by water from the springs at Broomlands.

In the Square the row of buildings which presently contains Hume's tailor shop was known as Innes Place, a name still visible on one of the buildings. Near it, behind the Cross Keys was a house called Tweed Lodge which has disappeared.

Finally the 1860 Ordnance Survey marks the site of two bowling greens in Kelso — one behind Grovehill House and the other in the Tofts.

16 Queen Victoria Visits

Often a place or an event is best described by an outsider. Kelso is no exception and many people, poets especially — like Burns, Leyden and Thomson, have put their feelings about the town on paper. Most of these have been so non-specific as to be virtually worthless in the way of saying much about the town. But one celebrated visitor did have something substantial to say. Queen Victoria visited Kelso in 1867. Here is an extract from her diary:

> We entered Teviotdale and descended it, entering the valley of the Tweed at St Boswell's. Between St Boswell's and Kelso, at Roxburgh Station, we crossed the Teviot again. We passed close under the Eildon Hills, three high points rising from the background. The country is extremely picturesque, valleys with fine trees and streams, intermingled with great cultivation. Only after half past eleven did we reach Kelso Station, which was very prettily decorated, and where were standing the Duke and Duchess of Roxburghe, Lord Bowmont, the Duke of Buccleuch, and Lord C. Ker, as well as General Hamilton, commanding the forces in Scotland.

Victoria was staying at Floors Castle with the Roxburghes but before she went there, she travelled in triumphant procession through Kelso:

> The little town of Kelso is very picturesque, and there were triumphal arches, and no end of pretty mottoes, and every house was decorated with flowers and flags. Fifty ladies dressed in white strewed flowers as we passed. Volunteers were out and bands played. At the Market Place the carriage stopped: an address was presented, not read [Victoria hated to be kept waiting, and in 1850 she spent exactly twelve minutes in Berwick Upon Tweed while she opened Robert Stephenson's Royal Border Bridge]; and a little girl was held up to give me an enormous bouquet. Immense and most enthusiastic cheering. We then drove on, admidst continued crowds and hearty cheers, up to the very park gates [Floors gates] where the old Sheriff, eighty five years old, was presented.

Queen Victoria's reception in Kelso was typical of the time and makes the kind of popularity enjoyed by modern royalty look muted and low key.

17 A Market Town

In 1871 the census showed that Kelso's population was 4,564 with 560 people living in the landward area of the parish, making a total of 5,124. This figure shows a stability which contrasts starkly with other Border burghs. As a result of the industrialisation of the textile and hosiery trade, Hawick and Gala were quadrupling their population at this time. People flooded into these towns from the countryside to what were regarded as well paid, regular jobs. Kelso did not experience this sort of population explosion and this had a positive effect on the shape of the town. Many of Kelso's older buildings survived because there was no large-scale factory building or the rapid construction of housing for workers.

In fact many of the town's institutions must have seemed positively mediaeval. In 1873 the local historian Fred Vernon records that the Town Hall bell was rung at 6am every weekday morning to call people to work and at 8pm to close the working day. This arrangement had replaced the men who marched around Kelso playing the drum and bagpipes at these times. Kelso was the last Border town to keep a burgh piper.

Rather than industrialisation, the town experienced a slow transformation into a market town offering good retail outlets for those who came into it from the country. Shops were established in the nineteenth century which survived for a long time.

On the facias of Kelso in 1873 were names like Hogg, Redpath, Gow and Croall. A Mr Middlemass employed several people at the jobs of cork cutting and the manufacture of aerated water. Redpaths were established in Roxburgh Street in 1812 and they employed between twenty to thirty people making 'hard' goods. They sent out salesmen all over the south of Scotland. Messrs R. Hogarth and Son were in business at Maxwellheugh Mill in 1873 as were Stuart and Mein (Seedsmen and Nurserymen). They had premises on the site of an old brewhouse in Woodmarket, which ultimately traded under the name of Laing and Mather. Whisky was blended and sold in a shop in the Square — Sheil the grocer. Messrs Croall and Kennedy established a coach building works on part of the Glebe Field which also made reaping machines.

In the second half of the nineteenth century Bridge Street emerged as a shopping area. Many of these Victorian shop-fronts are delightfully designed in a neo-classical style with fluted Ionic columns flanking their windows and lacy balustrades over their fascias. Although done in an old-fashioned architectural style —probably in imitation of Rennie's beautiful little toll-house at the end of Kelso Bridge — they were well designed with plate-glass windows forming part of the original composition. Not many present-day shop-fronts are as well designed. Consider the violence done to Kelso's townscape by examples of so-called twentieth century architecture like the appalling former electricity showroom in the Square or the supermarket in Horsemarket.

In the 1870s the Cross Keys was substantially altered so that very little survives of the Georgian built inn built by James Dickson. It acquired a new facade, in a style sympathetic to the shop-fronts in Bridge Street, and a balustraded 'promenande' on the roof. This was done by the owner, Mr Keddie, who also greatly increased the number of bedrooms.

18 More Mobbing and Rioting

This period of expansion and elegant building makes Kelso sound peaceful

Coronation Day 9 August 1902

and prosperous and indeed the town was just that, most of the time. Some of the time local people showed the sort of passion and spirt that was reminiscent of the toll riots at Kelso Bridge. At the general election of 1874 the Conservative candidate, Lord Schomberg Kerr (later to become Marquis of Lothian) had used persuasive, not to say coercive, tactics to persuade the electors of Kelso to vote for him. On polling day a mob of his political opponents capped him with a potato basket and threw wet rabbit skins and a dead cat at his supporters. In 1880 Sir George Douglas of Springwood, also a Conservative, offered himself for election and went to Kelso to address a public meeting. Whatever he had planned to say, the locals did not want to hear it and after howling him down they bundled him out of the meeting.

19 Rugby

Perhaps as a channel for all this aggression, Kelso Rugby Football Club came into existence. On 11 November 1876 the club was formed and matches were played against Kelso High School, and Gala. At that time rugby was played at Shedden Park. On 7 March 1879 the venue shifted to Springwood Park where a remarkable match was played against Earlston — remarkable because it was played under floodlights. Illumination was provided by two 'Siemen's dynamo electric machines' placed at either end of the pitch. Kelso had to wait until 1961 for its next floodlit game.

20 Population

Between 1871 and 1891 Kelso's population declined slightly from 4,564 to 4,184 and then again in 1911 it dropped below four thousand to 3,982. many of the crafts listed by Christopher Douglas in the *Statistical Account* of 1792, such as skinners, shoemakers and weavers had declined or disappeared. These were superseded by occupations which fitted the town's role as a major retail centre; Middlemas's soda and aerated water business, the manufacture of salmon rods, whisky blending and the new enterprise of photography. Although Kelso did not undergo an industrial revolution like Hawick and Gala, it was nonetheless an affluent town. In 1892 it had the largest number of telephone subscribers in Scotland (the telephone exchange was at the head of Mill Wynd), and when the City of Glasgow Bank (the local branch was in Innes Place next to Hume the tailor shop) failed in 1878, proportionately more Kelso investors were hurt by the bankruptcy than in Glasgow itself.

21 Improvements

A declining population did not discourage the new Town Council from making improvements in the burgh. In 1902 the re-paving (or re-cobbling) of the Square and Horsemarket was undertaken, as was the renovation of the Town Hall. In the same year the council bought numbers 19 and 21 Bowmont Street so that the site could be used for the building of Kelso's library with help from the Carnegie Trust. An isolation hospital was build at Angraflat (formerly Queen's House) and in 1904 the County Police Station was built at the corner of Rose Lane and Edenside Road. Improvement continued into the early part of the twentieth century with the opening up of Easter Kirkstile at Simon Square and the conversion of numbers 44, 48 and 52 Woodmarket into dwelling houses. In 1912 the Temperance Hall in Union Street (the Tin Kirk) was converted into Kelso's first cinema — but permission was given on the strict understanding that the projection equipment would be located outside the hall since the danger of fire from nitrate film was considerable. The following year the Town Hall Council bought number 63 Bowmont Street and numbers 28 to 30 Roxburgh Street for the building of a town yard.

By the outbreak of the First World War central Kelso had acquired the shape and character it has today.

22 The Seal

Perhaps symbolically the burgh seal, which was introduced in 1892 when the Burgh Police Act was adopted, is almost identical with the seal of the ancient burgh of Roxburgh. Like Kelso, Roxburgh bore the arms with a rose tree, the royal arms of Scotland and two birds. The birds on the Kelso coat of arms have been made into an eagle, the emblem of St John, and a dove, the emblem of St Mary. No single object sums up the history of Kelso better. As Roxburgh declined Kelso flourished around the abbey which took its name and was dedicated to the Virgin Mary and St John in 1128.

Part Eight

KELSO REMEMBERED

THE MOST VIVID sort of history is the sort related by people who have directly experienced it. When individuals have both feelings and recollections about what happened fifty or sixty years ago, it adds greatly to our sense of what the past was actually like.

The early twentieth century history of Kelso has almost, but not quite, outrun living memory. There is still a substantial group of townspeople who are old enough to remember events in Kelso before the First World War and in the twenties and thirties.

In this chapter eight Kelsonians have kindly agreed to share their memories of life in their town. Late in 1984 I made tape interviews with Sandy Blair, Rodger Fish, Will Ker, Jack Moffat, Mrs Helen Pettigrew, Donald Scott, Alan Smith and James Stewart. What follows is a written version of the spoken material they gave me. That means a text with a colloquial feel to it. I asked each person to talk about their own origins and, where appropriate, how they made their living in Kelso. The chapter begins with those introductions. I also asked the group to talk about specific events and institutions, like St James' Fair and the Hirings. Where one person had a substantial recollection of something specific, I have attached their name to it, but often all eight remembered something about most things and in those cases I have conflated their material.

In a general way it is important to realise that this concluding chapter deals not with written records (as in the rest of the book) but with the fabric of direct experience into which are woven personal opinions, prejudices and partiality. This does not diminish what is said — it heightens our sense of the recent history of Kelso because it makes it more familiar, more personal and because it shows clearly how much all these people love their native town.

SANDY BLAIR

I was born in Kelso in 1915 in an attic above a sweetie shop. The shop is called the old sweetie shop or Mitchell's and it's in the Dardanelles. Or people think it is, the correct address is actually East Bowmont Street. My father was away fighting in the First World War when I was born and when he came home, I was running about. He was very hurt because when I first saw him I ran to my mother shouting, 'A man, a man!'

Although I was born in East Bowmont Street I spent my young days in Roxburgh Street. We stayed in Beech Tent Lane which some people also called the Windy Gowl. I don't know where the name 'Beech Tent' comes from but perhaps there was a spreading beech tree there at one time, and perhaps its leaves and branches made a tent into which you could go. In the lane there was (and still is) a dairy then known as Lyle's Dairy. Its byres were down at the Winchester Row side.

I remember when Roxburgh Street was laid with granite setts. That was an improvement. Across the road was the Skinnery with its lime pits in Chalkheugh Lane. They dried the skins on the slopes of the terrace. There were open drains into the Tweed and the smell was terrible. On the Cobby Walk the grass used to be very high, not as it is now. Clothes were dried on the Cobby and each part of Roxburgh Street had its own days for hanging out clothes. Rugs and carpets were beaten there. I remember the cement base for the Pumping Engine that stood in the Windy Gowl. It took water out of the Tweed which people used to do their washing.

Where the Bus Station is now was a cycle shop and a chip shop which was owned by the Stoppani family. Turnbull's Garage was there as a base for the coal lorries which delivered around the town. He was the first agent in Kelso for Ford. Then Turnbull started to run buses out of his garage before the S.M.T. came along to take over the site. There's still an argument about a right of way through the garage.

RODGER FISH

I was born in 1911 in a flat in Bridge Street above Jock the Box's Entry. We were on the top flight. Jock the Box is the little tobacconist's shop with an entry through to Abbey Row next to it.

My first recollection of that place was my father going off to the War — the First War. The reason I remember it so well was that father was in the Volunteer Reserve and was called up immediately. As he was going downstairs, I stuck my head through the bannister railings, 'Dad, get the doctor because my mother's crying!' Then my head got stuck in the railings and they had to get butter or margarine to get me out.

I remember that, although we had a flush toilet in the house, there was no water other than that. We had to go down two flights of stairs and along Bridge Street to a place opposite Frank Frost's shop. This was the Pant and it was where you got your water by filling up your bucket. Every Saturday night mother and I went down and we got two buckets of water because you didn't go to the Pant on a Sunday. We had to carry those buckets all the way up. It was Pipewell water and we used it for drinking, cooking and washing. I remember there was another Pant opposite Will Ker's shop.

When I was a youngster in Bridge Street a wall went right along in front of what's now the entrance to the Ednam House Hotel. There was just a very narrow door through the wall. At the Weigh House, next to where the bar is now, there was a weigh bridge where carts coming into the town were weighed. They were given a ticket with the weight of their load on it. In Bridge Street a lot of shops have gone — Davie Scott the grocer, Lugton and Porteous who had a big shop which Bob Swan has altered (making a good job of it). Stempil's and J D Bews have both gone. I remember the Queen's Head and the Cross Keys had each a horse and carriage which went up and down to the Station to pick up customers and bring them down into the town. In the early days when we started in business we were at Maxwellheugh and I ran a hiring car. My job was to go up and meet the train in the hope of getting a passenger to take down to Kelso.

In those days we got a lot of commercial travellers who went everywhere by rail. They used to stay two or three nights at the Border Temperance Hotel. I remember a porter at Kelso Station. Somebody had sent a dog by train down to Kelso. The dog got out of the guard's van and ran along the platform. The porter was heard to shout, 'Stop that dog, it's a parcel!'.

My father was in the motor trade. He started with Croall and Croall, now Croall Bryson. Then he went to the Tweedside Motor Company which was run by Oswald Turnbull. My father had his car and it was reported in the *Kelso Mail* that 'Mr Rodger Fish had driven to Edinburgh and returned in the same day'. Another report in the paper said that an aeroplane had passed very low over Kelso at 2am. Actually it was my father — the exhaust had dropped off the car.

WILL KER

I'm 71 years old and I was born in the northern corner of Simon Square, near the Kirkstyle. That used to be a narrow opening but then they demolished the house on the left to make the road through from Simon Square to the Butts. Woodmarket and Simon Square have changed immensely since I was a boy. We used to have the pint-pitcher, as they called them, and go down to Rutherford Place where the Andersons had a dairy. Old Mrs Anderson had a big churn of milk and a ladle. She filled up your pitcher and you just walked home with it. That's how you got your milk in those days — no hygiene or anything, but we were all healthy.

Rutherford Place is down now, of course. It was a little cul-de-sac off Cross Street. Jacob Douglas stayed in there. Old Happy Wilson stayed in the corner house and he also had a dairy. Dames' house was where Rodger Fish built his garage and it had an entrance from Coal Market. Dames's dairy cows grazed in the fields next to Shedden Park. Every day they were driven up the town into the yard where they were milked.

This building where I have my business — I remember wanting to have it knocked down. It's an old building, rebuilt in 1794. I have the title deeds here in the shop. It belonged to a family called Jerdan. An Australian once came into the shop. His ancestors were born in Kelso and their name was Jerdan. I had to speak into a tape and say that we were both standing in the shop where his great, great-grandfather was born and that I was the present owner of the shop at Woodmarket.

Our business has been going on here since 1928 although my father was a watchmaker long before that, since 1910 in fact. He trained with old Clark the watchmaker at 34 Woodmarket before setting up on his own.

JACK MOFFAT

I was born in 1916 at 9 Union Street in a house which is still there. I think I was three when my mother and I moved to 10 Horsemarket. It used to stand on the site of the present supermarket. At one time there was a theatre there because in the houses behind you could see where the boxes had been — inside the houses. When I was ten we moved to 26 Horsemarket which is now Scrappy Henderson's showroom. We were next to Strathearn's Close. It's gone now but it led to Strathearn's yard where china and things like that were stored. It was between Elliot's Close (which is still there — next to the supermarket) and Kennedy's Close which led to Kennedy's Model Lodging House.

I left school when I was fourteen and was employed as an electrician with the firm of Chalmers. They worked out of Victoria Buildings in Horsemarket — that was opposite the Post Office. Chalmers had their garage in the old Sprouston Free Kirk which was in Shedden Park Road on the south side. I remember there was a cycle shop at Victoria Buildings. In 1936 we moved up to the new council houses at Orchard Park, number sixty.

MRS HELEN PETTIGREW

I was born in 1900 at 50 Horsemarket, where Hossack the baker is now. Nowadays I can't really ask anybody older than me about Kelso — but I do remember things away back very well, better than things that happened recently.

My family — the Brookses — came down from a young lad who was a page to the 4th Duke of Roxburghe when he came up to Floors for the season. The young man married a lass in Kelso and when the season ended he didn't want to go back to the London house. He asked the Duke to allow him to stay in Kelso, and that happened. His wife's name was Dodds and she came from the Townhead where her father was a carter. There have been Brookses in Kelso ever since.

In Horsemarket you had to go through a pend to get to our house. The bakehouse was there too and the flour store. Three families lived up that close. One of them was the Greens, they were orphans really. I remember one night the youngest wee lass got very badly burned. Jimmy Neil and my father took her up to the Cottage Hospital. But before he could get her to the hospital, he had to get his horse yoked in and my father wrapped the bairn in a blanket. He took her up to the hospital and the matron said, 'We can't possibly admit her at this time of night'. Jimmy Neil —a great big man — said 'Get oota ma road', and nearly knocked her flat. But the wee lass died hours later.

Out the back my father had a place where he kept the coke to heat the ovens, and cinders, and my mother's household coal. Behind that my mother had a great big drying green. Then you opened a door that was kept locked and it led through to the stables where we kept our own horses. From there you went into East Bowmont Street. The offices for Scrappy Henderson are where our stables used to be. When the carts (we called them vans) were loaded up with bread and everything else they went out into East Bowmont Street to go on their rounds.

I remember when my father had the top storey built onto our property in Horsemarket. We needed more room. My father had a beautiful bathroom put in when there was hardly a bathroom in Forestfield. He was asthmatical because of the flour dust. He was keen on his work. He liked the bakery trade but he did get anxious about things and so did my mother. Sometimes my father would overdo it and then he would have a bout of asthma. But he was a perfectionist, he had to have everything right.

We flitted to the Square (we were just in Bridge Street at Oven Wynd) in 1914. I was to go to the Art College but that was washed out by the War.

DONALD SCOTT

I was born above Scott the baker's shop at the foot of Roxburgh Street in 1914. My grandfather came from Gala to Kelso to start the business and he bought the shop from a man called Purves. Andrew Chatto of Mainhouse originally bought the building from the Duke of Roxburghe in 1743 and then sold it in 1746 to John Watt. He sold it to a tobacconist, James Robertson, in 1764. It eventually came into the possession of George Purves who died in 1885. His trustees sold the shop to my grandfather in 1902 when it became a bakery. He left it to my father in 1905. The present shop, not as a bakery, was built on the site in 1872 by Purves.

My brother Jack had the business and he wasn't married so he took in Neil Macarthur from St Andrews. Macarthur was a baker in St Andrews but the business only had room for one brother to take it over and there were two. So Neil Macarthur came to Scott's at Kelso.

In all that time the pies and the rolls have never changed —they're extremely good. My father's reputation was in bread making and the cakes and confectionery came later. I used to help in the shop and I remember at Easter making the crosses for the hot-cross buns with a pastry-stamp.

I remember my father used to have a bookshop in the corner of the Square where Jobson the Saddler is now. He gave up the bookshop to a Mr Smith who then sold it to a Mr Laing of Laing and Mather. Then it was MacDougall's shoeshop before it became a saddler's.

ALAN SMITH

I was born above Henderson the Grocer's shop in Roxburgh Street (also known as Gow's) and next to the pub called The Blazing Rag — above the Cassie! Now, where's that? Well, Roxburgh Street was cobbled up to Winchester Row and above that was the 'Cassie'. Don't ask me where the name originated. But everybody who was born above the Cassie was a Roxburgh Street Arab. No matter where you moved afterwards, you remained a Roxburgh Street Arab all your life! In fact in my boyhood we moved when I was two years old to Shedden Park Road, to those houses just by Rodger Fish's garage. They are still standing and are now mostly used by Hope's as stores.

My father started our business when he came back from the First World War. He served his time as a tailor and cutter with a firm in what is now Jock Hume's shop. It was Melrose's in those days. My father came back wounded in 1918, just before Armistice. In 1921 he started as a mens' and boys' outfitter in Roxburgh Street. He specialised in working for the estates where there was a tremendous lot of business to be had in those days. Now the estates have almost all gone, leaving really only Floors. Then there was Newton Don, Hendersyde, Pinnacle Hill, Broomlands. They all had a lot of grooms and servants who had their clothing provided by their employers. My father only got paid at the end of the year by the estates, so he was always rolling in money in the middle of January when all his bills were paid.

Even in my day (I started just before the Second World War in 1939) we still had a lot of estate accounts and that carried on until about 1948. Then the perks stopped when reasonable cash wages came in. In the old days I knew chaffeurs who had three or four suits that they'd never worn. Every year they got a new suit which, of course, lasted longer than a year. One old groom used to come into the shop and say, 'I've torn ma breeks, can ye mend them?'. I had two tailors working then; one of them was Tommy Simpson, Wilson Simpson's father. He would mend the old groom's breeks, even though he said he had five or six pairs of corduroys he hadn't worn yet. The same old groom used to exercise a horse for Robertson of Yetholm and he used to stop and go into the Plough for a pint instead of exercising the horse properly. When the owner went hunting up the College Valley and came back through Yetholm, the horse turned sharp left into the Plough. There was pandemonium that day at the stables.

JAMES STEWART

I was born in this house, number four Woodmarket. The business premises were downstairs and we lived in here right up to just after I got married. In fact this was our first house when we got married. Of course, the whole building is business premises now.

My grandfather started this business in 1886. He was a tinsmith with the firm of Hooper and Co, whose premises were in Roxburgh Street where the Clydesdale Bank is now. My grandfather set up as a tinsmith here in Woodmarket — making tin containers and things like that. My father joined him to start an ironmongery shop here. I was trained as an electrical engineer at Heriot Watt College (as it then was) and I brought in the electrical contracting side of the business in the mid 1930s. My son, Kenneth, trained in Edinburgh at the Heriot Watt University and he's now a partner with me. I suppose you could say that I'm semi-retired now.

THE HIRING FAIRS

Before the Second World War farmers employed their workers in a very different way. Each agricultural labourer and his family were contracted for (usually) one year at a time and beyond that they had no security of employment. In Kelso, as in other market towns all over Britain, there was an annual hiring fair where farmers came to inspect and employ labourers who had left their jobs after their contract or 'term' had expired. These were workers who, to use the operative phrase, had not been 'spoken to' by their previous masters, that is those who had not been asked to stay on.

The Hirings lasted for one day and before the building of Kelso's Corn Exchange, they were held outdoors in the Square. Whatever we may think of this institution in retrospect, it was an occasion which, in its day, brought tremendous business to the town and which was always celebrated. Although long gone the Hirings were clearly remembered by almost all the people who contributed here.

Jack Moffat
You have to remember that there were really two Hirings. The first one was on a Friday at the end of April sometimes into May. That was the main one where bargains were struck. A fortnight later the streets of the town were thronged with long carts piled high with furniture and drawn by horses. These were the farm labourers moving to the new places decided by the bargains struck two weeks earlier. On the second day there was some hiring done — of people who hadn't got themselves placed on the first day.

Alan Smith
On the two Hiring days we were tremendously busy. The shop opened at 7.30am and closed at 9pm. Not only the people to be hired came in, the whole of the countryside came into the town. Everybody met everybody else. Many people came into the shop saying, 'I've seen so and so, I haven't seen them since the last Hiring'. For people living thirteen or fourteen miles out of Kelso there was no means of getting in except walking, riding a horse or possibly cycling. That sometimes meant that workers living on a

remote farm only left it to come to Kelso once a year. I have a dim recollection of people coming into the town on the long carts. They brought their furniture after they had been 'spoken to' by a farmer and slapped hands. When farmers sold cattle they also hit hands to seal the bargain.

Our biggest trade in the shop was during the Hirings but with working people rather than the better-off. Lugton and Porteous and J D Bews looked after the toffs. We sold corduroys, britches, and a Sunday suit which was always tailored. My father had three tailors on the premises at the time as well as outworkers, usually in the country. I've cycled to Yetholm with stuff to be made up by a tailor, and then brought back the finished suit. My father did all his own cutting. By the time I got into the business all that was coming to an end. My father wouldn't let me serve my time as a cutter because he was far-sighted and could see that in the future clothes would be mostly sold off the peg and not properly tailored. He said that by the end of his time there wouldn't be a tailor in Kelso, and he was right. When I ran the business all my stuff went to Leeds.

Anyway we did well at the Hirings but by the time we closed the shop, Kelso was empty — by 9pm. The farm-workers didn't stay overnight in the town. It was nothing to walk a long distance in those days — to Leitholm, Yetholm or Morebattle. Many had bicycles and they had to carry home whatever they had bought in the town. Only the farmers, the lawyers and the nobility had cars.

I remember the bakers doing well at the Hirings. Sandy Sanderson's pies were famous and so were Willie Reid's — he was called Pie Reid. Brooks' did a marvellous trade and their foreman, Dave Murray, was called the Pie King.

Mrs Helen Pettigrew
The Hirings were busy days with all the bakers and grocers. Days before the day itself we had to get up early to start baking to have enough for everybody who wanted pies, cakes or bread.

I remember the farm workers standing in groups in the Square waiting to be hired. It was awful, very shaming for them. The first year we were up at the shop in Bridge Street it was a very wet day and the farm workers were waiting at the door. They came into Kelso on open carts and they hadn't the oilskins then. They stood in the street knocking at the shop door to get in. We had a tearoom in the shop and they just kept coming up the stair. The staircase came away with the weight of the folk. My father had to get the joiner to come down and mend it there and then. There were people who couldn't get down.

Will Ker
The Hirings were sometimes held across in the Corn Exchange. Now when I was serving my time with old Clark the Jeweller my job was to sell spectacles, — reading spectacles at 2/6 a pair. They were steel-framed and oval and old Clark had a hundred dozen pairs of different strengths. We used to put a copy of *The Scotsman* on the counter and they just tried them on until they got a pair to suit. And that was it, no eye-test, nothing. I'd sell a couple of dozen pairs on a Hiring Day.

James Stewart
We did tremendous business on those days. I can remember at our shop in Woodmarket we stored the farm workers' bicycles, completely filling the place. We charged sixpence for looking after them for the day.

Rodger Fish
The thing I remember is my relations coming into Kelso on the Hiring Days. My mother used to feed them; pies and broth. They used to spend a bit of time in the pub in between my mother's meals.

The highlight for me was when all the shows came to the Knowes. I'm a bit romantic. I couldn't stay out of the Knowes when they were building all these shows. I don't know where that interest came from — it must just have been in me, can't understand it. However, on the first Hiring Saturday night there weren't so many shows in, they really came a fortnight later. That was a big night — terrific. There was Murphy's Motors, the Cakewalk, Helter-Skelter, the Chairoplanes, all the shooting galleries, the hoopla stalls. They came every year and they were like old friends.

Now that was marvellous — but. The whole thing was rather awful, it was like a cattle market — except with people.

My mother used to sit at the top window in Bridge Street to watch all the carts coming past with the furniture piled up on them. This was when they were actually having to move, when they had not been 'spoken to' by their previous employer and they were going to another farm. They had long carts and the horses were all decorated with beautiful harness, and pom poms and little bells on their breast collars. Invariably the fellow driving the horse and the husband would be sitting on the side of the cart. At the back there was always the horsehair settee with the wife sitting on it with all her children alongside her. The wife often had her aspidistra on her knee. Mother used to say, 'Look, here's a nice one coming, with some good furniture too'.

When you think about it, they got all their belongings onto one cart.

ST JAMES' FAIR

As conditions of employment on the land improved so the Hirings disappeared from the calendar. Another annual event to fall out of use was St James' Fair which ceased to exist in the mid 1930s as the Border Union Show began to take its place. The Fair took place on 5 August and had been in existence at Roxburgh since the twelfth century. Some people remembered its dying days.

Sandy Blair

I remember the crowds coming up Roxburgh Street. There were many people from the country who came to the fair on a day's holiday. Bulman's the builder used to put up the bridge across the Tweed. That was up the Cobby near where the diving boards used to be and it took you across to the Fairgreen. Boys used to swim around the bridge and get pennies thrown by people crossing. On the green there were the muggers or tinkers selling ponies and horses. I remember plenty of arguments and fights. There were some stalls for hoopla and shooting galleries. Then people used to picnic up the back on the higher ground.

The Border Union Show took over and was at first held on the Fairgreen but further downriver at the Put.

It's sad that the Fair has gone and maybe it should come back in Civic Week. I've been approached by travelling people wanting to start the Fair again. It would be good to see the gipsy caravans come back. When I was a boy I was good at art and I remember once when I came back from St James' Fair, I drew a caravan. I remember they were all lined up on the green. It was a grand sight.

Rodger Fish

The Provost and others had to come down to Kelso from Jedburgh to open St James' Fair. Kelso couldn't because it wasn't a royal burgh and this was a sore point with us. One year we couldn't cross the wooden bridge because it was too dangerous, the Tweed being in spate. The Fair stopped because it wasn't needed. We had the Border Union Show instead.

Mrs Helen Pettigrew

My earliest memory is going to St James' Fair. My father took me and I was only four. I remember going across the bridge and my father gave me a penny to pay. I had to take his hand. I got to the other side but I don't

The Square after St James' Fair 6 August 1886

remember the shows or the muggers. I never went back. I couldn't because we were always so busy in the shop on Fair day. I remember my father saying once that the wooden bridge had been washed away.

Jack Moffat
On the day after St James' Fair all the gipsies and horse dealers assembled in Kelso Square because they had to be out of the town by 12 noon. As they drove their caravans out of the Square they were usually accompanied by several small carts which were decked out in bunting. I remember they drove at a very fast pace and I enjoyed watching their beautiful horses rattling along the cobbled streets.

Kelso people never liked the fact that St James' Fair was cried by the Jethart Town Crier — just because it was a royal burgh that stood close by after Roxburgh was destroyed.

Kelso's weekly markets have also gone but were well remembered:

In Woodmarket cattle were sold. This happened every Friday. The farmers used to stand in their places with their beasts; the farmer from Kerchesters would have ten or twelve animals to sell and next to them would be cattle from Kersmains and so on. After the market was over Hugh Ker, the town plumber and fireman, used to come with his hose and clean the street. In the Square local manufacturers used to display the agricultural machinery they had for sale. Both Scrappy Henderson and Storie's used to paint the harrows and reapers as brightly as they could so that they shone in the sun.

Howden's the ropemaker displayed his wares on the steps of his shops. In Horsemarket Bob Rush the horse-dealer used to run his animals from the Black Swan right down to where Rodger Fish's garage was. Sometimes they tied seven or eight horses together to compare and sometimes they ran two as a team. Where Hope's shop is now was a smiddy and farriery and it was always busy on market day. Off Horsemarket was Elliot's Close (where George Wright's shop is now) and it was where horsey people lived. Murdoch and Rush the horse dealers were there and there was a family of Prestons who were ostlers at the Cross Keys when it had stables. Sparks used to fly from the horses' hooves on the cobbles in Horsemarket on a Friday. Most of the bargains struck on that day happened over a drink in the Black Swan.

Although the 1930s saw the passing of some of Kelso's old institutions; the Hirings, St James' Fair and the market days, the town was developing a sense of its own identity in another way. Civic Week was an invention of

Picnickers at St James' Fair 1910

the 30s and Rodger Fish was in at the beginning:

Around about 1934 the Town Council decided to have a shopping week. That's how it started. The idea was that all the shops would make a special effort by decorating their windows and a prize would be given for the best window. This was to stimulate trade. I remember once at a local concert they held outdoors in Shedden Park, I made up a piece of poetry:

> Kelso held a shopping week to stimulate the trade,
> And the shopkeepers can't come tonight,
> they're counting what they made.

Then in 1937 Provost John Scott suddenly, completely out of the blue, attended a meeting in the council chambers with a flag and a sash, a blue and white sash. He said, 'I want a young lad to carry this flag around the town'. The councillors were aghast but there was nothing they could do since Provost Scott had simply gone ahead and done it. So that's how the idea of the Kelso Laddie was born, more or less. Well, that happened a fortnight before Shopping Week. So, they decided they would change the name to Civic Week seeing as they were having this lad with the burgh flag. The only boy who had a horse was Bobby Service so the councillors went out of the meeting, saw Bobby and said, 'Look, we want you to carry this flag around the town in Civic Week on the Saturday night'. Bobby was a bit taken aback but he agreed. He was an obvious choice, apart from the fact that he had a horse, because he was one of the most popular fellows in the town — a rugby player, you name it. He was a great guy.

He didn't really have much of a time since he only had a fortnight before the event. But they decided this was a great success — seeing the burgh standard carried around the town. They decided to do it again the following year. There were four wards in the town and so they asked each ward to put forward a candidate to be Kelso Laddie. I was put forward by Maxwellheugh. The public voted and I was fortunate enough to win. So then we decided — this was about three months before Civic Week was due to start — that I had to learn to ride a horse. Bobby Service taught me, he was a great horseman. If you could follow Bobby, you could ride a horse, I can assure you. David Clow, who was to become Kelso Laddie the next year, also learned to ride. Bobby said, 'What about us going up to Yetholm?' I said, 'That's a great idea and we'll go over to Halterburn and I'll see my grandfather'. So we rode up to Yetholm — there was maybe half a dozen of us. We went over to Halterburn and I saw the old man. But before we got to the house, Bobby said, 'Now, show off when you go up here.' My grandfather had seen us coming and he was waiting at the door. Bobby said, 'Put your horse into a gallop'. I did and I fell off right at my grandfather's feet. All he said was, 'Well, Rodger, that's not the way to get off a horse'.

Then Bobby and I thought why don't we incorporate this into Civic Week, and ride up to Yetholm and over the Border by the top of Venchen Hill. Mrs Gilchrist then came along and she said, 'I've discovered something. The Blue Bonnets were originally made in Kelso. Why don't you ride to Yetholm, cross the Border and wear a Blue Bonnet?' We thought, 'Why not *win* the Blue Bonnet and not get it until we'd done the ride to Yetholm, crossed the Border, taken a sprig off a tree or something like that, and then gone down to the Border Hotel.' So we did it. We got well tanked up at the hotel, it was very nice. Then we decided not to go back the same way but to go round by Linton. And so that's how the Yetholm ride was born, during my year as Kelso Laddie. When we did the ride we managed to get a few more riders; old Willie Gilchrist, Billy Service (Bobby's father) and one or two more. They all turned out on horses. I think there were either twelve or fourteen of us rode to Yetholm in the Civic Week.

When I see them going away from the Square now, I feel nostalgic about it. Three hundred horses from twelve. That's how it all started.

Many of the people I spoke to had vivid recollections of the small bit of Kelso where they grew up. Some of these places have disappeared and some have changed radically. The idea of tightly-knit neighbourhoods seems to have gone with those changes.

Alan Smith
The children in each part of the town were clannish and tended to stay in their part of the town. When I started rugby at the age of nine or ten, we played matches against other neighbourhoods —Shedden Park against the Mill Wynd. The Wynd were a very good side because they had all the Weatherstones and the Coulthards. Roxburgh Street had a team, as did Bridge Street and Belmount Place, and Horsemarket and Woodmarket.

The town has changed in that there were many people packed into the middle of the town. That sort of tenement living has almost disappeared from Kelso.

We lived in our patch, Shedden Park Road, up until 1921. The centre of our lives was Shedden Park itself and we spent our time there and at Bullet Loan and on Wooden Anna. In our summer holidays we fished for eels. There were a tremendous number of them in the river then. Every family in Shedden Park Road at that time kept hens — the Bryces, the Youngs, the Bennets, the Smails and the Darlings. There wasn't much to feed them

on so they got the eels. By jove those hens used to chase after the eels
—talk about fights. One hen pulling at one end and another on the other
end. I've always remembered that.

We caught the eels by forking them. We moved a stone back and forked
them as they came out. We also used cobbler's lingle (strong thread).
Cobblers used it to sew the shoes. What you did was to get a whole lot of
worms and bind them into the lingle (pronounced linnel) by winding them
and knotting them in. You threw that into the water and the eels went for
it. They caught their gills on the lingle and we just pulled them out. We
used to get dozens that way. There were a lot down by Haddie Tam's (now
called Wellwood) the fisherman's lodge at Hendersyde. There's an anna
that runs right down to the mill at Sharpitlaw. Just between it and the road
there seemed to be hundreds of eels in the channel.

We seemed to spend our boyhoods catching eels, playing football,
playing cricket and going to school — which wasn't a great attraction.

I remember in Shedden Park they used to have the guns from Lt
Shedden's ship. They stood right by the putting green; two guns and a
flagpole which used to fly Shedden's flag. At the lodge where they now
keep the putting sticks there was a resident parkie. By Jove he used to
chase us. Of course we never went in the gates like everybody else. Oh no,
we went over the railings at the top end. Many a time the parkie chased us
and somebody would catch their breeks and be left hanging upside down
needing to be lifted off to have their backsides kicked. They were high
railings, about five feet high with spikes on the top. They were taken away
during the last war.

There was a bandstand in the corner next to Mat Ballantyne's yard. I've
heard a band playing in it when I was young.

The Kelso Games were a great event in Shedden Park. Tom Black the
joiner erected awnings right down to the cemetery so that you couldn't see
in. There were no tennis courts then so they used the ground at the
bottom of the park. The tennis courts were laid around 1931. The games
gradually faded away and then the cricket took over. The first time I ever
saw a rugby match was in Shedden Park. This was in 1919 or 1920 before
Poynder Park came into use. I remember Spiers Black and Bobby Thomson
playing for Kelso in Shedden Park — and there was Jock Hume, Arch
Hume and Monk Hume, and the Tank (that was Robertson of Yetholm
Mains) so-called because he was built like one. I remember Hawick, Jethart
and Melrose playing in the park. I remember myself playing in a Border
League match in Shedden when Poynder was frozen. We just put up posts
and played — against Melrose. That was in the 1930s.

Going back to my boyhood I remember that Mill Wynd, the Pier Head and Vault Square was a tough part of the town. There were fights but no real viciousness. There was practically no crime. Theft and burglary were rare. I recall one bloke being arrested for stealing and he went to prison for it. When he came back to Kelso he was practically ostracised. The community was so small, so tight-knit, it could control it.

Pinching apples was different. That was OK. I once got caught outside Oaklands with a jersey full of apples by Sandy Baxter the policeman. What a lifter I got! He didn't bother with arrest or anything like that, he just used the boot — bang!

Just off Shedden Park Road there used to be a big smiddy; Allan the Blacksmith in Hermitage Lane. They were very busy with four full-time men shoeing horses, finishing cartwheels and so on. Opposite was Hogarth's, a big engineering works — where Ballantyne's office is now. Along from there, opposite the new Police Station was Chalmers' garage. It used to be the Sprouston Free Kirk and it was one of Kelso's first garages. They had a bus with hard wheels. It's owned by Ballantyne now.

My grandfather was 'Strong' Bob Smith and he worked with Maxwell's the blacksmith. They had a business behind Roxburgh Street where the Co-op grocery is now. That was a big firm. Bob Smith played rugby for Kelso, my father did and so did I — three generations.

Donald Scott

Roxburgh Street was very different in my day from what is there now. Scott the baker is practically the only business to survive. I remember Dan Ross had a toyshop opposite us. He was apparently a crack shot at the rifle competitions at Bisley. His daughter Lizzie Ross ran the shop and lived above it. Her nickname was Tib Toosh, a funny wee woman.

Next to that were the two Miss Youngs who had a shoeshop. They were characters. Above them in a flat was Miss Wood who had a sort of 11½d brother known as the Marquis. She always kept him indoors — never allowed him to go out. The property was pretty poor at the back and one day the leg of his bed came down through the ceiling of the Misses Young's kitchen while they were having breakfast. One of them looked up and said, 'Are we going to see the Marquis after all?'.

Kelso Museum was in Roxburgh Street. It's now the British Legion. I remember the stuffed crocodile at the bottom of the stairs. It was black and varnished. During the last war the Museum was used as a canteen for soldiers and then it became the British Legion. It was very stuffy because it had been an antiquarian place with dusty old stuffed birds. Very few people ever went in but I liked a nice little room it had upstairs. It had a gallery all around and I enjoyed walking there looking at the display cases.

After I went away to art college I lived and worked in Melrose. But now I've come back to Kelso to live up at the other end of Roxburgh Street at Walton Hall. It's an interesting house. It was built by Ballantyne the publisher in 1820 as a fishing lodge —that's why it's Walton Hall, after Isaac Walton the author of 'The Compleat Angler'. We're supposed to have fishing rights to the middle of the river. A previous owner, Miss White, built a fence across their land down below Walton Hall onto the Cobby and out into the middle of the river. She did it to protect her rights but probably mainly to spite the Duke.

Lady Bennet's Well is at the end of the little lane on the right of this property as you look at it. The lane has been overgrown by elder trees. There used to be the most awful smell of fish and I think it was poachers cleaning and taking the heads off their fish in the lane. It's now very wet and boggy. Mrs Mather next door diverted the spring and she has a little fountain in her garden that bubbles away all the time. Even when the Tweed flooded right over the wall you could still see it bubbling away so the spring must be pretty strong to maintain its pressure.

The Miss White who lived here with her sister must have been fairly eccentric. One of the ladies was a playwright and I believe she had her plays done in the West End of London. She used to rehearse the plays in Walton Hall and the actors were housed next door in what is now Mrs Mather's house. She had a bridge across the little lane for them to come over. This was in the early part of this century.

Sandy Blair

I remember going into the Kelso Museum in Roxburgh Street. It was looked after by a Miss Oliver and it was a very quiet place. There was a strange thing in there — a chicken with four legs. Miss Oliver used to bring it out in its glass case and show it to us. I think she was quite proud of it. There were stuffed snakes and flints and stones of all shapes and sizes. I still have a clock in the shop which my father bought when the Museum finished. Sadly most of the stuff has gone — goodness knows where. There are a few stone axes and bits and pieces from Kelso in the National Museum of Antiquities in Edinburgh, but that's all I could trace.

Down the other end of Roxburgh Street I can remember a place called the Crown Hotel. It was a lodging house — it was the building that Jamieson's Entry used to go through. People who couldn't afford anything better went there. We forget that at one time many people in Kelso were poorly off. Down the 'Pickie' (that was the name we used for Mill Wynd. We named it after Piccadilly in London because that was such a posh address.) was a poor area and people lived in there in terrible conditions —

one toilet for three families, that sort of thing. The buildings became broken down, and much of it, like Vault Square, has disappeared. I remember one place in particular where my father had his motor-bike and sidecar. It had a stone stair outside leading to a loft above his garage. People actually lived there. There was no running water inside and the people had to come out of there and go to an outside toilet. They got their water from a Pant. There used to be many outside toilets for the houses around the Square, in places like Oven Wynd. People lived hard down there.

Mrs Helen Pettigrew
Before the First World War Horsemarket was a lot different from now. We were a community and everybody was very friendly. I remember the family of Richardsons who had the Black Swan, especially young Sneck Richardson. They were Jews. His daughter Effie was a good singer and she sang a lot during the First World War. They had a good trade when they were in the Black Swan.

Then there was Charlie Forte, the first Italian in Kelso. I remember him coming to the town. He started his business in Horsemarket in the shop where Miss Neil had her dress-making and millinery department. That was next to where Claude Neil had his business.

Just along from there in the pend by Rodger Fish's garage there was a family called Roy who took in lodgers. One of them was our van man, Dan Easton. He wasn't much of a scholar. When the book-keeper at our shop asked him one day what tick he had to mark in after his round, he had this circle with dots inside it down in his book. Hilda, the book-keeper, said, 'What's this then Dan?'. 'It's a teacake, can ye no' see?', he said.

Just by the Roy's house was what's now Mairi Hope's shop. Part of that used to be an antique shop, owned by an old wifie, Mrs Radcliffe. On the summer days she had a favourite chair which she carried out onto the pavement. She sat there and spoke to everybody that passed.

There was Rutherford's the grocer next door. You could get a cup of lentils, an onion and a carrot, and if you were lucky a ham bone thrown in, all for three halfpence. Next to that was Hope's smiddy and round the corner in Cross Street the Salvation Army had two or three rooms in there. Grannie Ker used to live in Cross Street. She made this treacle toffee and sold lucky turnovers and that sort of thing. You just got it in a bit of newspaper for a halfpenny.

Every day, before we had our dinner, my mother took a glass jug and she went to the pump to get Pipewell Brae water. It was an old-fashioned long-handled pump that stood just between Erskine the plumber and the old Edenside Church — now the Roxy Cinema. There was supposed to be a fire station there but it was just a barrow. Hugh Ker was in charge. He pulled out the barrow with a tank on it and had to mend the punctures before they could get to the fire.

I remember there was a Pant in Bridge Street and two more in Woodmarket. The water was pure. There was also a trough at the end of the Inch.

It was a real change when we flitted from Horsemarket (mind you the old shop is still a baker — Hossack's) to the Square. After a bit my father bought the tenement next door to the shop and then later he bought Ednam House. Eventually every bit of property from our shop on Bridge Street right down Oven Wynd to the millrace was his. There used to be a library in Oven Wynd behind Pettigrew's. There was a staircase up to a room from one of the yards and you could get to it down a close between Tait's and the shop. It's all blocked up now.

Down Oven Wynd the title deeds talk about the accommodation people had, half-houses and quarter houses. God knows what that was like. But that's where people stayed in the old days, in the middle of Kelso and not spread out like now.

There used to be a lodging house at Peat Wynd; Shadrack and Nelson's. It was never empty. There were a lot of Irish people lived down Mill Wynd. They came for the harvest. And in Scott's Entry, you couldn't get past for Irishmen on a Sunday morning. They lived rough, in bad conditions.

They cleaned up that bit of Kelso right enough but they've really spoilt it as well. You could go for a nice walk down Oven Wynd or Mill Wynd and then to the Pier Head and down to the grass at the Cobby. Now it's all concrete and gravel.

Will Ker
I think the way of life in Kelso has changed immensely. We had to make all our own fun in those days. And in Kelso with its tremendous sports facilities, if you couldn't entertain yourself, well . . . In the school holidays it was Shedden Park, especially in this part of the town. We played cricket all summer. The kids who played up Roxburgh Street were water-rats. They spent the summer in the Cobby. Dr Willie Davidson and Billy Hall the plumber were the main instigators in building the old diving boards up the Cobby. They had swimming galas up there every summer with seating laid out for the spectators. They had races right down the Cobby to the Put and back up again. Mark Gleed was a great underwater swimmer. He was so long under the water, we thought he was away! He swam down to the Put and practically back up again before he surfaced!

Of course down at this end of town, in Woodmarket, none of us could swim a stroke, but we went up to watch them.

For six weeks in the summer holidays you went barefoot. And then in August you put your boots back on to go to the school.

Alan Smith

I started off in the Infant School at the end of Inch Road. There was the North Church which was demolished during the Second World War and it stood where the new part of the Infant School was built, the building that's now used as workshops. The old Infant School was next to the North Church and it had three classrooms. Of course the North Church manse is still there and it's used by the minister of Trinity North. But the school and the old kirk had no connection, they just happened to be on the same site.

Then I went to the Public School in Abbey Row and if you were clever at the age of twelve you got to go to the High School in Edenside Road. The Public School's now a community centre and the High School is demolished. Up until just after the First War the High School was a private school with fee-paying pupils only. When I first went to the High School it was a mixture of fee-paying pupils and the other kind, which included me. After they built the new High School in Bowmont Street, the old one was used by a knitwear firm, Lyle and Scott, as a factory.

Infants went to the school from five to eight and then eight to fourteen at the Abbey School and then fourteen to eighteen at the High School. Grove House was the headmaster's house. It was F P Shepherd in my time, the man who wrote the Latin grammar called King, Gillies and Shepherd. We used to have it rammed down our throats.

I left with a day school leaving certificate at fifteen. I wasn't thick but my brother was brilliant and my father couldn't afford to send both of us to school. My brother became Principal of Heriot-Watt University so I suppose it was worthwhile. My mother was a very clever woman and that's where my brother's brains probably came from. But the education we got at Kelso was a good one and many people at school in F P Shepherd's time went on to great things. Nowadays of course education doesn't mean so much and it's desperate for bright kids who can't get a job.

Jack Moffat

When I was at school I can remember looking forward to the things we did when we were *not* at school. At New Year, in fact on 1 January, there was a sort of party held in the old Temperance Hall in Union Street for the children of the Town. It was to usher in the New Year and we used to have to sing hymns and say prayers. For a penny we got the 'penny poke' which was a bag of buns and cakes and an apple and an orange.

Christmas Day used to be just an ordinary working day — it was looked on as an English holiday. The shops did open late —until 9pm — on Christmas Eve though.

At Easter there were picnics up at the Old Castle (old Roxburgh Castle) and at the Meadows. You needed a steep slope to roll your eggs down. There would be a bonfire to boil kettles for tea.

Kelso Races were held twice a year at Berrymoss. The first meeting was in the Spring and the second in the Autumn. Each meeting lasted two days. The race horses arrived by special horse carrying trains with padded stalls. They were unloaded at the old Station at Maxwellheugh with their handlers and then walked down the hill to stabling in the town.

The following day the racing fraternity descended on the town. The hotels and boarding houses were full and in fact every spare bed in Kelso was occupied. It was the only race meeting in the Borders conducted under rules. The Square was filled with crowds listening to the tipsters selling their predictions. They were flanked by an assortment of street traders offering everything from a 'gold' watch to cheap sweets to take home for the family.

I remember being impressed with the patter of these 'city slickers' and marvelling at their self-assurance.

Aside from special events like the Races the townspeople got their entertainment from lots of sources. The Pictures was popular; Davie Scott showed silent films in the Corn Exchange and a Mr Wade showed films in the Scout Hall. Willie Gilchrist was the most enterprising and he showed films on four nights a week at the Temperance Hall in Union Street. We called it the Tin Kirk and I remember being put out once for throwing a white pudding supper at the screen.

When the Talkies came the Pinders built the Playhouse in Havannah Court. That's the building which is now the Ednam Rooms. He ran eight shows a week there and so did Willie Gilchrist when he converted the Edenside Church into the Roxy. Of course in time the Pinders owned both cinemas.

Small concerts and plays were sometimes given in the town hall. The Corn Exchange was a favourite venue for professional touring companies offering opera and drama. It also housed the Buccleuch Hunt Ball every year and was known as the best badminton courts in the Borders. In other halls in the town, right through the winter, there used to be whist drives or beetle drives and small concerts. People had to make their own entertainment in those days.

Partly because there was no telly we used to live our lives much more out of the house than nowadays. As kids we used to see a lot of colourful characters around the town. I remember Puzzle Bobby, a little man with a two-wheeled barrow who made and sold wire puzzles and also sharpened knives and scissors. There was Old Yorkie or Tattie Shaw who tramped the countryside and slept in straw barns. And Jimmy Tongue or Tongo — he used to march down the middle of the road shouting 'Clear the way for Tongo!'. Or Highland Nancy who was usually accompanied by a man, but never the same one. I can remember pavement artists outside the GPO and some of them were very talented indeed. The characters that we remember as kids have obviously gone but I can't see anyone replacing them. Kelso has changed a lot and people seem quite a bit less outgoing, keeping themselves to themselves. Perhaps that has something to do with the way the town has physically changed with the shift of people away from living in the middle and into the council housing round about.

James Stewart
What I remember of Kelso in the 1920s, it didn't extend much further than the streets which emanated from the Square. Maxwellheugh was a small village with probably no more than a dozen houses. Obviously that has changed a good deal.

The population has been fairly stable. In 1921 it was down to 3,500 and then it gradually went up to almost 4000 in 1950. People were dependent almost entirely on agriculture and the various services that were needed for agriculture. In the past we had very few industries, only John Hogarth Limited at Kelso Mill, Andrew Dun & Son's bone mill at Maxwellheugh, George Henderson with the foundry and nail factory and Middlemas and Son making aerated waters. That was about all the manufacturing industry we had.

I joined the Town Council in 1955 because . . . actually because I always admired the people who did these jobs. I remember the Provosts, Arthur Middlemas and John Hill and John Tully. I thought that it was only right that we should try to put something back into the town. Of course at first I just took a back seat. Then after two or three years I was appointed Hon Treasurer of the burgh. I found that tremendously interesting. We levied the rates at that time. We did our best with housing and kept the rates at a reasonable level. The officials of the Town Council were part-time in those days, both the Burgh Chamberlain and the Town Clerk. We operated from a requisition from the County Council who looked after the major services like education and roads and so on.

Council housing was the main task of the council from about 1925 onwards. The first schemes were at the Tofts, a scheme at the top of Roxburgh Street, one at Hillbank Terrace and at Inch Road. In

Maxwellheugh there was Springwood Terrace and then in my time on the council we had the prefabs which were built at the end of the War. We then built quite a number of houses — at Inchmyre and elsewhere. We invoked the help of the Scottish Special Housing Association and really got on with a large programme. I remember opening the 2000th house owned and built by the Town Council. I was very proud of the revenue account because we were one of the few authorities to balance that account. It meant slightly higher rents but we took no more from the general rate-payer than the statutory amount.

When I joined the Town Council our great problem was to alter the economic base, to make Kelso more industrial. We didn't make much progress until the act of 1965; the government white paper on the Scottish economy, 'A Plan for Expansion 1965 to 1970'. That was followed by the Percy Johnstone Marshall report on the Borders. The whole thing co-ordinated with the appointment of a full-time Town Clerk in 1965. This was Mat Carlaw and he did a tremendous job for Kelso.

As I said, we wanted to broaden the economic base — the population of the town was only expanding through people coming in from the country — and we needed to create industry. We also took up a Glasgow overspill arrangement but never really made progress with that.

Following the government white paper where the Borders were made a development area, the Town Council purchased the Pinnacle Hill estate. We were very successful in attracting industry there, so much so that the population increased by 25 % between 1965 and 1975. This was really quite phenomenal. I feel that we led the Borders in this.

At Abbotseat the council housing was of such a high standard that many people thought it was private housing. And at Barony Park the Town Council bought the old auction mart, laid in the services and sold off plots to a private developer. This was a very successful operation indeed.

Our next move was to try to modernise our housing and also other property in the middle of the town. We tried to re-develop the housing lying between Woodmarket and Horsemarket. We couldn't quite manage that but there is a good new development at Rutherford Square with its sheltered housing and a day centre. We had difficulty with the centre of Kelso because we had to purchase property from many different private individuals.

One building in the town I've always liked is the Town Hall. It's a really splendid piece of architecture with its clock tower. I can recall the curfew bell being rung each night at 8pm. And on the first Monday of every month when the Town Council met, it was rung at 6pm. When the last meeting of the Town Council took place in 1975 I arranged for it to be rung for the last time.

I think Kelso lost out on the reorganisation of local government which happened as a result of the Wheatley Commission in the 1970s. The town lost its individuality. That was unavoidable. Kelso now only has two members on Roxburgh District Council and one on the Regional Council. Before that we were running the town with local people and local officials and I think the record of Kelso Town Council from 1892 to 1975 was very good. I would deprecate this very much and I said at the time that we would lose quite a lot. But there you are, that's progress.

What the eight people contributing to this chapter have given is a real sense of what life in Kelso was like in the recent past. They know about the town because they were born in it and have lived their lives there. No history of a living place can have a conclusion, it just stops at a point in time. But here are some postscripts to the story of Kelso so far:

Jack Moffat
Life in the town has changed a lot. People are better off, much better off even though there's so much unemployment. For example everybody now has a washing machine in their house — I should know, I used to mend them. So Kelso's 'Steam' or public wash-house probably won't ever come back into use. It was in Roxburgh Street near the end of Union Street. Inside the Steam were wooden stalls each containing two wash-tubs. You could pay extra and have your clothes spun in a centrifuge and dried in a press on hot rails. Then they were aired on a private drying green before we carried them home in a big basket. Across the road there was Lizzie Tillcock's laundry where you could get your clothes ironed. And there were other women in the town who took in washing just to make ends meet.

Sandy Blair
I've always thought Kelso was a friendly town. People will help you when you're in trouble. Lots of things are different now but I think that's still the same as it always was.

Will Ker
When I think about it I've not only stayed in Kelso all my life, I've never really moved out of Woodmarket so it's difficult to be objective. But being a shopkeeper and getting so many visitors in — they tell me I'm lucky, lucky to stay in a place like this. I don't argue with them.

Donald Scott
I'm so prejudiced because I like Kelso so much. I wouldn't know what to say about it, it's a part of me.

Alan Smith
Kelso doesn't have mills like Hawick or Gala. So it hasn't grown much but it has remained an open town without the great mill buildings in the middle of it. Kelso's always been more dependent on its district and more involved in it than the other Border towns. Also we always had relative prosperity and never a series of ups and downs. The agricultural background has always held the local economy steady. There have never been any slumps like in the mill towns or any real highs either. Maybe that's why we're all so easy-going.

James Stewart
What would help Kelso in the future would be a Community Council with some teeth, with a local full-time official. If it could raise some revenue perhaps we could look after local affairs like parks, street-cleaning and things like that.

Mrs Helen Pettigrew
In Kelso I think some things have changed very much for the better. I can remember poor people in Kelso, many more than now. In the past if you were poor and you hadn't a relative to look after you and no income you were just taken off to the Poorhouse in Inch Road. I remember that every Thursday one man, Champie Lamb, had a day off from the Poorhouse. He came into town and he would walk about in Bridge Street until he saw my father. Or if I saw him out the window I'd phone through to the bakehouse and tell my Dad. Champie got two newly baked pies and my father went across to Frankie Frost's and bought him an ounce of tobacco, and gave him enough money for two glasses of beer.
  I'm glad that's gone now.

Rodger Fish
A few years ago you couldn't walk up the street without saying hello to virtually everyone you met. Now I can walk up the street and I don't know anybody, they're strangers, new people. Many of the youngsters have left Kelso because of the lack of work. Now there's a bit of industry and new people come in.
  But there's one funny thing I can't understand. I quite like it. I see kids in the town that I don't know and they'll say, 'Hello Rodger.' And I think

'how does he know my name's Rodger and why does he say hello to me?' It must be a passed-on thing, but I quite like it.

Subject Index

Index of Names